For most of his career, **Stephen Green** has been an international banker, who has lived in East Asia, the Middle East and North America. From 2011 to 2013, he was trade minister in the British government. He is a member of the House of Lords and is Chair of the Natural History Museum and of Asia House in London. He is an ordained priest of the Church of England.

He is the author of *Reluctant Meister: Germany and the new Europe* (Haus Publishing, 2015) and of *The European Identity: Historical and cultural realities we cannot deny* (Haus Publishing, 2015). He has also written on business values and is the author of *Good Value: Money, morality and an uncertain world* (Allen Lane, 2009). He lectures regularly on the cultural, geopolitical and environmental challenges that face the increasingly connected and urbanized peoples of Europe and Asia.

The Human Odyssey

Stephen Green

East, West
and the Search for
Universal Values

First published in Great Britain in 2019

Society for Promoting Christian Knowledge
36 Causton Street
London SW1P 4ST
www.spck.org.uk

British Library Cataloguing-in-Publication Data
A catalogue record for this book is available from the British Library

ISBN 978–0–281–08113–4
eBook ISBN 978–0–281–08115–8

1 3 5 7 9 10 8 6 4 2

Typeset by Falcon Oast Graphic Art Limited
First printed in Great Britain by TJ International
Subsequently digitally reprinted in Great Britain

eBook by Falcon Oast Graphic Art Limited

Produced on paper from sustainable forests

For my grandchildren: Heather, James, William,
Andrew, Samuel, Hannah and Phoebe.
May they grow into their full individuality
in this connected world

Contents

Preface

I have had the great privilege of living in different parts of the land mass we call Eurasia, and of travelling extensively over three decades throughout many of its countries.

It has been a period of extraordinary change: the emergence of entire new cities, the spread of mobile telecommunications and the whole digital revolution. As this has happened all around us, I have seen and heard many things that tell of the new struggling to break out from the old – or of the endless human search for beauty and worth – and of the numbing force of human evil.

I have seen families struggling to get their children educated for a better future in remote rural villages of Myanmar and Cambodia. When I ask one young girl through the interpreter what she wants to do after the schooling her parents are working tirelessly to pay for, she shouts out – in English – 'I want to be an engineer!' At the same time, I have seen people living in prosperous Europe, in Singapore and in Japan, who have forgotten how hard it used to be and who struggle with the crises of affluence; and I have also seen enclaves of fabulous personal wealth in India, in Hong Kong and in the Gulf – enclaves where lives are lived that beg all the obvious questions.

I have experienced the extraordinary beauty of every culture of Eurasia – from soaring European Gothic cathedrals to ethereal Russian icons, from the exquisite geometry of Turkish mosques to the exuberant Hindu temples of South India, from Buddhist cave frescoes in China to Kyoto temples where time seems to have stood still. I have seen gentle groups of colourful worshippers on pilgrimages in rural India – as well as gangs of noisy young men in the grip of religious fervour, protesting a court decision to allow women of menstruating age into Sabarimala, dedicated to a bachelor deity and the most visited temple in the whole of India. The moving and the unnerving.

And I have been to places that are heavy with the evils of human history: I have seen the Yasukuni Shrine in Tokyo, where some of Japan's convicted war dead are buried. I have also been to the Peace Park in Hiroshima and seen the watch that is stuck at exactly a quarter past eight – the moment when the bomb exploded above the city. I have been to Yad Vashem in Israel, where the intoning of children's names must surely melt the most hard-bitten of hearts; and I have made my pilgrimage to Auschwitz – a place I am glad I have seen once, but never want to see again.

I have also sensed the gradual degradation of our environment over the same period. Where I grew up you could hear the skylarks on the nearby hills every summer; now they are all gone. I have seen the smoky haze caused by the burning of tropical rainforest in South East Asia. I have seen the huge flares of burning gas lighting up the night sky above an Iraqi oil field in the desert outside Basra. And I have seen photographs of dead pangolins, an endangered species of mammal illegally trafficked in large numbers to both China and Vietnam, where their meat is a delicacy and their scales are thought to have medicinal properties.

And so on. What a piece of work is this *Homo sapiens*, which has produced such an astonishing variety of the sublime and the mundane, the precious and the pointless, the hopeful and the dreadful. So where are we heading? I look at my grandchildren who, on present rates of life expectancy, will live to see the next century. This is not just an academic question: it is one that involves those I love. It is for them and their friends that I write this book.

Several people have gone more than an extra mile with me in this project: Helmuth Bahn, Martin Donnelly, Werner Jeanrond, Ana-Maria Pascal, Stephen Platten and Michael Winckless all read the whole of the first draft, and their comments led to significant enhancements. I am permanently grateful and in their debt. Philip Law and the team at SPCK have been enormously helpful in bringing the book to its final fruition. And the person who has gone with me, not simply an extra mile or more but on the whole odyssey, is Jay – whose contribution is greater than perhaps even she is aware.

Introduction

The long human odyssey of self-discovery has now reached a crucial stage: everything we do affects everyone and everything else – *and we know it*. The next hundred years will bring more change than we can easily imagine: more opportunities for more people to achieve the fulfilment of a good life, and more risk of catastrophe and harm to the whole planet than we have ever known before.

All the greatest challenges of the next hundred years will centre on Eurasia – the land mass that includes Europe, Asia and the Middle East, and which is the largest and most crowded continent on the planet. We are used to thinking of Europe and Asia as two separate continents, but there is no geographical reason for this. Eurasia is a single land mass and we cannot make sense of its present and future without understanding that its past has been woven together for a long period of time. It is where all the world's great living cultures first emerged. It is increasingly closely connected, physically and virtually. All the world's great powers of the twenty-first century are Eurasian, except one: America. All are inextricably entangled there – including America. Human experience in Eurasia is becoming, for better or worse, more and more intensively shared; and because of its sheer scale and complexity, what happens in Eurasia will affect the whole world.

Most Eurasians now live in cities and, by the end of this century, virtually all will do so. Everywhere, our societies are being changed utterly by the transient life of the city. In the midst of the change it is easy to lose sight of just how radical, how fast and how recent this change is. However, the common experience of connected urban life has not produced any emerging sense of common purpose, let alone shared identity. On the contrary, the cultures of Eurasia – each with its own traditions, histories, memories, beliefs and aspirations – are in many cases becoming more, not less, assertive as they jostle together. Throughout much of

1

Eurasia – perhaps with only the Europeans as exceptions – the consciousness of nationhood is at least as strong as ever. And digital connectivity,
so far from making old histories fade and old barriers crumble, seems to
nourish these cultural identities as never before.

So a new balance of power, based on the same fundamental principles
that determined relations among the European powers in the nineteenth
century, is coming into being, only this time *on a Eurasian stage*. In the
twenty-second century, there may well be other great powers on the world
stage, but not yet. The new geopolitical order of this century is a Eurasian
one. It is subject to the same sorts of stress that the old Europe was. In
particular, one established global power (America) feels challenged by a
big new rising power (China). Does this mean that they will inevitably
clash? Will the next spiral of history remind us of the terrible hundred
years in Europe that finally ended only in 1989?

If this seems like a familiar pattern of history, something else is
occurring that is not. For better or worse, the experience of urban
life is changing all those cultures of Eurasia. For, under the impact of
urbanization, humanity is slowly but surely discovering its individuality.
The breakdown and disappearance of older pre-urban social structures
and the broadening knowledge horizons of city life mean that we are
gradually becoming more and more individual. There is no possibility
of reversing this trend in human experience, because there is no possibility of reversing the trend of urbanization. No culture, however deeply
rooted, will remain immune to this change.

The risk is that we confuse individuality with an individualism that
makes the self the subject of every sentence. The hope is that we will
gradually learn, through experience and observation, how impover-
ishing such self-centredness can be, both for the individual and for the
communities and the cultures of which all individuals are a part. That
is the point of the human odyssey: the more we learn about one another,
the more we discover the commonalities of human experience, and the
more our own individuality is fulfilled – not through a naked individualism, but at its deepest level of being. *For we discover ourselves fully only
as we discover the other.*

Viewed geopolitically, the main question is whether or not and how
the world views of the two most important and influential powers on the

Eurasian stage – China and America (the one fundamentally Confucian, the other essentially individualist) – can be constructively synthesized. At a deeper level, though, the great question is how the irreversible fact of urbanization will nurture the growth of human individuality in every society, such that the wisdom of others transforms and enriches *all* those great Eurasian cultures. This book explores those questions, with all their implications for the human spirit, and with all their risks and possibilities for our grandchildren.

1

Eurasia: the next hundred years

Eurasia, and its continental shelf, stretches from Ireland in the west to the Bering Strait in the east, and from Franz Josef Land in the north to Sri Lanka in the south. It includes the South East Asian archipelago. It is a third of the world's total land mass. Both the Arctic Circle and the Equator run through it. It includes virtually every kind of climate and geographical environment known to humanity. It has the highest mountains, the largest steppe, the largest area of tundra, the largest inland sea, the largest body of fresh water, some of the longest rivers, one of the three largest tropical rainforests, and the largest known reserves of hydrocarbons anywhere in the world. It is also home to two-thirds of humanity.

There is no single all-purpose definition of Eurasia: geologists and natural historians may well, for example, have a different perspective from social historians or from political scientists. For the purpose of history, geopolitics and culture, Eurasia clearly includes the Indonesian archipelago. Australasia is effectively part of the story too, although it plays a relatively marginal role and would not normally be thought of as being geographically a part of Eurasia. At the other end of the land mass, what about Iceland? Geologically, it straddles the great Atlantic divide, but in human terms, it is very obviously part of the European story rather than America's. Like Australasia, only even more so, it plays a marginal role, though its importance in the history of north European culture is out of all proportion to the small size of its population.

The big question is about Africa. In deep geological time, it was part of the same great land mass as Eurasia. And from the earliest beginnings of *Homo sapiens*, there has always been interaction between the two great continents. For much of recorded history, that interaction was limited by the almost impenetrable barrier of the Sahara Desert: had it not prevented any significant southward movement of people, Africa might

5

well have become the demographic centre of one of Eurasia's greatest cultures – Islam. As it is, Africa's interaction with Eurasia was largely confined, through most of recorded history, to its northern regions and some trading links down its eastern coast. Five hundred years ago, that began to change, and with the huge growth of shipping, air links and digital connectivity, Africa has been reconnected ever more intensively with Eurasia. Africa's impact on Eurasia will grow enormously through-out the coming decades. If present demographic trends continue, Africa's population may be almost as large as that of Asia by 2100. In the longer-term future – but perhaps not until the next century – Africa may be home to some of the world's most powerful states. But not yet. The truth is that, for the rest of this century, the world's agenda – whether polit-ical, cultural or spiritual – is going to be determined, for better or worse, mostly by Eurasia.

The world's centre of gravity has shifted back from an American-led West to the Eurasian East, where it was for most of human history. Increasingly, Eurasia will be dominated by its two great behemoths, China and India. All the world's biggest risks and opportunities lie now in Eurasia. It produces around two-thirds of the world's economic output. It is also the origin of all the world's great cultures and spiritual traditions, and so it will be the testing ground of all the great challenges facing humanity for the next century. In Eurasian history – past, present and future – what we see is nothing less than the evolution of the human spirit. Looking backwards, we can see the tracks of a journey with many detours; looking forwards, the most important question facing us all is if and how that human odyssey will continue. The answer will lie, to a large extent, in how humans relate to one another and deal with one another on the Eurasian land mass. The impact will be felt globally, not only in Eurasia's near neighbour Africa but also in the Americas, already deeply influenced not only by Europeans but also through Asian immigration, and now increasingly by Asian investment too.

Some argue that this is the wrong question – that it is outdated due to the digital revolution. They have foreseen a different future, one in which all the great human opportunities and challenges will present them-selves, not in a geographically determined form, but in a digital realm of consciousness, in which physical limitations and geographically based conceptions of identity will become increasingly irrelevant. With the predicted emergence of such a new '*noosphere*' – to borrow the ingenious terminology of Teilhard de Chardin, who (writing long before the digital era) saw shared thought and reflection as part of the essence of a new humanity[1] – goes a loss of interest in the past as a source of identity and meaning. Geopolitics takes on radically new forms: the old order is passing away and, depending on the visionary's penchant for optimism or for pessimism, either our grandchildren will enjoy a new and freer world or a new beast is slouching towards Bethlehem to be born.[2]

But reports of the death of the old world of geographically based identities, geopolitics and cultural histories are – to use Mark Twain's famous words – an exaggeration, as we shall see in Chapter 4. Yes, the digital realm brings significant new, non-national actors into geopolitics (as did capitalism in the last three centuries, by bringing into being international businesses that seemed to have no national home or loyalties). And, yes, digital connectivity makes it much harder to put barriers round people's thought worlds. Yes, too, artificial intelligence will surely transform our life experience in the coming decades, as well as posing a whole new series of questions about values and ethics (how long will it be before we determine that an artificial intelligence has moral or legal rights?). But, no, we are a long way from shaking off our materiality. Even in the next century, we will not have reached the questionable utopia of pure digital existence (because we never can; even the cloud depends on hardware). In the meantime – and probably for much, much longer – we will live with all the joys, pains, stresses and stimulations that come from being what such diverse figures as Confucius, the Buddha, Aristotle, the apostle Paul and countless others down the ages have always known: a mysterious mixture of the material and the spiritual.

The empires of Eurasia

Humans have done well in Eurasia. From very early on, they made their presence felt. They hunted the mammoths and may have contributed to their extinction. From the ice ages onwards, they left their stencilled handprints and their figurative and abstract art on the walls of caves from one end of the land mass to the other. They built monuments, the purposes of which we can in some cases only guess at, and these have dotted the land mass for at least the last six thousand years. They learned how to produce workable metal. They domesticated animals, namely dogs, sheep, goats, cattle, poultry, camels and the all-important horses. They domesticated wheat and rice. They moved gradually from hunting to pasturing their flocks, to growing their crops and to founding cities. From a very early stage, contact over large distances increased, helped by their camels and by their horse-drawn chariots, which first appeared over four thousand years ago.[3] In this way, small hunting groups evolved into nomadic pastoralists, into settled farmers and into urban trading societies, with each of these shifts enabling a dramatically increased population density. All these ways of existence overlapped, even into modern times.

By the turn of the Common Era, Eurasia was home to the vast major-ity of all the world's human beings. No one had travelled from one end of the land mass to the other, but many of them knew at least something about other Eurasian societies that they never saw. The Romans and the Chinese knew of one another's existence and the insatiable Roman appetite for silk was a major impetus for an emerging East–West trade over very long distances – a trade that was named for the silk but also came to include precious gems, copper, spices, chemicals, glass, saddles and horses, plus weapons.

Close encounters were all too often violent: witness, above all, the centuries of wars between Greeks and Persians, both before and well into the Christian era (a contest that, in a sense, mutated later on into the great struggle between Christendom and Islam). It is one of the oldest cultural fault lines in all of human history. The epic stories – told to us mainly from the Greek side, from Aeschylus and Herodotus onwards – are, however, only part of a broader pattern recurring throughout Eurasia. One clan, or tribe, or nation, would move or expand, at the expense of less-energetic, less well-endowed, less well-organized neighbours. Over the millennia, empires and civilizations have waxed and waned, most leaving traces visible only to archaeologists and philologists, but with a few leaving deep imprints even on modern cultures, as we shall see.

Some reached degrees of sophistication that are extraordinary given their antiquity. Thus, for example, the Harappans of the Indus Valley left not only their remarkable city outlines (as well as treasures such as an exquisite bronze statuette of a dancing girl from four thousand years ago) but also an indecipherable script and tantalizingly little evidence of how they developed and why they went into decline. Over the centuries, others – some nomadic, some settled – came and went, rose and fell, were decimated or just absorbed by the next group of people whose star was rising: the Scythians in the area north of the Black Sea; the Kushans to the west of Tibet; various Indian kingdoms; the Huns; the Alans; the Khwarezmians; the Kharakhanids; the Ghaznavids; the Seljuk Turks; the Vikings; the Xiongnu; the Xixia. It can all seem like a continuous swirl. Cities and states sometimes lived and let live, and sometimes went to war. Nomads sometimes traded with and sometimes raided the settled communities (they were an age-old scourge of China, Iran, Russia and Europe). Above all, there were the Mongols, whose incredible and terrifying explosion across the land mass brought them nearer than anyone else before (or since) to ruling Eurasia from sea to shining sea.

For much of history, all this turmoil had very little to do with ideas. Great powers expanded because they were good at it, because they had leaders with vaulting ambition, because economic pressures pushed them and/or because there was wealth to be had – the Greeks under Alexander, for example, as well as the Mongols – and perhaps also because of a Darwinian sense that they had to conquer or succumb (this was surely the main impetus behind the growth of Republican Rome through its existential struggle with Carthage). There is something elemental about all this: the drive to feed and reproduce, to dominate territory and to control the group is widespread in the animal kingdom too.

But there were some movements of history that were impelled by ideas, beliefs and aspirations that went beyond such primal drives. The first empire with any sort of idea or programme underlying its expansion was arguably Persia. The new idea that conquest could be a civilizing duty – or at least that it would confer civilizing benefits on the conquered – might be said to be the legacy of Cyrus and Darius (the former being famously accoladed as the Lord's anointed by a tiny people with their own rather special sense of calling, as recorded in the Jewish Bible[4]). At its height, the Persian empire was at least three times larger than present-day Iran; its rulers described themselves as 'Kings of Kings';

and they constructed the world's first bureaucracy and communications system to run their empire.

Others would follow. Ashoka took his Indian philosophy of just rule deep into Central Asia. His edicts, carved in rock and scattered all over his empire, proclaim a Buddhist-inspired code for living (the tone of which also sounds surprisingly like the voice of Confucius). The apogee of the Roman idea came, ironically, after the death of republicanism: it was the moment when the Emperor Caracalla granted full Roman citizenship to all free men of the Roman Empire in 212 CE. Although he intended it as a tax-raising measure, this Roman idea is effectively a harbinger of what became the concept of Christendom and provided the potential basis for a European identity. Then came Islam – the most spectacular explosion created by a new idea in all of history, not only up to that point but also for over a thousand years thereafter (until a very different explosion at one end of the Eurasian land mass triggered by the French Revolution in 1789). Islam reached the Pyrenees and the gates of China within its first century. Its control and transformation of the lands central to Eurasian communications ensured the emergence of the most sophisticated, cosmopolitan and creative culture the world had yet known. The cross-fertilization of ideas – Chinese, Indian, European, Iranian – that took place under this Islamic aegis made it one of the greatest times for the human spirit in all history. Then there is China itself. Though not the world's oldest continuous civilization, China is certainly the world's oldest continuous identity, founded on the bedrock of an holistic cosmological and terrestrial philosophy that saw its emperors as having 'the Mandate of Heaven to rule all under heaven'. Then, when Europe was in the ascendant, the Habsburg Emperor Charles V ruled over domains that covered much of Europe as well as huge swathes of a new world and stretched all the way round to Manila. His empire was the first in human history on which the sun literally never set. His motto was *plus ultra* – 'there is more beyond'. His faith and commitment to his role as Holy Roman Emperor was deep and personal.

But in all these cases, what was potentially a universalizing vision ran out of steam, either because they ran into adversaries who brought them to a halt or just because sheer extension became unmanageable. Ashoka's domain didn't long survive him. Islam found its high-water mark in Europe at Poitiers in the eighth century and soon thereafter began to break up into separate polities. China had sought to extend its tributary relationships around the Indian Ocean in the early fifteenth century, but then retreated to the mainland. And Charles V retired to his monastery, exhausted by the burden of his mission.

Even the fearsome Mongols also reached a high-water mark: they were stopped in the end from totally overwhelming Islam by the Egyptian Mamluks (who also finally defeated the Crusaders) at Ain Jalut in 1260. Soon after defeating a Polish-led army at the battle of Liegnitz and a Hungarian army at the Battle of Mohi in the same week in 1241, they turned back from moving further westwards (scholars have debated the reason: the death of the Great Khan back home may have been the decisive factor; but they may also have been daunted by the unfamiliar and uncongenial forests that blocked their progress westwards towards the Atlantic). A generation later, a 'divine wind' or *kamikaze* protected Japan from Kublai Khan's invasion force in 1281 (an intriguing parallel with the storms that saved England from the Spanish Armada in 1588).

Since then, others have sought dominant positions in various regions of Eurasia: the Ottoman Turks, who built an empire on the ruins of Byzantium and established a new caliphate in Constantinople; the British, whose trade drew them into empire in India; the Russians, who moved into Siberia and into the vacuum left by the Mongols in the centre; the Japanese, who emerged from more than two centuries of isolation to erupt into Eastern Asia just at the time when the Qing Dynasty of China was losing the Mandate of Heaven; and lastly the Americans – the first non-Eurasian power to play a role (and a decisive one) in the land mass, at both ends of it, in the wake of the Second World War. In all cases, the motives were mixed: the drive for geopolitical supremacy, economic advantage and cultural assertion all played their part.

Connections and tensions

Over the millennia since *Homo sapiens* first came to Eurasia, the human spirit has developed immeasurably. All the great cultures of the world originate from there. Connections have been established and broadened, knowledge of our context and of one another has deepened, the life experience of people everywhere has become enormously more complex and sophisticated. Apart from a small number of epic journeys by medieval travellers such as Xuanzang, Marco Polo and Ibn Battuta, few saw much of the land mass before modern times. Now we can cross it by air in fifteen hours. Railway maps of Eurasia over the past hundred years and projected over the next few decades show extraordinarily rapid proliferation. Only two hundred years after the first railway opened in northern England, there are now thousands of rail freight journeys between east and west in Eurasia every year, with much more growth to come.[5] Rivers are being bridged, tunnels bored through mountains and islands connected to their mainlands. China's so-called Belt and Road Initiative (of which more later) will see massive amounts of capital being mobilized for investment in new infrastructure, which will further enhance the connectivity of the whole land mass. On top of all this, shipping lanes round the continent are becoming ever more crowded, while millions of flights criss-cross it every year.

The upheavals of the nineteenth and twentieth centuries have produced a geopolitical map of the land mass that has over eighty different sovereign nations, all jostling to make their way in this increasingly connected twenty-first century Eurasia. Inevitably, though, the geopolitical balance on the Eurasian stage is dominated by a handful of great powers, each of which has an identity rooted in its own history and self-understanding. By the dawn of the new millennium it was becoming clear which these dominant powers were: China and India – the one soon to be the largest economy in the world, the other the largest by population; Russia, geographically the largest country in the world and the only major power that straddles the traditional divide between Asia and Europe; the Europeans, prosperous and finally at peace after centuries, but struggling to achieve cohesion; Japan, the largest island society in the world, with its uniquely impenetrable social dynamics; and America – the only non-Eurasian power to be engaged in and around the Eurasian land mass, both to the west and to the east. Others too have aspirations for cultural or regional influence: Turkey, Iran and Saudi Arabia.

All of these occupants of the Eurasian stage are uncomfortable with their position, sometimes more than they will admit (even to themselves).

China exudes confidence internationally, but knows it is riding a tiger, because its authorities fear a domestic pluralism that could so easily turn into debilitating instability. America fears China, as an established leader always fears a new and assertive rival; it fears its economic strength and the military power thereby made possible; and it is unsure how to respond to China's ideological challenge on the world stage. India is obsessed with China's success and strength, and it has nightmares about encirclement. Russia seethes with resentment at the humiliation of the collapse of the Soviet Union; it is ill at ease with all its neighbours. Europe is deeply unsure of what it stands for, and the European Union is struggling to find a new vision and impetus for its seventy-year-old project of integration. Japan chafes more than America appreciates under its post-war tutelage; and it becomes increasingly nervous about Chinese resurgence with every passing year. Finally, there is an unanswered question about the Muslim world, always conscious of the *ummah*, the commonwealth of Islam, but criss-crossed by divisions and tensions reflecting its separate cultural and national histories and identities, particularly those of Turkey, Saudi Arabia and Iran.

As a result, growing connectivity and interaction have not – or at least not yet – produced any sense of common purpose or shared destiny. In fact, this looks increasingly like what became known in the context of European history as the Westphalian order. The treaties signed in Westphalia in 1648 became the basis of geopolitical relationships as the modern era dawned, as we shall see in Chapter 6. From Westphalia onwards, states – some of which already thought of themselves as nations in an increasingly modern sense – began to identify with and define themselves by their cultures. In the mid-seventeenth century, this meant their religion: few were yet prepared to recognize a distinction between their culture and their religion. Hence the Latin watchwords that summed up the essence of this new order: *cujus regio, ejus religio* – that is, the ruler determines the religion of the people. But as religion faded from public life over the following three centuries, this principle morphed, in effect, into a broader requirement to 'live and let live'.

Yet such a system is not stable. Henry Kissinger has demonstrated that a Westphalian system has no direction of travel.[6] It depends on what he calls legitimacy, which boils down to mutual trust and acceptance of the status quo. It also depends on balance – that is, on there being no member of the dominant group of powers too expansionist and too powerful to be constrained effectively by the others. The European system was always fragile and was repeatedly threatened during the eighteenth century, before being blown apart by the French Revolution. At a stroke, this destroyed the old basis of trust and, with it, the old balance. The resulting convulsions brought the Russians on to the European stage for the first time, before a new balance was established at the Congress of Vienna – only to be thrown into play again by the unification of Germany.

But it was not only the balance of the European system that was shaken in the nineteenth century and then finally destroyed in the twentieth. It had also lost the old basis of its legitimacy, and this too contributed to the huge tragedy that unfolded. The settlement in 1648 arose not only from economic exhaustion but also from a growing weariness with the old narratives of religious dogmatism. The newly emerging idea of the time was one that, unlike the political settlement of Westphalia, did have a direction of travel – or, rather, several. This was the European Enlightenment. Unique in Eurasia, we shall see in Chapter 8 how it was destined to be a challenge to every Eurasian culture and polity (and, indeed, throughout the world). The Enlightenment did not appear out of the blue: it owed to the Christian humanists of the Renaissance more than it often cared to admit. But religious belief in Europe was being privatized and religious institutions of all stripes over the next two centuries were to lose much of their moral and social authority. In fact, the whole hierarchy of society was being undermined by this new spirit. In the context of the new Europe struggling to be born in the eighteenth and nineteenth centuries, this meant that legitimacy could not for much longer be that of an interconnected courtly elite, of the kind who put together the Westphalian settlement and then the Metternichian settlement after the final defeat of Napoleon at Waterloo. Although 1848 was a year of failed revolutions, the voice of the *demos* was beginning to be heard, and intellectual seeds – sown even before the elemental violence of the French Revolution – began to blossom into beliefs and identities that would eventually destroy such a socially limited legitimacy, irrevocably transform the whole of Eurasia and shape the modern world.

All this is a reminder that there is nothing inherently stable about today's Westphalian Eurasia. The European settlement was brought down in the first decades of the twentieth century by ethnic and cultural nationalism (virtually everywhere), borderless ideas (notably, communism) and a rogue state that had no interest in the status quo (Serbia in the years leading up to the First World War). At that stage, the rest of Eurasia was, like Africa, largely a playground in which European rivalries were fought out. Now Asia is resurgent, the Middle East is in turmoil, while Europe has exhausted its passions and is preoccupied with its internal cohesion and its identity. So now it is different: the new stage is a Eurasian one, but all the elements that made for the European tragedy are still there and are visible now on that Eurasian stage. Now, as then, its actors include countries of very different sizes, stages of economic development and cultural histories. Some seethe with ancient, and not so ancient, resentments against others. There are at least one, possibly two or three, rogue states and this time they have nuclear pretensions. Borderless ideas thrive like germs in the atmosphere; not all the same ones, but just as destabilizing. And cultural nationalism is taking on a new lease of life in all the major Eurasian powers.

All these three points are worth dwelling on.

Rogue states like the Serbia of pre-First World War Europe matter to others when such states believe they can act internationally with impunity, either because they deny the legitimacy of the international order and/or because they believe they have a protector in one of the major powers. For several decades, North Korea has seemed to fit this bill perfectly. There are also non-state actors ready to use extreme violence for a cause. The parallels with the pre-First World War Balkans are uncanny and uncomfortable.

Second, a Westphalian balance will always find it difficult to cope with borderless ideas. The last century has known three such powerful ideas. All three have sought to give direction and impetus to human spiritual, cultural, political and economic development. All three have had a deep impact on contemporary Eurasian affairs. One is now a spent force, but the other two are not.

Communism, with its Marxist–Leninist intellectual apparatus, was the forced life experience of over a third of the entire Eurasian population.

Its legacy is profound: Russia, China, Vietnam, the Korean Peninsula, Central Asia and East Europe will never be the same again. Leninism has now been rejected everywhere and could surely not again achieve the sort of dominance – or produce the sort of horrors – we now associate with the Soviet Union of the Bolsheviks. Mao's 'mistakes' – to use the rhetoric of the modern Chinese Communist Party – are also recognized for what they were: disastrous experiments in social advancement and ideological purification that cost tens of millions of lives. Yet, although there is barely a single true-believing traditional communist any-where in China, the Communist Party is still unwilling to slough off its Marxist metaphysics, even as it deliberately borrows Confucian termin-ology to express its vision and objectives. In effect, it still claims the Mandate of Heaven, and the deeper basis of its newly found moral authority is much more robust than some Western ideologues may care to admit. That mandate of the Chinese Communist Party has, in fact, morphed into 'socialism with Chinese characteristics for a new era', now known officially as Xi Jinping Thought, the significance of which is still not fully appreciated in the Western world. The question – which we will return to shortly – is whether that mandate any longer has the univer-salizing thrust either of the ancient imperial claim to rule over all under heaven or of the communist vision of a new global order brought into being by and for the workers of the world.

The other two borderless ideas in the Eurasian atmosphere are very different. Islamism – the movement to assert a fundamentalist version of Islam, through militancy and violence if need be – is one. In varying degrees, it has had an impact on all the major Eurasian cultures except one (Japan). All have had to witness Islam's struggle with the questions of modernity: some – notably the Europeans – have had to face their own questions about identity as a result. All have had the experience of being the witness – and sometimes the victim – of the violence un-leashed by fundamentalist Islamism. This hydra has many heads, but it is theocratic and conservative, both socially and intellectually. Notoriously, some dream of a new caliphate, but a very different one from the historic caliphates of Damascus, Baghdad, Cairo and Cordoba, which saw the efflorescence of the greatest glories of Islam. So the struggle for the soul of Islam is real. This is sometimes portrayed as if the struggles of the

European Renaissance and Reformations were being transposed to a new era and on to a new world stage. This precedent is of limited value, however, except in one respect perhaps, in that it reminds us such transitions within a religious culture can be violent and long-drawn-out.

The other borderless idea? It is, of course, the liberal democratic order that found its most dedicated and powerful protagonist in America, and triumphed in the end in Europe, as well as taking root in several other Eurasian powers (and increasingly in Africa and Latin America). But this liberal democratic order has had troubles of its own. In the immediate aftermath of 1989, it came to be understood as a political order very closely dovetailed with a liberal approach to economic development and management – and that it would take the world by storm in the wake of the fall of the Soviet empire.

This confidence was badly shaken by the financial and economic crisis in the first decade of this century. And in any case, the evidence was that liberal economics and pluralism did not automatically lead to democratic politics: China, in particular, gave the lie to that easy implication.

Moreover, liberal economics has been challenged at the philosophical level by East Asians, by Indians and by Muslims, and on several different grounds. For one thing, it had shown itself to be based on a fundamental fallacy – that markets were essentially self-correcting and, therefore, like a kind of gyroscope, would always return to balance after any shock. Second, throughout the world many have felt a revulsion at the inequality that seemed to be its inevitable concomitant. Third, many have bridled at the transactional individualism and the materialist implication that the value of everything is reflected in its price.

The liberal democratic order is, finally, uncomfortable with its own heritage in the European Enlightenment. It is ambivalent about the legacy of the Enlightenment (which was the intellectual parent of Karl Marx as well as of Adam Smith); and as a creature of a secularizing age, it is also unwilling to recognize its own debt to Christian humanist thought. Conversely, Christian social thinking has never been wholly at ease with the claims of the liberal democratic order. It also jars with more holistic Asian (especially East Asian) understandings of the roles and obligations of human beings. Indeed, Christian movements in East Asia – which are some of the most extraordinary examples of entirely peaceful new

17

religious growth, without any imperial compulsion or support, since the early era of Christian expansion in the Roman Empire and of Buddhism in China – sit much more comfortably with the modern Confucian ethos propagated by China than their Western brothers and sisters usually recognize.

All this points to an uncomfortable possibility: *that there may be cultural differences deep enough to put in question whether there are universal ideas or values at all.*

This, in turn, reminds us of something else: the endurance of nationhood as a force in human lives, as we will see in Chapter 4, and the cultural nationalism that is indeed sweeping across Eurasia in our time, which we will explore further in Chapter 5. China's Communist Party is, in fact, a motherland party and no one can overlook the assertive patriotism on the streets and in the social media of modern China. Russia's Putin is consciously playing the role of tsar and seeking to base the modern Russian identity on older but still recognizable foundations laid by Ivan the Terrible, Peter the Great and Catherine the Great. Meanwhile, Turkey under Erdogan and India's Bharatiya Janata Party (BJP) – for all their obvious differences – represent strikingly similar projects. They both aim to dismantle the secularizing principles on which their states were founded. Erdogan has sought to take Turkey back to its Islamic and Ottoman roots; the BJP wants India to assert its ancient Hindu traditions as its dominant identity. The one is taking on Kemal Atatürk; the other is taking on Jawaharlal Nehru. Last, but not least – in view of its economic weight and technological sophistication – Japan has always had a more nationalistic streak in its identity than is usually recognized by others (except by the Chinese, for whom the Japanese remain far too unwilling to come to terms with their actions during the Second World War).

And what of Europe? Europe is rare among Eurasian cultures in nurturing claims about universal values that it sees as the standards by which its own behaviour *and that of all other cultures* should be judged. It no longer sees itself in imperial mode, of course. It has never fully recovered from the disasters it inflicted on itself; it is older, chastened and determined to learn the lessons of its own terrible past. The last thing it wants to do is slide back into the nationalist nightmare, but it is profoundly unsettled about its identity. Indeed, does it indeed have a shared identity at all? If so, is it not based on principles worked through painstakingly from the eighteenth century onwards: a commitment to rationalism, democracy, individual rights and responsibilities, the rule of law, social compassion and so forth? If so, then are those principles not universal? Those principles are, in fact, subject to increasing challenge, not just from Asian voices but also even from within Europe itself: populists raise the spectre of mass Muslim immigration from Europe's chaotic hinterland and call for protection of what they see as Europe's ancient identity. More thoughtful critics raise the question of whether or not Europe can ever be true to its identity if it consistently refuses to recognize its past as Christendom and if it insists on deifying the Enlightenment. As a result, it is perhaps not surprising that Europe seems to lack either confidence or courage in its convictions; and it certainly lacks the cohesion to promote its world view effectively and energetically.

All of this highlights the vulnerabilities among the increasingly connected – yet perhaps also increasingly divergent – identities on the continent of Eurasia. And if this were all there is to be said about the next hundred years, it would not augur well. As noted, the Westphalian parallel is not a reassuring one. What might still be hoped for, and worked for, would be painstaking consensus on matters of shared interest – on the environment and climate change, on scarce natural resources, on international terrorism and on nuclear non-proliferation. These are not trivial gains, of course. Nevertheless, this would suggest that, at least for the foreseeable future – for the next century, let's say – we would be approaching some limit to the human journey of self-discovery through encounter with others. And we would be reaching that limit at a potentially dangerous moment in history.

A contest of world views and values?

We are, in fact, on the threshold of an era that will see two different perspectives on the human self-understanding contest for legitimacy on the world stage. They are, in effect, the world views, and the deeply rooted instincts, of the two great powers that will dominate the Eurasian, and world, stage for the rest of this century: America and China.

The American world view sets the inalienable subjectivity of the self at its core. It came originally from Europe and it lies at the root of the borderless idea of liberal democracy; it is what is encapsulated in those great watchwords of the founders of America: life, liberty and the pursuit of happiness. This, in turn, is a reminder that, despite all the doubts about, and philosophical challenges to, the liberal democratic consensus during the last ten years or so, we are dealing with a view of human identity that was not just the invention of Adam Smith but rather, is deeply rooted in the European exploration of the nature of the human self. By contrast, the great alternative on the world stage of this century – the Confucian culture that is the bedrock of the Chinese world view – is not primarily focused on the autonomy of the self. It sees the individual in a wider familial, social and even cosmic context, so it has much to say about the purposes and obligations of life, as we shall see in Chapter 3. The great question that matters to us all is how can those two world views, each of which has a very long trail of history behind it, be dovetailed into some kind of a synthesis over the course of this century? This question matters for the peace of nations; it matters for successful economic and social development; and it matters for the sustainability of life on our fragile planet.

Since China's evolving world view and self-understanding are less familiar than America's, we need first to look at the road China has been on in recent years, which has brought it to that point. Thirty years ago, in the early stages of opening up, Deng Xiaoping famously said that China should hide its capacity internationally, that it should bide its time, that it should be good at maintaining a low profile and should never claim leadership. This was Deng Xiaoping's China in the 1990s. As time moved on, that position began to shift. China spoke of taking a more active role in international affairs and working to make the international order more just and equitable. Specifically, China spoke of recognizing a 'community of common destiny' in its regional neighbourhood. In 2014, Xi Jinping took the next step forward when he spoke, not merely of recognizing China's neighbourhood as a community of common destiny but also of turning it into one. Then, in 2017, he began to speak on the international stage of working together to build a 'community of shared future' for all humankind.[7]

In other words, this was China's foreign policy going global. It is certainly not a detailed blueprint for how China plans to act internationally over the coming decades, but it is, to use a business school cliché, a vision statement – something of a statement of purpose in terms of the way in which China intends to engage over the next generation. In his speech, Xi Jinping conjured up the promise of 'an open, inclusive, clean and beautiful world that enjoys lasting peace, universal security, and common prosperity'. We should not overlook how he articulated that general vision: he talked about the need for countries to respect one another and discuss their issues as equals; he spoke of the need to promote trade and investment and grow international connectivity through business relationships; and he spoke of the importance of recognizing and respecting the diversity of civilizations, with 'estrangement replaced by exchange, clashes by mutual learning, and superiority by coexistence'. It is worth savouring some of those words. The reference to diversity of civilizations and clashes deliberately calls to mind Samuel Huntington's famous book *The Clash of Civilizations*, which we will come back to in Chapter 6.[8] The crucial point to notice here is that China's newly articulated vision is fundamentally national and societal rather than individual. The actors in its version of the drama are countries; the vision is not of an emerging global citizenship of individuals. Its starting point is Confucius, not Locke (and is also certainly more Confucius than Marx). The contrast with the strong individualist instinct that underlies the American view of the world is unmistakable.

This is sometimes seen as the great debate between America and China – or between East and West – about the individual and the collective. But the issue is much deeper than that, for the individual has, of course, always been significant in all human cultures. We may have little idea of the self-awareness of individuals in the communities who painted the walls of Eurasian caves forty millennia ago. For most of history, the vast majority of humans have left no record of their feelings, but human beings have never seen themselves just as soldier ants. Even in the most structured hierarchies, where slaves had no rights and women had few, humans have always been individual selves. They have had names, they have places in the order of things, they have known about their mortality and, indeed, through most of history, humans have prepared for some form of afterlife.

21

The individual's place in the order of things

As a result, the metaphysics of all Eurasian cultures have explored the place of the individual human soul or spirit in the scheme of things. There are three major dimensions of difference. First, between those metaphysics (largely Indian in origin) that presume transmigration of the soul and those which do not (including Confucianism, all three Abrahamic faiths and all mainstream modern post-Enlightenment thought). Second, there is the difference between those that see the human self as an initiating ego with a degree of autonomy (as does most Western thought as well as Confucianism) and those – most venerably in some of the most ancient streams of Buddhist thought, but also in some modern Western schools of philosophy – that see consciousness as reducible to a bundle of perceptions, such that the self is basically illusory. And third, there is a difference between those metaphysical approaches that see the individual as the primary subject, such that all relationships are viewed from the subject's perspective (typically the Western approach, and fundamental to the American self-understanding) and those which see the individual primarily from the perspective of the whole (which is the essence of the Confucian world view).

However, metaphysical musing about the soul is not the same as the exploration of the living self. It is in art and literature that humanity has always explored its actual experience of being – in all its life, its joys, its loves, its losses, its hurts and its transience. The creativity this has called forth is to be found all through Eurasian culture and down the ages from very early times. There are many differences in specific contexts and perspective, of course, but some of the greatest achievements of Eurasian creativity have a strange universality and timelessness about them – as we shall see in Chapter 7. These achievements deal with human experience in a way that reminds us of what we all share because we are all descended from those same human ancestors of forty thousand years ago.

There are other commonalities too. The human religious instinct to explain, and perhaps control, the unknown and mysterious also manifests itself again and again across cultures and down the ages. It is born of a belief that we are part of a natural order of things that we only partly understand. The sense of enchantment – the sense the natural world is our spiritual home – is ancient and pervasive. That is the instinct of both Chinese Daoism and of traditional Japanese Shinto, and in both China and Japan it continues to live on in strength in the modern era. It has a long pedigree in the Christian, Muslim and Hindu worlds too. Much later in human history, the European Romantic instinct of the nineteenth century is its descendant. Modern post-industrial urbanism has by no means wholly abolished the fear of spirits and has added, especially for the intelligentsia, a yearning for the lost paradise.

In fact, one way or another, all the major Eurasian cultures have exhibited a continued yearning for the transcendent, expressed through mysticism and/or ritual. That sense of the One beyond/within the many – of our Oneness with the Being of the cosmos – has been manifested in every culture: Christian, Muslim, Chinese, Indian (though the Japanese stand out as different in this respect as in so many others). Mysticism is a (mostly) individual journey inwards and upwards, rather than outwards. It is evidenced in such key figures as St John of the Cross (and many others in the Christian tradition, both European and Russian), Rumi (and many others in Islam) and Zhuangzi in China. But the Indians are the masters of the cosmic consciousness: from the *Rig Veda* onwards, through all the endless cycles of *karma* and *dharma*, the pursuit of *moksha*, or absorption into the One, has been quite extraordinarily diverse and colourful. This theme has some resonances in European, Russian and Muslim thought too, but it never became the dominant mode of speculation or worship in either Christianity or Islam, and even less so in the Chinese and Japanese thought worlds.

Will the instinct for mysticism survive in an urbanized modernity? Perhaps only for a small minority. Probably more durable is the human religious instinct for ritual – the reverence of the sacred, expressed through symbolic actions and words. Manifest, again, in every culture down to the present day – Chinese, Islamic, Hindu, Christian (and, in this case, definitely including the Japanese) – it lies at the heart of Islam and Judaism in particular. Also, more so than mysticism, this instinct may well survive the impact of urbanization, not least as a psychological or spiritual mark of identity.

Finally, there is the instinct for self-discovery and self-assertion. For many in all cultures, this may amount to little more than a defiant indulgence, an Epicurean equation of happiness with pleasure, but for some, it is more than that: it is an existentialist assertion of the significance of the individual in action. In the post-medieval European context, this became the journey from Milton's Satan through Goethe's Faust to Nietzsche. In the Buddhist East, this was the strange journey from the Four Noble Truths through the Chan Buddhism of China to the Zen of the Japanese samurai. It is always potentially a dangerous option, taken explicitly only by a few but implicitly by many, wherever power is in play (especially in commerce and politics?)

Patterns of history?

In our unending search to express the human experience, we will continue to become ever more aware of how much we share such instincts as human beings across cultures. The question is: does all this mean that the human journey of self-discovery will continue? Does this mean that, in the end, there can be no enduring Westphalian stasis? Is there, in fact, a direction of travel – even if the journey ahead is long, just as the journey so far has been?

Down the ages, of course, people have tried to discern patterns and even purpose in history – from the early Christian conviction that they were living in the last days, through Chinese millenarian movements of Buddhist (and, later, Christian) inspiration, to Shia Muslim beliefs in the secret Imam to be revealed in due time, to the medieval Christian mystic Joachim of Fiore and his three ages of history, to the most enduringly influential of them all: Hegel. His concept of Absolute Spirit realizing itself in the struggles of history was radically transformed by Marx, then surfaced in mutated form again in Mao's thought, as we shall see in Chapter 9. Even the liberal democratic order has centred on a belief in individuality and progress that implies a direction of travel in history. It expects there to be roadblocks and wrong turnings, just as there have always been. But it presumes that the direction cannot be reversed, that the potential for growth is limitless, that we may never in practice reach a point of satiation, but that it will not be possible to settle where we are.

The question is, are there indeed patterns in history that justify the narrative of a human journey – an odyssey which, for all its twists and turns, is a journey of learning and growth – towards maturity? Such journeys of exploration do not have a precise and predetermined destination and are not guaranteed success. Is this, in fact, the deep story of what is under way over the next century? We know that such journeys can be painful; but we also know that, as long as we keep on going, they are always fruitful. The essentials are basically the same for individuals, for societies, for cultures, for nations and, in fact, for any form of human identity. We also know what they are: coming to terms with our pasts; taking responsibility for what we are and do; looking for the human in the other; and always looking to learn. In no case is the journey ever quite over; in no case have we arrived. In many cases, the individual cannot face the trials involved; in many cases too the state – or the *demos* – may seek to control or impede the journey. Indeed, such controlling or blocking behaviour is widespread, as we know all too well, but the question is, will such resistance, in the end, succeed or fail? Will the journey of exploration continue – for each one of us, for all the wider identities we are part of, and for humanity as a whole?

But that is to get ahead of ourselves. We first need to explore the human condition as it is revealed in the Eurasia of the early twenty-first century. To do that, we need to begin by looking at what is by far the most fundamental change in the human condition to have swept through the continent since the time of the Mongols. Beginning around two hundred years ago, picking up momentum in the last century, and now gaining the force of a whirlwind, this change is altering our physical environment, our societies and our individual consciousness. The next chapter looks at the phenomenon that has changed – and will continue to change – our very experience of existence: urbanization.

2

Cities: immediacy, connectivity, freedom, alienation – and identity?

I remember standing at the border fence separating Hong Kong from the Chinese mainland in 1984. At that time, Hong Kong was Britain's last significant colonial outpost, but the moment when it would have to hand it back to China was nearing, as the lease on most of its territory ran out in 1997. Hong Kong was already a vibrant modern city, growing fast but anxious about its political future. It was one of the densest urban environments on the planet.

The view from the border fence was into a different world. Most of the flat landscape was covered with duck farms and paddy fields. In the middle distance you could see the small sleepy town of Shenzhen, home to about twenty thousand people.

Shenzhen is now – less then forty years later – a city of ten million. With its huge boulevards, massive skyscrapers, a world-class technology infrastructure, and an economy that is as sophisticated and successful as anywhere on the planet, Shenzhen is the modern face of China. It is larger and growing faster than present-day Hong Kong and exuberantly self-confident. There is still a border, but looking across towards Hong Kong from the top floor of one of its luxurious hotels, it can be hard to see where that border is. Driving from Shenzhen to Hong Kong, you know you have crossed from one to the other mainly because everything in Shenzhen looks that much newer, because the traffic signs in Hong Kong are all in English and in old-style Chinese characters, not in the new, simplified ones familiar to the mainland – and because Hong Kong drives on the left, not on the right.

The urban transformation of Shenzhen is one of the most dramatic anywhere. It was aided by deliberate Chinese policy and by the proximity of Hong Kong, whose entrepreneurs were its most important source of capital in the early stages of its opening up.

There are other examples, no less extraordinary. In that same year when I stood at the border fence between Hong Kong and Shenzhen, I also paid my first visit to Dubai. At that time, Dubai was a small, traditional Arab creek town, much of it still consisting of single-storey mudbrick dwellings with their characteristic towers designed to catch the breeze and cool the interior. There was one single tall building, the ambitiously named World Trade Centre, and it stood out in the desert, looking like the perfect example of a white elephant. Nowadays, the World Trade Centre is still there, but it is dwarfed by the hundreds of newer skyscrapers that make up what has become one of the world's best-known urban skylines.

Shenzhen and Dubai are two of the most successful urban transformations of the last few decades, but there are hundreds of others. Urbanization is the visible sign of the fundamental change in most people's lives compared with those of their parents and grandparents. In fact, it is the most important change in human experience since the move from nomadic pastoralism to life in settled agricultural communities. With virtually no exceptions, urbanization is changing people in every continent. But because Eurasia is home to most of the world's cities, and all of its oldest ones, cities have played a dominant role in the history of Eurasian cultures and hence in the development of the world's cultural life. The evolution of Eurasia's cities reflects the journey of the human spirit.

To appreciate the extraordinary significance of urbanization for developments in the human sense of identity and for the journey of the human spirit that lies ahead, we need to look first at the raw facts; then at the social and political role of cities as they have evolved over the centuries; and finally at their psychological and spiritual impact on human experience.

The facts, to begin with, can be baldly summarized in statistical terms. The year 2008 was when humanity passed a major milestone: more than fifty per cent of the entire global population now lives in cities. In 1850, only two or three cities had populations exceeding one million. Now there are more than a thousand. There are at least twenty-five cities with populations of more than ten million, and at least ten with populations of more than twenty million. The total global population of cities is around four billion, or 55 per cent of the world's total population. By the year 2050 – in less time from now than it took Shenzhen to transform itself from the small town surrounded by duck farms into today's huge metropolis – the world's urban population will have risen to around 6.5 billion. That increase represents more than the entire population of the world at the end of the Second World War. It will also be more than the total world population growth over the same time frame. By 2050, 65 per cent of all humanity will be living in cities. Well over half of that growth will have taken place in the newer Eurasian economies: very few cities in developed countries will show any growth at all.[1]

The transition from an agricultural to an urban economy has had dramatic consequences for society and for human life experience everywhere. In fact, there are no known exceptions to the rule that development and modernization is associated with urbanization. Britain in the nineteenth century was the first country to embark on this change. In 1800, up to 80 per cent of its population lived and worked on the land. By 1881, that percentage had already shrunk to about 25 per cent. Now, some 90 per cent of Britons live in towns and cities; only just over one in a hundred is employed in agriculture (and the pattern is similar in other major European economies; even in France with its famously powerful agricultural lobby, fewer than 3 per cent of the population actually work in the sector).[2] The folk memories of rural life may persist; but the reality has largely disappeared for the vast majority. Japan shifted equally radically from a largely rural to an overwhelmingly urban profile over the century or so from the Meiji Restoration in 1868. By now, fewer than 6 per cent of Japanese jobs are in the rural economy. Russia achieved the same transition, only even faster, by very different means. Forced industrialization and the brutal collectivization of agriculture – begun by Lenin, tempered for a while in the 1920s, and then accelerated under Stalin – brought about the same huge shift as in Britain, in just thirty years.

China, India and other Eurasian countries are on the same journey of rural to urban migration. They have some way to go, but the pattern is familiar. In China, the urban population is rising towards 60 per cent. Already, the countryside is dotted with villages denuded of their working people, inhabited by the old and the very young. The drift to the cities will continue for at least another generation and will involve at least another two hundred million people. India has further to go on this journey, with an urban population in the early twenty-first century of less than 40 per cent. Throughout India, rural overpopulation is obvious even to casual observation; and over the next few decades, all India's cities will continue to expand inexorably. But in contrast with China, which has more effective means of managing and controlling the change (such that there are no visible slums in Chinese cities), India's urban growth is to a large extent unplanned and uncontrolled. As a result, few Indian cities are adequately prepared for the influx; slums proliferate in and around the big conurbations; infrastructure is poor; and pollution and filth are pervasive.[3]

The Indian experience is neither exceptional nor wholly new. No country's journey of urbanization is identical to any other country's – there are too many specifics about history, economics, governance and demographics that affect each country's experience. But there are certain underlying commonalities too: the pattern of change in modern Indian cities is not so different from what happened – as described in graphic and moving detail by Friedrich Engels – in Manchester in the 1850s.[4] The pollution that bedevils Chinese and Indian cities used to blacken the buildings of Paris and London, and made the air unsafe to breathe in Tokyo. We forget too easily what earlier generations had to endure, just as we also forget the rampant poverty and insecurity of rural life, which have so often driven people to seek a better life in the cities.

In fact, cities have always been a magnet for human beings, from ancient times. The Eurasian land mass is dotted with sites of the very earliest urban communities. Some are now nothing more than traces in the landscape, silent ruins yielding their secrets only to patient arch-aeological investigation. Others are still cities today, with the remains of antiquity buried beneath the bustle of modernity (and in some cases be-neath the horrors of violent modern conflict). Mohenjo-daro, the ancient citadel of the Harappan civilization in the Indus Valley, was a planned city built well over four thousand years ago in brick on a grid system, with public buildings, drainage facilities and a central market place. Its scale and sophistication are extraordinary for its age. Little is known about its people: their city went into an apparently rapid decline some four thousand years ago, and they remain one of the enigmas of history.

Other ancient sites have lived on, though, to tell more continuous stories of human achievement and destruction. Aleppo and Damascus, for example, both of which have suffered terribly in Syria's brutal civil war, are two of the world's oldest continuously inhabited cities. Their histories are layers of political, commercial and cultural change, all the way down to the tragedies and upheavals of the twenty-first century. Rayy, now a suburb of Tehran, is almost as old as these Syrian sites: Neolithic pottery as well as fortifications dating back to the time of the Medes tell a story of thousands of years of human endeavour and strife. Luoyang – one of the ancient capitals of China and one of the earliest centres of Chinese Buddhism – has been continuously inhabited since Neolithic times and is at least four thousand years old as a city. Varanasi is India's oldest (as well as most sacred) city. This huge, sprawling city on the holy Ganges river is at least three thousand years old, and Hindu legend has it as much older than that.

All these cities, and the many others that became major centres of human civilization before the premodern era, were situated in geographically prominent positions, for strategic control of a region and/or for ease of trade and communication. They were designed to dominate the surrounding country or to control river traffic. They were from the earliest times (as is clear from the design of Mohenjo-daro) centres of power and of trade. Their rulers always faced two fundamental challenges: to maintain themselves in power against any contestant, whether internal or external, and to provide security for their inhabitants and for the surrounding country that fell under their sway and provided their food. That was their basic task; their reason for existence.

Many failed. Eurasian history is laced with the tragedies of cities overwhelmed and laid to waste by outsiders who destroyed their architectural glories, seized their treasure, defaced their images, burnt their books and slaughtered, raped and enslaved their people. Sometimes the violence was motivated at least in part by a ruthless quest for booty, as were Mahmud of Ghazni's notorious campaigns at the turn of the first millennium in northern India (which may have been the *coup de grâce* to an already declining Indian Buddhism – of which more later). Sometimes, it was a coolly calculated and methodically executed strategy to set a completely devastating example to any other victims tempted to resist.

The past masters of such behaviour were the Mongols, who were known to wait around near the ruins of a city they had razed, so as to finish off survivors days later as they emerged from their hiding places.[5] From Jerusalem in 587 BCE, to Persepolis in 330 BCE, to Luoyang in 189 CE, to Nalanda in 1193, to Baghdad in 1258, to Delhi in 1398, to Magdeburg in Germany in the depths of Europe's Thirty Years War, and on through right into the modern era, one urban cultural centre after another fell to this perennial human lust for destruction.

There is surely nothing more heart-rending than the accounts down the ages of the fall of great cities. From the oldest stories onwards, they stir and trouble the imagination, precisely because everyone from the ruler to the poorest slave, from the hero to the most hapless child, is caught up in the horror. Whatever our life conditions, we can imagine ourselves somewhere in the midst of it all. The stories conjure up in us the same sense of human anguish – of heroism, venality, betrayal, grief, anger, fear and, in general, the pity of it all. Some are told in unforgettable poetry, some in laconic prose, some in methodical detail: the fall of Troy in the *Iliad*; the fall of Jerusalem in the book of Jeremiah;[6] the forced evacuation and burning of Luoyang in *The Romance of the Three Kingdoms*;[7] the fall of Baghdad to the Mongols in the account by the Iranian historian Rashid al-Din;[8] the fall of Constantinople in Runciman's classic narrative;[9] and the sack of Magdeburg in Schiller's essay on the Thirty Years War.[10] There are also compelling visual images: the sack of Vladimir by the Mongols as unforgettably envisaged in Tarkovsky's film portrayal of the icon painter Andrei Rublev; the real images of the Russian conquest of a shattered Berlin in 1945; or the fall of Phnom Penh in 1975.

Cities and the human spirit

The very fact that these disasters have become part of the nightmarish folklore of Eurasia reminds us of something profoundly important about cities and their role in human development. It is precisely because of the essential role of cities in the cultivation of the human spirit that the many stories of their destruction throughout Eurasia are so numbing. Because they were centres of power and trade, cities became wealthy; and the wealth made possible the cultural life that always emerges where there is enough stability and enough economic surplus to support a creative intellectual life. Hence cities became centres of culture in every civilization; of a community life that produced religious and civic architecture of spellbinding beauty; of learning and the precious books which cultivated the human spirit; as well as of popular human expression through dance, poetry and theatre. In fact, it is probably the case that in times of stability, cities have seemed to have more in common with one another than with their rural hinterland.[11]

When a city died, all this was so easily lost too, alongside the countless human lives. There were indeed immeasurable losses, and the ruins still visible today of such great centres of human splendour and creativity as Merv and Nishapur give us a poignant glimpse of what has gone. But the story is nevertheless one about survival and renewal, not just about waste and destruction. Totemically, Aeneas emerges from the burning ruins of Troy, carrying his old father Anchises on his back, and heading out to sea on a new journey that takes him to Latium in Italy, where he founds the eternal city of Rome. This completely fictitious myth by the great Roman poet Virgil serves to remind us that the story of human cultural creativity is never finished. (It also served to explain the destruction of another great city – Carthage – in terms more elevated and more moving than simply as a narrative of all-out war to the death between two competing Mediterranean powers.)

It was true for Islam too. The fall of Baghdad to the Mongols in 1258 was not the end of the glories of Islamic culture, whose centre of gravity had already been shifting away from Baghdad as the Abbasid Caliphate gradually lost its ability to control its vast domains. Particularly in the Shia world of Iran, there was more philosophy to come – as well as some of the greatest poetry the world has ever known – in the centuries after the demise of Abbasid Baghdad. In India, there was more to come too. The Mughals would, in later centuries, make their majestic impact on the architecture of the great North Indian cities, as well as nurturing the graceful Persian/Indian miniaturist art that entranced the more discerning European travellers from the seventeenth century onwards. Later too, Constantinople was to have a second life as the centre of a great Islamic empire. Adorned by the spectacular beauties of Ottoman architecture, it became a magnet for people from all round the Middle East, the Black Sea and the eastern Mediterranean.

China's story is different in specifics, but the overall theme is the same. China's ancient cities were repeatedly sacked and burned during the centuries of weak central control between the Han and the Tang dynasties and between the Tang and the Song, and then again at the hands of the Mongols; but the civilization with its enduring Confucian sense of order lived on through it all because of its endless – and very urban – propensity to write things down. In short, throughout Eurasia the destruction was repeated and widespread, but it was never enough to bring city life and human cultural development generally to a stop.

Even the Mongols, in fact, had a constructive vision, despite their dreadful reputation. Genghis Khan's historic mission was to bring peace and unity to the world by extending Mongol domination in all directions (even if they were also interested in booty to adorn their tented palaces and to clothe themselves in silk). His sense of authority was born of a shamanistic belief in the divine sky – the Eternal Heaven – giving him strength and protection, as well as the mandate to rule all under heaven (a Chinese idea that he may well have gained from Chinese advisers to his court).[12] For him and his sons, this vision meant global domination. They carried out that mission with a fearsome thoroughness and destructiveness which has become legendary. But the broader truth is that the *pax mongolorum* led to renewal of urban life all over Eurasia and, indeed, to their own absorption into the very civilizations they had savaged on their mission to rule all under heaven. Recent scholarship has brought to light the extent of the involvement by Mongol rulers in the details of administration in their sprawling domains.[13] It was their traditional way of life, on the vast steppe between the sky god and the earth, that faded into insignificance, not the urban life. The urban life was the primary locus of all human spiritual and cultural development.

By the time of the next (and last) great horse-borne military explosion in Eurasia – that of Timur (Tamburlaine) almost two centuries after Genghis Khan – the ferocity was still there, but this was a leader who presented himself as from within the civilized world of Islam. He styled himself as the Sword of Islam, dedicated to strengthening and politically unifying the Muslim *ummah*. He saw himself as a determined patron of arts and learning. He met, and recognized the importance of, the brilliant Arab historian and historiographer Ibn Khaldun; and he is said to have engaged in the sort of repartee with the great Iranian poet Hafez that Shakespeare attributes to Henry V, as a way to demonstrate his wit and humanity. He was the grandfather of Ulugh Beg, sultan, astronomer and mathematician, who ruled in Central Asia in the early fifteenth century and built Samarkand and Bukhara into great centres of learning; and his great-great-great grandson Babur founded the glorious Mughal empire in northern India in the early sixteenth century.

In short, for all the upheaval and the horrendous loss of life, the threads of human cultural development continued to be woven across the urban centres of Eurasia.

For cities have never been just agglomerations of people. Up until the last two centuries, only a small minority of people lived in cities; yet such cities have always been home to the vast preponderance of human cultural and creative activity. Indeed, several of the great religious movements and metaphysical systems that have deeply imbued all the major cultures of today's Eurasia have their origins in urban life experience. Buddhism, Christianity and Islam all have urban roots, and so does Chinese Confucianism. Even the learning facilitated by the monasteries of the Christian Middle Ages in Europe, and of Buddhism as it spread from India into China and Japan, was closely dependent on urban connections for its nurture and dissemination. Cities, in other words, were where the human spirit made its greatest strides. It is no coincidence, for example, that the three great thinkers of the high Middle Ages who were the paramount influences on the intellectual frameworks of Islam, China and European Christianity respectively – al-Ghazali, Zhu Xi and Thomas Aquinas (all of whom we will consider later) – were each subject to the magnetic field of the great urban centres of their times (in fact, in one way or another all three found this relationship with urban power difficult, even potentially dangerous).

That intellectual life was further enriched by the connections that trade brought to the cities, as, along with the precious goods from afar, came inspiration. Thus, Buddhism filtered into China along the Silk Road and gained its foothold in Chinese culture through patronage by the Eastern Han court in Luoyang in the first century of the Common Era. On its way into China, Buddhism may have been influenced by Iranian patterns of thought that brought to it a new symbolism of light and luminosity;[14] Classical Greek thought – including especially its geometry, geography, medicine and philosophy – was taken boldly into the Islamic world on an almost industrial scale by the so-called translation movement based in Abbasid Baghdad, which was becoming the centre of a vast trading nexus throughout the *ummah* and beyond from the late eighth century onwards. Indian mathematics penetrated the Islamic thought world over broadly the same timeframe, and thence found its way to the European and Chinese worlds. And the thought world of Christian Europe was opened to the fruits of Islamic intellectual work on its own lost Classical Greek inheritance through another translation effort – this time from Arabic into Latin – made possible by the Christian conquest of Toledo in 1085. This was an important impetus to a new ferment of intellectual life in Europe, which saw the founding of Europe's first universities, most of them in cities that were prospering from the development of trade connections. This new ferment marked the early stage of a spiritual re-birth we have come to call the Renaissance, the later confluence of which with the Reformation created the great incoming tide of the modern era, which, in turn, was to change not just Europe but the whole of Eurasia and the wider world in the nineteenth and twentieth centuries.

Indeed, in many of Eurasia's cultures, visions of perfection were visions of the city. For Virgil and Ovid, Rome was the eternal city – and the name has stuck to this day. In Christian imagery, the story of salvation is one that takes human beings from the Garden of Eden to a New Jerusalem described in vivid and mystical colours in the book of Revelation:

> And I saw the holy city, the new Jerusalem, coming down out of heaven from God, prepared as a bride adorned for her husband. And I heard a loud voice from the throne saying, 'See, the home of God is among mortals. He will dwell with them; they will be his peoples, and God himself will be with them; he will wipe every tear from their eyes. Death will be no more; mourning and crying and pain will be no more, for the first things have passed away.' . . . The city lies foursquare, its length the same as its width . . . The wall is

built of jasper, while the city is pure gold, clear as glass . . . I saw no temple in the city, for its temple is the Lord God the Almighty and the Lamb. And the city has no need of sun or moon to shine on it, for the glory of God is its light, and its lamp is the Lamb . . . Its gates will never be shut by day – and there will be no night there.[15]

Augustine's monumental and hugely influential *De Civitate Dei* (*The City of God*) sees the whole of human history as a universal struggle between good and evil, expressed in terms of a great conflict between the City of God and the Earthly City. It ends with an overwhelming sense of the full, finally undiluted bliss of the heavenly city, which he describes, however, not in physical imagery but in terms of the transformed experience of the blessed souls who come to experience it. Some of what he says almost sounds like a description of the ideal secular city of a much more recent thought world, when he writes, for example, of a city 'where there will be no inactivity or idleness and yet no toil compelled by want', where there will be 'no distinctions of honour and glory', and where 'there will be freedom of will – one and the same freedom in all'.[16]

The Chinese, characteristically, have a more earthly – even prosaic – image; it is of existing city life, not of some future utopia, but it is an image of urban splendour nonetheless. For them, the quintessence of the civilized urban scene was the famous scroll painting, created sometime in the early twelfth century during the Northern Song Dynasty, of the Qingming festival at Kaifeng, which was then the capital of the dynasty. It shows the city set in its surrounding countryside, a hive of activity, crowded with people from all social strata – scholars, monks, fortune tellers, beggars, innkeepers and shop workers. Strikingly, although this is the festival when all Chinese families were supposed to visit and tend their family graves, there is no sense of the sacred or sombre about the painting. In fact, there is no more sense of the other-worldly about this scene than there would be on a British urban high street on a present-day Easter Sunday. But the significance of the painting is complex. Although it seems like a depiction of Confucian social perfection, the centre of the scene shows a boat heading towards the bridge without having lowered its mast and in danger of crashing; watchers on the bridge are gesturing frantically and lowering a rope to the crew. It is not clear how this should be interpreted but it may well be a parable of how onlookers should behave when others are seen to be in trouble. If so, it is an echo of the teaching of that most humanist of the great Chinese sages, Mencius. A later (and less interesting) Ming Dynasty copy of the painting shows the boat being guided carefully and safely under a taller bridge – thus removing the element of drama and the implied sermon on civic duty.

Seven hundred years later, Wordsworth extols the beauty of a London as yet untransformed by nineteenth-century modernity in his famous sonnet 'Composed upon Westminster Bridge':

> Earth has not anything to show more fair:
> Dull would he be of soul who could pass by
> A sight so touching in its majesty:
> This city now doth, like a garment wear
> The beauty of the morning; silent, bare,
> Ships, towers, domes, theatres and temples lie
> Open unto the fields, and to the sky;
> All bright and glittering in the smokeless air . . .[17]

Wordsworth wrote these lines in 1802, just before the impact of the Industrial Revolution was beginning to make itself evident in the physical appearance of cities. Half a century later, the scene would not have been open to the fields, nor bright and glittering in the smokeless air. As the world moved from the pre-modern to the industrial era, so the nature of cities and the experience of city life changed. Cities were centres of regional or national power and of trade. Inevitably, therefore, they were also the main sources of both tax revenue and financial credit.[18] They became the centres of a new manufacturing industry that changed the pattern of work, killed off craft industries, pulled people off the land, radically altered the physical shape and appearance of many existing cities, and spawned whole new ones. Birmingham, Essen and Shanghai are all the creations of this period; none had a population of more than about five thousand before the nineteenth century. In Britain first, then in Germany and other European countries, in America and in Japan, and even in notoriously backward Russia, industrial city life became the reality for more and more people. Ways of life that had endured for centuries

37

in small rural hamlets were lost within a generation, as people moved from the relatively open and small-scale life of agriculture to the much more regimented and controlled existence that was factory labour. The factory with its chimney stacks belching smoke and fumes into the city air became a new icon. Its very ugliness came to have a certain fascination for both writers and artists (such as Dickens, Zola, the French Impressionists and L. S. Lowry).

The rise of the bourgeoisie and the proletariat

The resulting emergence on the social stage of two new groups – or classes – of people, the bourgeois and the workers, fundamentally shifted the balance of power, radically altered city life, and thus brought into focus entirely new themes for cultural expression.

The European bourgeoisie owed the beginnings of its pre-eminence to the trade that had been burgeoning even in the high Middle Ages, but particularly from the sixteenth century onwards. Wherever political conditions favoured commercial enterprise – especially, as that perceptive observer Montesquieu noted in the early eighteenth century,[19] in the Dutch Republic and in an England that had begun the journey towards constitutional monarchy – the new class gained wealth and influence. In both countries, this new group was self-conscious. Its members were outward-looking, reared on a diet of austere and individualistic Protestantism (but which in many cases was already by Montesquieu's time morphing into deism under the impact of the Enlightenment); and they were enthused with the excitement of a new technical curiosity about their world. This was the time of Birmingham's lunar men (the dozen inquisitive minds who met at one another's homes once a month on the Sunday nearest the full moon – so that they could get home afterwards by the strong moonlight – to discuss scientific experiments). Such people were becoming the new urban elite; slowly but inevitably, the older ruling elites – the monarchy and the aristocracy – would have to allow them the freedom to flourish commercially and socially, perhaps even take on their outlook, or simply make way for them.

The rise of the bourgeoisie represented a challenge everywhere in

Eurasia. Traders had traditionally held a lower social status than the warriors who became the great landholders and the clerical orders who controlled education and the culture. In India, for instance, the priestly caste and the warrior caste – the Brahmins and the Kshatriyas – dominated the caste system throughout history (and have by no means yet lost all their disproportionate influence even today). The Vaishyas – the skilled traders and merchants – were the next layer down, above only the Shudras, the unskilled workers. In Confucian China, the trader was the subject of patronizing disapproval by the bureaucracy and could never be considered a sage. In Islam, the picture is complicated by the fact that the original Arab momentum behind the expansion of the *ummah* was provided by a group of traders; but this did not in the end prevent the cultural domination of Muslim societies by dynastically inclined absolute rulers, by their bureaucracies and their military, and by an increasingly powerful clerical class. In Japan, again, the merchants were looked down on by the aristocracy and by the warrior class (the samurai). For all the obvious differences and historical contexts across these cultures, the similarity in the standing of traders everywhere in pre-modern Eurasia is very striking.

Only in parts of Europe where cities had, for complex historical reasons, enjoyed a degree of autonomy were commercial interests able to make social headway in the late Middle Ages.[20] In Italy, the contest between the Holy Roman Emperor and the Papacy for supremacy weakened both of them; as a result, some cities found themselves relatively free from central control, and well positioned to take advantage of Mediterranean trade flows. They grew rich, and their wealth became the economic base for the glories of the Renaissance. Some cities in Germany benefited in a similar way from weakness at the centre. The trading cities of the Hanseatic League were a proud example; they ran the trade across the Baltic Sea, again making themselves wealthy in the process. But in the end, it was the Atlantic that mattered more than either the Mediterranean or the Baltic (just as cities in Asia with easy access to the open ocean came to prosper at the expense of the inland trading cities of Central Asia[21]). French cities had never enjoyed the degree of autonomy needed for a vibrant trading mentality. Instead it was England and Holland whose cities seized this new opportunity. London had settled on arrangements with the Normans that gave it a high degree of autonomy right from the start in 1066; the vestiges survive to the present day in the pomp and circumstance surrounding the colourful office of the Lord Mayor. And the Dutch cities clustered around the mouth of the Rhine broke away from Habsburg overlordship in the sixteenth century, just as trade with the Far East was gaining significant momentum. Both countries saw the rapid emergence of a wealthy and confident bourgeoisie, whose influence in politics and in culture was to become increasingly dominant in the seventeenth and eighteenth centuries.

The power of the bourgeoisie, particularly in England, was growing because their very business was evolving, under the impact of industrialization. Where seventeenth-century entrepreneurs traded precious goods and delicacies across the oceans, the eighteenth century discovered the power of steam and began to make things. Capital had found a new use, nearer home. And it found its new intellectual champions: above all, Adam Smith, who set out the classic philosophy of the market, the division of labour and the famous invisible hand. Before his time, there had been little useful systematic thought in any of the world's principal cultural traditions about the role of economics in human societies. From Aristotle onwards in the European thought world, and from Confucius onwards in China, concepts of money, capital and productivity were rudimentary, naive and infected by the same moral stance that saw trade as demeaning to human worth. Money was barren – to use the Aristotelian conception – and the value of any object lay in the labour required to produce it. This in turn meant that traders (and lenders) who made profit without apparently having to labour for it attracted a degree of suspicion that fuelled the ancient and almost universal prejudice against them.

Smith never simply jettisoned the culturally widespread and deep-seated notion that value is determined by the human labour involved in production; but he certainly recognized its limitations in explaining actual economic activity in an increasingly mechanized world. Gradually, a new concept of value was established that is now such an intrinsic element in the way we think about the modern world, we no longer recognize its origins in the new urban industrial age that was then dawning. The change was, in fact, fundamental and had far-reaching implications for the modern human identity (as we shall see later). In the thought world ushered in by Smith, value is not somehow intrinsic in the nature of an object and the amount of labour required to produce it, but it is determined by the interaction of supply and demand through the mechanism of competition. Moreover, it became increasingly well understood that the value of inputs, and not just of outputs, was determined by the interaction of supply and demand; and that this applied, in an industrial world, to labour, to land and to machinery. The competitive market, which balanced supply and demand, was the arbiter that valued everything – including a person's work. Lastly, it was recognized that time had a cost, because no person's time is infinite: what is available now has a greater value than what is available later. Thus the concept of capital came into clear focus, enabling a common measure of value – determined by supply and demand – of all the different sorts of input (including land, labour and machinery) over the time required by a production process. This concept was the essential intellectual framework for the collectivized and mechanized work that the new technologies of the Industrial Revolution demanded.

And so the factory was born. The collectivization and mechanization of work in the factory was built on the principle of efficient division of labour, as memorably explained in the opening lines of the very first chapter of *The Wealth of Nations*:

A workman not educated to the business [of pin-making] which the division of labour has rendered a distinct trade, nor acquainted with the use of the machinery employed in it . . . , could scarce, perhaps, with his utmost industry, make one pin in a day, and certainly could not make twenty. But in the way in which this business is now carried on, not only the whole work is a peculiar trade, but it is divided into a number of branches, of which the greater part are likewise peculiar trades. One man draws out the wire; another straights it; a third cuts it; a fourth points it; a fifth grinds it at the top for receiving the head; to make the head requires two or three distinct operations; to put it on is a peculiar business; to whiten the pins is another; it is even a trade by itself to put them into the paper; and the important business of making a pin is, in this manner, divided into about eighteen distinct operations, which, in some manufactories, are all performed by distinct hands, though in others the same man will sometimes perform two or three of them. I have seen a small manufactory of this kind, where ten men only were employed, and where some of them consequently performed two or three distinct operations. But though they were very poor, and therefore but indifferently accommodated with the necessary machinery, they could, when they exerted themselves, make among them about twelve pounds of pins in a day.[22]

In other words, Adam Smith starts out on his revolutionary analysis with a very practical example – drawn from his own personal observation – of how enormous increases in productivity could be achieved by the factory. A complex interplay of push and pull factors moved more and more workers off the land and into factories built where steam power was readily available, which meant in turn that the factories clustered where coal and transport were easy to access.

And these factories brought a new urban working class into being. Much of the history of the nineteenth century in Britain, but also in France and in Germany, was to be about the way power relationships within society would have to adjust to accommodate the two new urban social groups – the capitalist bourgeoisie and the working class. The urban working class was to become for a century or so the largest group in the population, as the balance of the economy shifted from rural to urban industrial employment. The proletariat's struggle for the right to organize, and to achieve parliamentary representation, became a leitmotif of European politics in the nineteenth century. With their numerical superiority, the proletariat became what urban craftsmen, slaves and (above all) the peasantry had been for urban power elites from Roman and Chinese Han times onwards: essential but always potentially dangerous. In earlier times, the nightmare had been of urban mobs, slave rebellions or peasant uprisings (the latter in particular were a recurrent feature of European, Chinese and Japanese history). Now these fears were being replaced in Europe by the spectre of the proletariat.

At the same time, a German philosopher named Karl Marx evolved a new theory, which – through all the twists and turns of twentieth-century history – was to become a major metaphysical and ideological competitor of Smith's law of the market. Marx, unlike Smith, put the value of labour at the very centre of his system. He took over from Hegel the view that human beings release their essence through labour; and he saw human labour as the only true source of value. In the mechanized urban industrial world, the worker sells labour power to the capitalist, who in turn exploits that labour power as thoroughly as possible for profit. But the capitalist system is doomed to destruction by its own intense competitive dynamics; the rate of profit falls even as its exploitation of labour power becomes more aggressive. Eventually, it will collapse under the weight of its own contradictions. Marx identified the proletariat – the class whose labour power has been so ruthlessly exploited by the increasingly desperate capitalists – as the group destined to precipitate a new revolution. This revolution would in effect create a modern, materialist version of Augustine's City of God. It was to transform the whole of human experience: it would usher in nothing less than a new economy, a new society and a new and better human nature. We shall return to this later. Suffice it here to note that both the two great ideas about the human economic and social order, which were so radically to change the whole of Eurasia – the liberal market of Smith and the proletarian-led revolution of Marx – were born into and conditioned by the new urban context of European industrialization.

No other Eurasian culture shared for the first hundred years or so this new urban industrial experience. Mechanization and industrialization sat uneasily with the complacent, backward-looking Chinese Confucian order; Russia remained a vast, illiterate peasant society dominated by an autocratic conservatism reinforced by a subservient but culturally powerful Orthodox Church; India had run out of creative energy during the long and religiously conservative reign of the last of the powerful Mughals, Aurangzeb, before succumbing to British trading interests for which the country was both a source of supply for the lucrative tea trade and a large market for its manufactured goods; and most of Islam was under increasingly sclerotic autocratic rule, while the theology then in the ascendant in its thought world was every bit as backward-looking as the official Confucian ideology of China – and just as deeply suspicious of the European Enlightenment.

The Japanese exception

In one Eurasian culture, however, at the same time as the modern era was dawning in Europe, another new urban culture was being born that was not industrial, but nevertheless created the conditions for entry into modernity by a unique route. Japan in the Tokugawa era, which began at the start of the seventeenth century, might seem to have almost nothing in common with the Europe of the same era. After decades of feudal warfare, the Tokugawa Shogunate had established peace under a highly centralized regime that lasted for two and a half centuries. Where Europe was opening up and crossing the oceans, Tokugawa Japan was closing out foreign influence, particularly from Europe (although it is possible to exaggerate the degree of isolation: throughout the seventeenth and eighteenth centuries, Japanese traders maintained a substantial presence in Hội An on the coast of Vietnam, which was then one of the major entrepôts of the Asian sea trade and a bustling meeting place of Chinese, Japanese, European and local traders of everything from food to spices and porcelain). The new regime was happy to take from China a Confucianism, recast in a highly conservative form, to underpin its social authority with an ideology of order and obeisance. It suppressed the relatively newly arrived – and initially remarkably successful – Catholic Christianity of the Jesuits, with a ferocity and efficiency unparalleled before the twentieth century. It also persecuted the Nichiren school of Buddhism (which proclaimed a social gospel in the rural areas and was feared by the authorities in rather the same way that European rulers feared radical Protestant movements). It controlled the movements of regional aristocrats with a precision and intrusiveness that made Louis XIV of France seem like a ruler with a very light touch. And it turned the famous warrior class of medieval Japan – the samurai – into state bureaucrats paid in rations of rice whose size depended on the harvest.

On the face of it, Tokugawa Japan was a very different place from Europe's new centres of bourgeois influence. This was no liberal society: it was an autocratic, efficient police state whose eyes were everywhere. Yet precisely because there was peace, the social order was changing, and the culture changed with it. The cities grew, especially Edo (Tokyo), Osaka and Kyoto. Over the decades of the seventeenth century, the samurai saw their economic status eroded, while the merchants they had always despised grew rich. All that the samurai could hang on to were their pride in absolute loyalty to the unapproachable emperor, the powerful sense of duty that had infused their *bushido* code, and the Zen Buddhist ethos of meaning-in-action, which was the closest they came to a religious outlook on the world. For it was the traders who gained from the Tokugawa peace. They ran the supply chains needed to support all the comings and goings between the court at Edo and the regional cities. And, as was the case everywhere from Renaissance Italy onwards, they were the source of the credit others needed when they fell on hard times. They also provided the market for the services of what became known as the 'floating world' of Edo's pleasure districts. Their tastes created kabuki, *ukiyo-e* art and the geisha. The result was an astonishing efflorescence of subtle, intricate visual arts, theatre and literature that the rest of the world did not discover until the nineteenth century. Japanese woodblock prints – classic products of this new culture – have become well known throughout the world since the nineteenth century; but too few non-Japanese are familiar with even the names of the great literary figures of this brilliant Japanese era – of Monzaemon Chikamatsu, for instance, the great playwright who at the turn of the eighteenth century was writing some of the greatest love tragedies of any culture, set in an urban context for a bourgeois audience.

Thus a world of rigid social control, internalized among the samurai bureaucrats in particular as an intense – even sacrificial – commitment to their duty, coexisted with a parallel world of pleasure where money was more important than class, and where the aesthetics and sentimentality of a new bourgeoisie blossomed into a rich popular urban culture. This strange combination of control and creativity, of duty and feeling, goes some way to explaining a deep contradiction in Japanese cultural life that has survived to this day – between, on the one hand, the loyalty and self-denial manifest in the military of the mid-twentieth century and in company workers ever since then and, on the other, the wild art of manga and of make-believe video games. This cultural bifurcation was to prove astonishingly effective, as the country began to modernize in the late nineteenth century, and then very dangerous in the twentieth century.[23] It is a reminder that urbanization always changes society, but that the way it does so can vary sharply with the cultural context – a point we shall come back to in the Chapter 3.

Estrangement and the backlash

But first, we need to notice how the progress of industrial urbanization generated its own intellectual backlash. For it produced – perhaps for the first time in human history – a deep ambivalence about what city life was doing to human beings. Down the ages, the urban elite of every culture had yearned every now and then for the peace, quiet and spiritual calm of the country. From Roman aristocrats to Chinese bureaucrats, from Muslim *wazirs* to the Japanese court figures of the Heian period around the turn of the first millennium (so vividly portrayed in the world's earliest novel, *The Tale of Genji*), or to Russians like Pushkin, who regularly escaped St Petersburg in the summer months to his country estate (there to compose some of his most extraordinary poetry), everywhere the well-connected and influential had their countryside retreats. That was the point, however: these places were retreats, not their homes. As for the unprivileged people of the cities – traders, craftsmen, slaves – their voice was rarely if ever heard; they just got on with their lives.

As the momentum of the Industrial Revolution grew, bringing with it a new economic and social configuration of cities, all this began to change. The reaction began in Europe, because it was there that the huge impact on the physical face of cities, on traditional societies and on individual life experience was first felt. In particular, the European Romantic movement gave powerful voice to what might be described as the revolt of human feeling against the cult of reason that had propelled the European Enlightenment towards urbanization in the eighteenth century. (In the words of the German liberal Protestant theologian Ernst Troeltsch, writing in the early twentieth century, this was indeed a revolution: 'a revolution, above all, against the whole of the mathematico-mechanical spirit of science in Western Europe, against a conception of natural law which sought to blend utility with morality'.[24])

Above all, it found a passionate cause in the loss of the human sense of oneness with nature. The same Wordsworth who celebrated the urban glory of the view from Westminster Bridge wrote another sonnet, 'The world is too much with us', in the same year, 1802, which is, however, a world away in its sentiment:

> The world is too much with us; late and soon,
> Getting and spending, we lay waste our powers.
> Little we see in Nature that is ours;
> We have given our hearts away, a sordid boon!
> This Sea that bares her bosom to the moon,
> The winds that will be howling at all hours,
> And are up-gathered now like sleeping flowers,
> For this, for everything, we are out of tune;
> It moves us not . . .[25]

The origins of this estrangement are complex, and indeed culturally specific to Europe (neither in China nor in Japan as they later modernized themselves would anything analogous manifest itself). Over many centuries, Christendom had largely – albeit not completely – succeeded in taking the mystery out of nature. For the Christianity of the high Middle Ages, nature was subject to the human and the human was subject to God. The task of the species was – in the language of the book of Genesis – to be fruitful and multiply, to fill the earth and subdue it.[26] It would not have occurred to anyone to see this mandate as giving rise to any sort of spiritual tension between the city and nature, or between the city and our (true) nature. Only relatively recently, as part of their Renaissance, had Europeans begun to discover – or rediscover – a sense of the mysterious, a sense of themselves, in nature. A famous milestone on this journey of discovery had been the letter written by the Italian poet Petrarch, describing how he and his brother climbed to the top of Mont Ventoux in Provence on 26 April 1336. He writes that he had with him a copy of Augustine's *Confessions*; at the top, he opens it and finds himself looking at a passage, which reads:

Human beings go out and gaze in astonishment at high mountains, the high waves of the sea, the broad reaches of rivers, the ocean that encircles the world, or the stars in their courses. But they pay no attention to themselves . . .[27]

For Augustine, as we shall see later in Chapter 5, this was the precursor to a reflection about the importance of imagination and memory in the formation of the human self, rather than a celebration of the spiritual value of natural splendour. For Petrarch, too, it was the occasion for silent contemplation of the importance of history and tradition for the inner life of the human being, precisely because his eye had been drawn to that particular passage in Augustine. By the nineteenth century, however, Petrarch's experience had become a pointer to the way humans can find their true selves in and through nature.[28]

No one was more aware of this than Wordsworth, whose own 'confessions' – in *The Prelude*, as well as his famous 'Lines written a few miles above Tintern Abbey' – were steeped in what was for him the formative mystery of nature. It was not that nature was simply a source of recreation, of a calm peacefulness to quieten the turmoil of an overstressed soul. For the Romantics, nature is the disturbing experience that fills the spirit with an overwhelming sense of awe and mystery. Wordsworth describes this as:

> A presence that disturbs me with the joy
> Of elevated thoughts; a sense sublime
> Of something far more deeply interfused,
> Whose dwelling is the light of setting suns,
> And the round ocean and the living air,
> And the blue sky and in the mind of man . . .[29]

And it followed from all this that urbanization impoverished the soul, by sundering its relationship with nature. England's green and pleasant land was being covered with Blake's 'dark Satanic Mills'. What was this doing to people's spiritual being, to their identity? Blake's poem *Jerusalem* seeks the answer in a strange apocryphal story of the young Jesus coming to England in its ancient and pristine purity, before its despoliation by the Industrial Revolution; but his mystical call to build the new Jerusalem means little now to the vast majority of those who happily sing his poem to the rousing tune Hubert Parry composed for it. The truth was that a radical change was underway, which was unstoppable and would indeed alter people's view of themselves and of their place in the world. The

Romantics might call attention to the loss of the human place in a natural order of things that Europe had so relatively recently discovered for itself, but they had no realistic manifesto for reversing the direction of travel.

In any case, it was not just the human bond with nature that was being lost through industrial urbanization. Many were at least as concerned about the effect of the upheaval on family and community life. Already, Adam Smith had drawn attention to the human psychological – or even moral and spiritual – implications of the new urban paradigm that set the division of labour at its core. In *The Wealth of Nations*, he notes that:

> The man whose whole life is spent in performing a few simple operations . . . has no occasion to exert his understanding or to exercise his invention . . . He naturally loses, therefore, the habit of such exertion . . . The torpor of his mind renders him not only incapable of relishing or bearing a part in any rational conversation, but of conceiving any generous, noble or just sentiment, and consequently of forming any just judgement concerning many even of the ordinary duties of private life.[30]

To a modern reader, this seems a rather patronizing passage, but it was an expression of a fear, which many held, that there was something dehumanizing about the new urban economy. It was – to use a term that Karl Marx made much of – *alienating*. For the Romantics it alienated human beings from their natural environment. Marx was no more interested than Smith in the human relationship with nature; rather, he was concerned about human relationships in community with other people and, still more importantly for him, a person's relationship to work and what is produced. How could Adam Smith's pin-maker sustain any satisfaction or pride in what was produced by the minute division of labour he describes? How could this be anything other than profoundly degrading and alienating? Marx, like Smith, saw this as fundamentally damaging to the human being as a person, even if it was the inevitable consequence of technological developments:

> Individuals have always regarded themselves as the point of departure; their relations are part of the real process of their lives. How

can it be, then, that their relationships become independent of them, that the forces of their own lives gain control over them? The answer, in a word is – the division of labour, which depends on the extent to which productive forces have developed.[31]

There was no answer at the individual psychological level to this question about the needs of the human spirit for a healthy identity. Neither Smith nor Marx saw any road back to a more integrated past. Smith answers his own dilemma by calling for the government to promote education of workers; and indeed, most nineteenth-century reformers pursued this and other familiar policy goals designed to better the lot of the urban poor and generally to humanize the new urban society. Marx was different: he finds the resolution in a way that was entirely characteristic of the German philosophical tradition in which he had been nurtured.

Marx evolved a metaphysical approach to history and its processes, as a framework for interpreting what had brought the Industrial Revolution into being and for predicting how it would develop. The basic concept of his metaphysics he inherited from Hegel, while also introducing a radically new dimension. Like Hegel, he sees history as a sequence of movement and countermovement, always leading to a new state that absorbs the previous phases and then becomes the start of a further sequence. This was the famous historical dialectic, summed up as the triad of thesis, antithesis and synthesis – although Hegel himself preferred a different set of terms: the abstract, the negative and the concrete. This sense that history is a journey which is necessarily conflictual, that *negativity is intrinsic to progress*, is arguably Hegel's most profound and enduring contribution to human thought, and we shall come back to it later in Chapter 9. Marx took it over as the basis for the resolution of the dilemmas of industrialization and the impending collapse of the capitalist system based on the alienated labour of the proletariat. But he also inherited, particularly from Feuerbach, an adamant rejection of Hegel's highly speculative conception of history as the realization of Absolute Spirit. For Feuerbach – and for Marx, even though he was fiercely critical of Feuerbach in many respects – there is no god, no absolute spirit and no external motive of the historical process. Specifically, Marx sees the base of all human consciousness, not in the world of ideas at all, but in the economic system:

> The imaginary creations of the human brain are the inevitable sublimations of the material process of existence, which can be observed empirically, and which depends on material causes. Morality, religion, metaphysics and all other forms of ideology and the related forms of consciousness thus lose the independence they appeared to have. They have no history or development of their own; it is only people, developing their material production and mutual material relations, who as a result come to think different thoughts and create different intellectual systems. It is not consciousness that determines life, but life that determines consciousness . . . and all consciousness is that of live individuals.[32]

It is the economic dialectic that is the base of all human history. It was his term dialectical materialism that was to become very familiar as a watchword of twentieth-century communist ideology. In relation to Hegel's triad, it enabled him to see the capitalist phase of history as the great negativity that will end in collapse, giving way to a next – and final – stage of the dialectic when a new community, based not on exploitation but on a common life of shared goods and well-being, would come into being. Moreover, this was no apocalypse – in the sense of a vision of a new Jerusalem descending from the heavens or materializing out of nowhere. It was the outworking of human history: the concrete synthesis that would be ushered in by the convulsive end of the phase of negativity, which was the inevitable result of the self-contradictions he saw in the new urban capitalism.

But there was an ambiguity buried in all this. Was history inexorably determined to take its course or did there need to be decisive action to unleash the revolution? Marx was neither a detached academic nor a determinist. Though he believed that action should work with the grain of history, he was clear that theory without praxis was idle. This was not simply academic analysis: for him, disengaged thought lacked integrity. The point, famously, was not to understand the world but to change it. And it was the historic destiny of the proletariat to do that, because they had suffered most and had least to lose from the violence of revolution.

Lenin dispensed with any ambiguity. He led the Bolsheviks in a successful coup – not by, but in the name of, the proletariat – in Russia in 1917. His success was by no means either predictable or inevitable. Were it not for the effective militarization of the Russian labour force under Lenin and Trotsky, and then for Stalin's equally successful totalitarian consolidation of power from the mid-1920s onwards, and for his victory in the life-and-death struggle with Nazism, it is questionable whether Marxist metaphysics would ever have had such an extraordinary life on the geopolitical stage as it did throughout most of the twentieth century. Mao certainly used the language of Marxism; but it did not fit Chinese circumstances any more than it had been relevant to a highly rural and backward Russia. In any event, China's urban transformation has achieved most of its momentum and economic success only after Mao, by which time the Chinese Communist Party was openly talking of 'socialism with Chinese characteristics' and pursuing a policy of economic flexibility that owed more to Smith than to anything that could be described as authentically Marxist (although neither Smith nor Marx would have allowed, in their respective schemes, for the role played by the modern state-owned enterprises of China).

Marx's argument that capitalism was destined steadily to impoverish the proletariat, and that rampant competition among the capitalists would lead to widespread ruination of the bourgeoisie and a collapse of the system, has never been borne out by the facts – though capitalism has certainly produced growing inequality and undergone occasional periods of financial convulsion. And he never envisaged a stage of development in which the traditional proletariat would decline to the point where it is now just a small minority of the workforce in the developed world. Yet the irony is that Marx the philosopher created a metaphysic which was just as impervious to the awkwardness of facts as the German idealist metaphysics he so vehemently rejected. Like most such systems (including much theology), it has proved itself highly malleable and syncretistic – enough, in fact, to continue to be useful as the conceptual framework even for a twenty-first century Chinese Communist Party wrestling with some very modern challenges.

The forces unleashed by urbanization

From one end of Eurasia to the other, societies are now either already highly urbanized or in the process of becoming so. We do not yet fully understand the implications of this for modern societies and for the individual. Already the transformation is dramatic: slowly but inexorably, urbanization is – to highlight one of its most fundamental effects – bringing about the empowerment of women (a phenomenon of our times that is so profound and wide-ranging in its effects that it is beyond the scope of this book to explore fully). This most radical of changes is still not complete even in the most developed societies; and there is a long journey ahead. But one bastion of male privilege after another is being undermined and then brought down, and half the world's population is gradually being freed to make their own life choices. No culture will remain immune to this incoming tide.

Simultaneously, the role of cities is continuing to change: from the pre-modern era when cities were centres of power and culture but their rural surroundings were the main base for (agricultural) production; to the industrial era when cities themselves became production centres of much greater economic value than the countryside (and underwent radical transformation as a result); to the era of offices and commuters (who may live in semi-rural settings but whose lives are dominated by their urban working environment); to a new era already dawning when the digital revolution in general, and artificial intelligence in particular, will change city profiles yet again, making more and more shop-floor and office jobs unnecessary.

We know that artificial intelligence will close the path towards affluence which has been followed since the Second World War by so many countries (from Japan in the 1950s to China in the 1990s) by removing the cost advantage of cheap and efficient labour, as it makes more and more low-skilled jobs simply unnecessary. We also know from the experience in mature European economies how hard it is to manage urban decline due to the death of old industries. At the same time, we know too that urbanization is a one-way street: neither economically nor socio-psychologically will it be possible for any significant numbers of people to be reabsorbed into the rural world. Indeed, the drift to the cities will continue everywhere except in very mature societies such as in western

Europe and Japan where urbanization is already largely complete (and where rural life has effectively been 'urbanized' by the ease of transport and by the intense connectivity of the digital era, such that there are very few pockets left of old rural ways and attitudes).

Three huge common challenges are predictable in this context. First, the social fluidity of the modern city poses questions about identity and value for individuals. This is the real issue underlying the alienation that so troubled Smith and Marx. As they perceived it, alienation was the product of the technology of production; but regimentation is receding as an important mode of social organization, in either economic or in political life. Fluidity rather than structure is becoming the dominant characteristic of urban life, so the question that becomes ever more insistent everywhere – from Shenzhen to London – is a new and deeper one. But the exact form of the question – is it, 'Who am I now?' or is it, 'Who are we now?' – begs its own question. Another question is also becoming more insistent: are the answers basically the same in all modern urban cultural environments or do the answers vary from one culture to another?

Second, were the Romantics right to be troubled by the loss of empathy for the natural environment? Was this just a European preoccupation of nineteenth-century literati and aesthetes yearning for something so recently found and then lost again? Or does urbanization pose a deeper and more general threat to human well-being in all societies as they modernize? If so, what impact does it have on the great cultures of Eurasia?

That question about the human spirit and its natural context opens out into a third and wider concern: in a crowded and increasingly urban world, we face the problem of the commons. The human impact on the planet was felt first in Eurasia. It was Eurasians who first hunted animals to extinction; it was they who first made the move from hunting to agriculture and who first cleared the primeval forests. For nearly two centuries they have produced the most urban pollution. They have had the largest impact on the oceans through overfishing and now through plastic pollution, and on the climate through their carbon emissions. Increasingly, this problem of the commons is one that the Eurasians share, not only among themselves but also with the wider world. How will we measure up to this challenge, and what will be the implications for the development of the human spirit as manifested in the great world cultures that have their roots in Eurasia?

These questions are for the rest of this book. As we explore them, we will find ourselves facing one other question: does the connected urbanization, which is becoming the reality of life experience for us all, create in the end a deeper commonality than we have so far known – and what would this mean for those great Eurasian cultural traditions that have been the pathways of the journey of the human spirit so far?

Next, then, the question about urbanization and the human spirit. What is all the new social fluidity doing to our self-awareness? Who do we now think we are?

3

So who do we think we are now?

Most of us now live in cities; and within a few decades the large majority will do so. Soon there will only be folk memories of the rural or small-town life in which most of the presently living grandparents of the world once lived.

And because we are still in the midst of the process of urbanization, *many of us are migrants now* – in the specific sense that a large proportion of people no longer live their lives out in one place, as was the normal experience for most of human history. In some countries, this is the new life experience of the clear majority. Many of those who move still feel a special attraction to the place where they first saw the light, which is the focus of memories that come flooding back, and where they would perhaps like to be buried when they die. Others turn their backs on a home that was constraining and brutal and shake the dust off their feet as they leave. In many cases, of course, they cannot go back. Desperate poverty makes this an unattainable dream; or political upheaval has driven them out, perhaps for ever.

Most of the migrants who make up so much of today's urban population are willing migrants, of course. And the majority have migrated *within* the country where they were born. In particular, both China and India have huge internal migrant populations (with the important difference that vast numbers of Chinese have moved to the cities for specific jobs, leaving families behind in the village and returning home annually for the Lunar New Year, in what may be the largest movement of people on the planet). Some countries also have large extended communities of their citizens living and working in other countries round the world, such as India, Pakistan, Poland, the Philippines and Britain.

Patterns of migration, both within and across borders, take many forms. Some are young middle-class people who move for education and then for lucrative jobs in the big city. Many move across borders for jobs in service in the prosperous societies of Europe or the Gulf States of the Middle East. Others move with no specific prospects, because rural life is hard and limiting and because they are lured by the bright lights and opportunities of the city. They come in search of temporary jobs, they rent cheap accommodation, they find a bed with someone from the same extended family or from the same village, they drift into the slums, or just sleep on the streets. Many end up in grinding, insecure work. Not a few end up in what amounts to slavery. Even internal migrants often face formidable cultural barriers: they may not speak the language of the region they have come to (this is a difficulty in India in particular); they may be totally unfamiliar with the ways of the city; and they often face barriers, either blatant or subtle, of class, ethnicity or religion. And what is true for internal migrants is true all the more forcefully for those who cross borders.

The experience of a middle-class migrant – from, say, Scotland to London or from Japan to Britain – is of course a very long way from that of a rural Chinese from a remote western province migrating to one of the industrial cities on the east coast, or from that of an orphaned boy from India's south who ends up on the streets of Kolkata, let alone of the Syrian migrant who has fled from terrifying destruction and ended up in a hostel in a town in eastern Germany. The political, social and economic context is utterly different. As for the cultural challenge, the middle-class professional moving for a new job may complain about unexpected costs, unfamiliar bureaucracy, strange local ways, and the difficulty of finding a suitable apartment. But all this pales into insignificance beside the dangers and traumas of the trafficked orphan or of the refugee who has nothing in common with the new hosts – not even language – and who yearns for a lost home.

For all the profound differences, there is one commonality: all these people are migrants. By one means or another and for one reason or another, they have come to the city from somewhere else. In most cases they have come from a small town or from a village. They did not start in the city, and it will be a long time – if ever – before they see the city in the deepest sense as their home, and this in turn means that it may well never become a central part of their identity. To take just two examples:

57

London has been a magnet for people from all over the British Isles for centuries and, in addition, more than a third of its residents were born overseas; overall, it is probable that more than half its population was born elsewhere. Who, then, is a true Londoner? Can you be one without having been born there? And what does it mean to be a Hong Konger, in a city where 40 per cent of residents were born elsewhere? But although the specifics differ from city to city, this question of identity is now very widespread; for many urban people, the city they live in is not, to use a revealing phrase, where they're *from*.

Their children will probably have a different perspective. Looking back over the big migrations, forced or otherwise, of the modern era – of Europeans to America in the nineteenth century, of Chinese into South East Asia at the same time, of Russians into the steppes of central Asia in both the Tsarist and Soviet empires, of Germans from eastern Europe after the Second World War, of Indians and Pakistanis at partition – we can see how subsequent generations come to settle spiritually into their new setting. They may still sing the old songs and dance the old dances; they may attend clan gatherings; and they may take their own children to see the village their grandparents came from. But they no longer yearn for it; they gradually lose the old language and the past has become a foreign country. Their city becomes their home and part of their identity. Or, to be more exact – and to allow for the many who will readily move from one city to another in pursuit of advancement – cities in general, rather than one city in particular, will become for many people a core part of their identity. The modern era is creating the footloose urbanite.

The rupture has been profound. It is a break not just from a traditional home; it is typically a break from a rural life lived in close proximity and in harmony with nature. City children often have little knowledge of where their food comes from or how it is produced. In poorer districts, many children never leave their surroundings and grow up never having seen the open countryside that was all around many of their grand-parents when they grew up. For the first time in history, most people have no living connection with the wider natural environment.

In earlier times, even those who lived in cities knew about the cycle of agriculture. They also had a vivid awareness of the stars. There was no light pollution; so the educated city dweller could take an interest in astronomy (and astrology). Kant, the great German philosopher of the European Enlightenment, who died just after the dawn of the nineteenth century (at a time when Wordsworth was in his prime, and before the Industrial Revolution began to light up and pollute the cities), famously wrote: 'two things fill my mind with ever increasing wonder and awe, the more often and the more intensely I contemplate them; the starry heavens above me, and the moral law within me.'[1] Kant could see the panoply of the stars from his home in the city of Königsberg. Today, a city dweller would need to make a special journey some way out of town to do so. (And it is arguable – as we will see later – that the connected urban life of the modern era has also made it harder to detect the 'moral law within me'.)

The loss of the human place in the natural order of things

All this is a reminder of something we feel we have lost. We are no longer part of an integrated order of things, and the rupture is intimately related to urbanization. For most people down the ages, the sense of being part of the natural world was not some remarkable new epiphany; it was simply a fact of their lives. They knew they had to catch, graze or grow their food, and that their water came from the heavens and flowed in the rivers and streams of the lands they lived in. They also shared the world not only with plants and animals but also with spirits, and they knew that certain mountains, or rivers, or groves in the woods were especially haunted, or especially sacred. The realm of the animate extended much further, in both directions, than it does for us in the modern era. In one direction, things we consider inanimate were for them alive; in the other direction, there were disembodied animate beings – spirits or gods – in waiting behind every rock or tree or, in the case of the Arabian world that was to be the setting for Muhammad's vision, in the winds that swirled the sand into dunes in the desert. Virtually everywhere, from one end of the land mass to the other, this sense of the permeability of the world – of the intricate interplay of the seen and the unseen – had been a vital part of the human consciousness since the beginning of history.

Most could never imagine any alternative to this sense of oneness. They had their own unquestioned place in the natural order; any important question about their place in the world always had an answer in their folk stories. These stories were not about themselves; they were about the superhuman beings and heroes who dominated this order. The stories might answer implicit questions about fate and destiny; but the language they used to tell these stories was always in the third person. In short, so far as their own lives were concerned, most people just lived them out; they did not have to think about them, in the way that has become – to use a significant phrase – second nature to us now.

Even the names they gave people, animals and things were not just signifiers of particular individual beings or things, as they are in modern usage; rather, they were marks of place in an order that both the named and namer were part of; the names of individual beings and things represented their essence, their animus, their relationship to the whole and hence to those who named them. (This gave naming a significance we no longer easily appreciate, but we detect its influence in the cultural worlds of Christianity and Islam, through the role played in the origins of both by the Jewish Bible, which shows clear signs of how the names given to people, animals and places had spiritual significance; and we can also detect it in the very different context of early Chinese thought, in the focus in both Confucian and Daoist texts on the rightness of names.)

From ancient times there have been gifted thinkers who have sought to articulate a metaphysical framework to account for this sense of being inextricably involved in a wider natural order, above all in China. The Chinese Daoist tradition is ancient. Although the very different ethos of Confucianism has – as we shall see – been the dominant orthodoxy of China down to the modern era, Daoism has fed directly into the stream of consciousness of the Chinese for more than two millennia. Furthermore, its indirect influence through its impact on Chinese Buddhism is hard to overestimate.

Little is known about Laozi (Lao Tzu), the man who tradition sees as the author of the *Dao de jing*, the classic text of Daoism. He was almost certainly a real person who lived sometime in the fourth or fifth century BCE. Beyond this, it is probably unnecessary to try to sort out the truth from among the tangle of obvious legend and possible facts about him. Whether or not the story told by Sima Qian, the great Chinese historian from the first century CE, is true – that the sentry at the city gate refused to let him leave on his journey to a hermitage at the age of eighty until he wrote down a summary of his wisdom – what we have is this remarkable book of only about five thousand words, which has been as deeply influential in China as any other single text. As the twentieth-century Chinese scholar, Wing-tsit Chan, put it, 'no one can hope to understand Chinese philosophy, religion, government, art, medicine – even cooking – without a real appreciation of the profound philosophy taught in this little book.'[2] He goes on to provide a summary of the essence of Laozi's teaching that has never been bettered:

> Whereas in other (Chinese) schools Dao means a system or moral truth, in this school it is the One, which is natural, eternal, spontaneous, nameless and indescribable. It is at once the beginning of all things and the way in which all things pursue their course. When this Dao is possessed by an individual thing, it becomes its character or virtue. The ideal life for the individual, the ideal order for society, and the ideal type of government are all based on it and guided by it. As a way of life, it denotes simplicity, spontaneity, tranquillity . . . and most important of all, non-action.[3]

But non-action does not mean inaction; it means allowing Nature to take its course. Thus Nature takes a central place in this view of the cosmos and of the basis for virtue. The secret of the good life is to live with the grain of Nature – although it is essential to recognize that this is a much more all-embracing idea than the relatively simple naturalism which has charmed the urban middle classes and their poets in more recent times. From the *Dao de jing*:

> Humankind models itself after Earth,
> Earth models itself after Heaven,
> Heaven models itself after Dao,
> Dao models itself after Nature.[4]

Such a construct dovetailed perfectly with the life experience of the deeply rural societies that characterized China (and everywhere else too) at that time.

A century or so after Laozi came another highly influential Chinese thinker who took the metaphysics still further – Zhuangzi. As in Laozi's case, little is known about him; but Sima Qian describes him as a minor official in a remote small town who once turned down a summons to live at the court because all its pressures and expectations would constrain him from being his true self. However that may be, he gave his name to a book which sits alongside the *Dao de jing* as the wellspring of Daoism down the centuries.

Zhuangzi took Daoist expression in a more transcendental direction than did Laozi; he is at once more mystical and more individualist. But the same sense of essential belongingness – that humanity is part of the wide order of Nature – infuses both these two remarkable products of human creativity. Laozi and Zhuangzi are the intellectual counterparts of that pervasive popular sense in pre-modern societies that humans lived in an enchanted world. Zhuangzi sets out the metaphysics in a way that links Nature to our nature, and our nature to what is good for us:

When things are produced in accordance with the principle of life, there is physical form. When the physical form embodies and preserves the spirit so that all activities follow their own specific principles, that is nature. By cultivating one's nature one will return to virtue. When virtue is perfect, one will be one with the beginning . . .[5]

Yet there is also a seed of something new in Zhuangzi – a seed that would lie dormant for a long period but had the potential eventually to germinate into a rather different view of the human place in the order of things. For his individualism is as striking as his metaphysics of nature. He knows how human moods seem to dovetail with nature, in a way that would resonate with European Romantics over two thousand years later:

Pleasure and anger, sorrow and joy, anxiety and regret, fickleness and fear, impulsiveness and extravagance, indulgence and lewdness,

62

come to us like music from the hollows or like mushrooms from the damp. Day and night, they alternate within us but we don't know where they come from.

He then continues with a highly significant question:

Without these feelings, there would not be I. And without me, who will experience them?[6]

This is one way of putting an enduring human question: 'Am I the sum of my feelings and experiences or am I more than that and, if so, who am I?' It is also Zhuangzi who tells the famous story of how he dreamt he was a butterfly. When he awoke, he was left unsure whether he had dreamt he was a butterfly – or whether the butterfly was dreaming it was him. At one level, that story can be seen as calling into question the reality of the individual, and as blurring the distinction between subject and object. But at another level, it is asking that same – very individual – question again: 'Who am I?' We will see later how this question reverberates down the ages and across the cultures of Eurasia. But for now, suffice it to note that this sense of the self does not sit entirely comfortably with the central emphasis on belongingness. Hence, some of the potential implications of this were unwelcome to the Confucian orthodoxy that became the underpinning of Chinese society for a thousand years from the Song Dynasty onwards. But that is to get ahead of ourselves.

No other culture evolved a metaphysics so closely integrated with the basic circumstances of life-in-nature and became as influential as Daoist ideas have been in China. But all pre-modern societies were characterized by that same life-in-nature, because it was the universal experience of humanity before the Industrial Revolution. So all cultures evolved world views based on an order of things that, one way or another, encompassed that human experience of belonging in the natural environment and the cosmos.

In the case of three of Eurasia's great cultures – China, Christian Europe, and Islam – this involved a specific intellectual challenge: that of integrating an understanding of the nature of things and of the human place in the macrocosm with a particular, very dominant social and political orthodoxy. In each of these three cultures, the pre-modern period produced brilliant minds who took this challenge on. They were the great medieval synthesizers who, in very different contexts – and with varying degrees of influence in their respective cultural traditions – sought to produce a rational account of the natural order of things that would be consistent with, and reinforce, the dominant orthodoxy. The intellectual achievements of these synthesizers – all in a relatively short period of about three hundred years from the turn of the first millennium of the Common Era – were (and are) remarkable. But they would not endure, because that integrated life-in-nature of the pre-modern era would, in the end, be fragmented everywhere by the rise of the city and the new questions this posed (which were, however, not so new, as we have seen in the way that Zhuangzi had already posed them).

For Christianity, the One was revealed and personal; the task was to give a coherent account of the created Many and its relationship to this One. For Islam the philosophical task was essentially the same (except that it avoided the added theological complication of needing to articulate the mysterious nature of the One who was also Three in One). Both started from their own revelations – from the New Testament and from the Qur'an respectively – in their reflections on the One. And both turned to the classical Greek world, and to Aristotle in particular, as the starting point for an understanding of the Many. Aristotelian thought saw the world as permanently in motion, and developed concepts of matter, form, potentiality and causality to account for the existence of the multiplicity of particular things. As an element in this conceptual structure, it embraced a sense of purposiveness in the material world – a sense that nature has its ends – which was not so far distant from the Chinese instinct, and facilitated a holistic account of the many as more than just random particularities, more than just the random movement of molecules.

The culmination of such reflection in the Muslim thought world was the philosophical work of Ibn Sina (Avicenna), who lived around the turn of the first millennium. He was an Iranian polymath of extraordinary brilliance, who had learnt the Qur'an by heart by the time he was ten years old; he was a physician and an astronomer as well as philosopher and theologian; he wrote voluminously on all these topics.

He had been born into the cultured family of a small-town administrator near Bukhara. He spent his life in the service of one regional ruler after another, providing medical services and general scientific advice, once falling into sufficient disfavour that he went into hiding, and once being imprisoned. But his enduring place in the pantheon of human thought is due to the way in which he sought to integrate a theological understanding of God, which was anchored in the Qur'anic revelation, with a philosophical rationale for the necessary existence of a First Principle – of the One – as essential to the existence of all being.

Ibn Sina's synthesis incorporates ideas from a Greek neo-Platonist thought world, which had been carefully studied by his Muslim predecessors, to reflect on the One and to explain the transition from non-being to the being of things through creation. To account for the multiplicity of the Many, he refined and developed Aristotelian modes of thought about the nature of existence. He sought with these arguments to set out a rational account of how God creates and interacts with the created world, and thus to provide an answer to the question about the One and the Many in a way that underpinned the Islamic revelation. As part of that project, he argued for the necessary existence of God in a way which was to be influential not only in Islam but also in Christian Europe.

Ibn Sina also developed a philosophy of the soul – following Plato rather than Aristotle (for whom the soul was neither immaterial nor immortal) – that was to be influential in Christian as well as Islamic thought. During his spell in prison he conducted a famous thought experiment involving a 'floating man', to focus on human self-awareness and to argue for the immateriality of the human soul. He imagines himself as a man floating freely in the air, such that he has no sense perception about anything, not even about his own body. In such circumstances, he would still be conscious of his own self, which must therefore exist as an immaterial soul apart from his material body. This argument can be seen as, in effect, a distant echo of – and a possible answer to – Zhuangzi's question.

In the European Christian world, Aristotle began to have significant influence only a century or so later, as the intellectual window on the Greek classics and on the Muslim philosophers was opened in Spain towards the end of the eleventh century. So the apex of the Christian work of synthesis came later, in the thirteenth century, in the enormously influential work of Thomas Aquinas. Thomas was born into a minor southern Italian noble family who failed (after trying everything including incarceration in the family castle) to prevent him from joining the Dominican order. He eventually taught and wrote in Paris, Rome and Naples.

Like Ibn Sina, Aquinas believed it was possible – indeed, it was necessary – to understand the ways of God and the nature of the created cosmos through human reason. He too produced arguments for the existence of God that have generated endless debate ever since. He evolved a conceptual framework that brought nature and virtue together, based on the fundamental Aristotelian idea that all things have ends. In particular, the rational animal that is the human being has a true nature with its ends and purposes – its *telos*; perfection is realized in the fulfilment of those ends; and the virtues are necessary to – and a manifestation of – this perfection. To Aristotle's *telos*, Aquinas adds divinely ordained law (as did both Islam and Judaism). And to Aristotle's concept of error, Aquinas adds the concept of sin.[7] He was, of course, also convinced that God was the source of love and he was never going to reduce his system to any kind of pantheism or to a deistic humanism (both of which were to find their voice later on as the integrated thought world of the pre-modern era began to break down). The result was the most sophisticated and authoritative natural theology that Christianity ever knew. Aquinas became embroiled in a theological controversy with Etienne Tempier, the Bishop of Paris, which may have cost him his health. At its core, the issue was about whether the sovereignty of God could be restricted by the principles of rationality that underpinned his metaphysical system. However, Aquinas' legacy survived the attack by the Bishop and his system went on to become pre-eminent in the Christian thought world for at least the rest of the pre-modern era.

There were other thinkers in both the Muslim and the Christian worlds who contributed to this stream of thought, of course. And there are differences – some obvious, some very subtle – between Ibn Sina and Aquinas (and between both and Aristotle). But there is an underlying similarity of outlook and instinct that is equally striking. It derives from two facts about them and their cultural context: first, they were both devoted theists and gifted theologians; and, second, they both flourished in pre-modern societies whose dominant characteristic was that of life-in-nature. The result was an integrated metaphysics that sought to dovetail the divine with that life experience, and thus relate the One to the Many in an intellectually satisfactory way. It was a synthesis that would prove vulnerable as that life experience itself changed.

Meanwhile, in China, the challenge was at one level quite different, because Chinese thought had never been theistic. But at a deeper level, the context was the same: of life-in-nature in a pre-modern society. China, in the first few centuries of the Common Era, had seen a remarkable intellectual and spiritual ferment, stimulated by Buddhist ideas filtering in from India, by the growing influence of Confucius and Mencius in imperial circles, and by the continuing importance of Daoist instincts and meditative practices. As Confucianism was becoming dominant during the Song Dynasty from the tenth century onwards, the intellectual task was to integrate all this and to provide a rational account of the One and the Many, in a way that was consistent with the ethos of Confucius and Mencius (for both of whom the many was largely the human many, rather than the many of the whole natural order, and whose whole outlook was positivist and practical rather than contemplative or mystical).

It was Zhu Xi, China's greatest medieval philosopher, who achieved this synthesis most authoritatively. He flourished in the twelfth century, a hundred and fifty years after Ibn Sina, and almost a hundred years before Aquinas, and in a very different thought world from either. Zhu Xi was an imperial bureaucrat who had a politically tempestuous career, which brought him obloquy because of an embarrassing tendency to speak his mind about incompetence and corruption, and nearly ended in his execution. His writing has a combativeness to it that is still detectable today, even through the prism of translation; but his legacy is enormous. He stabilized the Confucian canon, and provided it with an articulated metaphysical framework that owed significant elements to Daoism (notably its account of the source of the life principle in the unknowable and nameless One, and its focus on the way this finds its outworking in the particularities of the many) as well as to some strands of Buddhist thought (importantly, the idea that every particular unit reflects the totality – such that humanity, and each human, is a microcosm that reflects the macrocosm).[8] While thus drawing carefully from the different well-springs of Chinese thought, he established a confident Neo-Confucian orthodoxy that knew how to differentiate itself from both Daoism and Buddhism. His impact on the Confucian order in China was profound, above all through the use of the canon he defined – the Four Books, including the *Analects* (of Confucius), the (writings of) *Mencius*, the *Great Learning* and the *Doctrine of the Mean* – as the basis for the imperial examination system for the next eight hundred years.

As the core of his praxis, Zhu Xi focused strongly on what he called 'the investigation of things' – an approach to the understanding of ends and purposes in both the natural world and in human society that has an obvious resonance in the Aristotelian themes reflected in both Ibn Sina and Aquinas.[9] In fact, the question of how far Zhu Xi resembles Aristotle has generated some abstruse scholarly debate.[10] But in the last analysis, the commonality lies in a rationalistic, and largely this-worldly, focus on the nature of material beings and on the nature of human beings in particular that determines what makes for human well-being and virtue. Once again, the result is an integrated world of metaphysics, life-in-nature and social norms that ran with the grain of human life experience in the pre-modern world.

All three of these intellectually integrated systems had their challengers. Of the three synthesizers, Zhu Xi was the most influential in his culture, and Ibn Sina was the least. In fact, only Zhu Xi's Neo-Confucianism endured into the modern era, because it was the only one that was firmly embedded in a system of governance (which lasted in China until 1911).

But even in China, Zhu Xi did not reign supreme and without question. In particular, the human yearning for personal authenticity was never truly satisfied by the Confucian intellectual system. Its most effective challenge came from two sources: one from within the Buddhist stream, in the shape of Chan (Zen) Buddhism (which, however, eventually proved more influential in Japan than in China), and the other from within the Neo-Confucian thought world itself. Wang Yangming was an almost exact contemporary of Luther. He was one of the elite of the Chinese imperial system at a time when the Ming Dynasty was on the wane into decadence. He was a successful general as well as a bureaucrat who ended his career as governor of Jiangxi province. In his youth he had flirted with Daoism, and then returned to Confucianism – but gave it a very unorthodox stripe. He became the leading opponent of the Zhu Xi system, essentially on the grounds that its core praxis of the investigation of things had become a desiccated routine and had missed the real point: that the human mind had an innate knowledge of the good and that it could and should naturally extend this knowledge into action. Where Zhu Xi was rationalistic and analytical, Wang was forthright and spontaneous. Sincerity of will was prior to the investigation of things: commitment and action were of the essence. Wang was very influential, if controversial, during the remaining life of the Ming Dynasty, but his views never succeeded in dethroning Zhu Xi, whose legacy was secure in the imperial examination system for as long as the empire lasted.

In the world of Islam, by contrast, the philosophical tradition represented at its greatest by Ibn Sina came under sustained attack – essentially on the same grounds as the attack on Thomas Aquinas by the Bishop of Paris: that it illegitimately curtailed the sovereignty of God. Ibn Sina had never become the moral authority of an entire empire, unlike Zhu Xi. And unlike Aquinas, the legacy of Ibn Sina had a far stronger opponent than the Bishop of Paris, in the person of al-Ghazali. Born about twenty years after Ibn Sina died, he was also of Iranian origin. He set out an assault on rationalist metaphysics in his enormously influential work *The Incoherence of the Philosophers*, picking away at many of Ibn Sina's arguments in their own terms. The core of the issue is one that haunts Islam – as well as parts of the Christian movement – to this day: can a free-ranging philosophy coexist with a specific theology? A philosophy of religion is clearly possible, but can there be a true philosophy of *a* religion? One way in which this question poses itself involves the meaning of words: is God an agent in the created universe *in the same sense* that human beings act (in accordance with our ordinary understanding of cause and effect) – or does agency have a different meaning when used of God?[11] Al-Ghazali took his stand on the straightforward meaning of the word – lest the role of God get lost in abstruse philosophical argument about meanings.

Al-Ghazali's impact on the Islamic consciousness is huge but ambivalent: on the one hand, he championed a highly respectful approach to the interpretative traditions embodied in the Hadith (the collections of sayings of the Prophet and of his Companions) as the source of moral and practical wisdom – an approach that gained momentum in subsequent centuries and is now dominant in Sunni Islam; and on the other hand, he turned to Sufism later in life as an expression of his own deepened experience of faith. (His own story of his conversion, told in his book *Deliverance from Error*, is one of the greatest expressions of religious faith in any culture, and inevitably recalls Augustine's moving account of his conversion seven centuries earlier.)[12] The tension between these two instincts – the traditional and the mystical, the corporate and the individual – has been a feature of Islam ever since. Sufism became a powerful vehicle for the expression of Iranian Shiite consciousness in particular; but it was gradually marginalized in the majority Sunni Muslim thought world, as revelation and tradition began to be woven into the sharia that came to dominate the life of the community. (Sufism was subsequently, in the later seventeenth century, to suffer severe persecution in the Iran of the Safavid Dynasty: the ultimate beneficiary of this was the official Shiite clergy, which was to become so powerful in the late twentieth century after the fall of the Shah.[13])

Al-Ghazali did not seek to bring all Muslim philosophy to a halt, but he did reset the balance between reason, scripture and tradition. His attack on rationalist metaphysics foreshadowed a debate that was to take place later in Christian Europe too, but the outcome of the debate was different, as we shall see shortly. Al-Ghazali's legacy changed the direction of Muslim philosophy – away from the rationalist search for an integrated metaphysics of being, towards a spirit of enquiry that was subtly but importantly different. Muslim philosophy became both less rationalist-metaphysical and also more mystical. This is best and most beautifully represented by the early seventeenth-century Iranian Shiite philosopher Mulla Sadra. For him, existence always had metaphysical primacy over essence (that is, the existence of different things is what gives rise to abstract concepts about things, and not the other way around). But he had a mystical sense that the more we appreciate the subtle layers of difference discernible in reality, the more we appreciate the mystical truth of the underlying unity of everything. He saw the human spiritual journey in four phases: the original fall into the diversity of the many; the individual earthly journey of existence, shot through with the unavoidable pain of separation; the ascendance through mystical experience towards home; and the final coming into the presence of the divine. There are obvious echoes of this in medieval Christian mystical experience.

One way or another, the basis for synthesized systems of rationalist metaphysical thought was beginning to fragment, at the levels both of intellect and of instinct. In the Muslim world, Ibn Sina represents the high-water mark of synthesis. Thereafter the mood – even among philosophers – was increasingly to focus on the realities of existence rather than on the metaphysics of first principles, essences and abstract concepts. In other words, the project of an all-embracing rationalist metaphysical architecture was no longer a priority. And the same tendency was taking hold in the European Christian world too – helped, ironically, by the influence of the last great rationalist metaphysical philosopher of the Muslim world, the Andalusian Ibn Rushd (Averroes), whose detailed commentaries on Aristotle had introduced a whole new generation of European intellectuals, including Thomas Aquinas, to this seminal Greek thinker. Here, in fact, was a double irony: Ibn Rushd had almost no influence in a Muslim thought world that was becoming dominated by the interpretative traditions of the sharia; while in Europe, his rigorous focus on the fundamentally materialist categories of Aristotelian thought helped to unleash a new spirit of enquiry about the cosmos which eventually disposed of those same Aristotelian categories and ushered in the age of empirical science.

One of the most significant representatives of this new spirit was William of Ockham, an English Franciscan who was born around a hundred years after Ibn Rushd died and just a few years after the death of Thomas Aquinas, and who was one of the Black Death's most prominent victims in 1347. His famous 'razor' essentially argues that the structure and nature of being should be explained in the simplest terms possible.[14] It is therefore tantamount to an argument for the primacy of existence and of existing things over essences and more universal categories of being; and it is a major milestone on the journey away from Aquinas' integrated metaphysical approach to interpreting reality and its divine context. Thus in both Christianity and Islam, there was a turn away from the attempt to find an intellectually elegant solution to the question of

71

the One and the Many within their respective theist revelations. But the nature of the turn was very different: in Islam, theology asserted its supremacy over philosophy; in Christian Europe, philosophy gradually wriggled free from its chains.

Then came an explosion in the European atmosphere that had no parallels in either the Islamic or the Chinese thought worlds. Where the Muslim world yearned for interiority, it turned to that Sufi mysticism that was so important to al-Ghazali and infuses Mulla Sadra's thought. Where the Chinese yearned for the personally authentic, they could listen to Wang Yangming. Mysticism was in the Christian atmosphere too – in particular, the German Dominican friar Meister Eckhart, who was a generation older than William of Ockham, wrote of the need for the human soul to become totally empty of self so that 'God comes completely out of himself' for love of the soul.[15] As we shall see in Chapter 8, these ideas resonated well in the Japan of the twentieth century, which discovered Buddhist affinities in them. But in Christian Europe that same yearning for authenticity also produced Martin Luther – in particular political circumstances that made him a central, and not a marginal, figure. This triggered explosively centrifugal cultural and political forces, from which Europe never recovered until late in the twentieth century. Even now, as we shall later discuss, it is not clear that Europe has succeeded in recovering a clear sense of cultural identity.

Plainly, therefore, these cultural journeys were all very different. China's synthesized central orthodoxy survived until well into the modern era, although it certainly did not help China to prepare for the challenges posed by an increasingly connected urban world; and the awakening, when it came in the nineteenth century, was brutal and humiliating. The prestige of al-Ghazali endured too. But he had put an end to efforts to achieve intellectual synthesis; and as the mystical tradition that he had championed receded, in the majority Sunni world at least, the twentieth century would see the very conservative sharia-based approach of the central Arabian Wahhabi movement become its dominant orthodoxy. It is unlikely that al-Ghazali (let alone Ibn Sina) would have approved. Meanwhile, European Christianity broke up; the religious domain fragmented ever further as Protestantism divided and redivided like a river delta; and the political world fragmented with the rise of nation

72

states and the crumbling of the Holy Roman Empire. Thomist thought remained authoritative for many in the Roman Catholic Church; but it began to lose its status as a dominant intellectual orthodoxy in Europe's important polities from the seventeenth century onwards.

And yet, for all the differences, these cultural journeys had something profoundly important in common. In the end, all three syntheses failed. The underlying reason for this was that urbanization was in the process of ensuring there *could not be* any ruling orthodoxy that offered an integrated metaphysics and world view, of the kind all these pre-modern synthesizers had striven for. Life-in-nature was gradually giving away to a more ruptured life experience, as the cities grew and as human curiosity began to examine the world in more detail.

The new norm: ruptured life

For the world was moving on from one *episteme* – to borrow a term from ancient Greek philosophy that the influential modern French philosopher Michel Foucault used to refer to cultural mindsets. In classical Greek, the word *episteme* refers to knowledge that is theoretical or scientific. Both Plato and Aristotle (in *The Republic* and *The Nichomachean Ethics*, respectively) contrast it with *phronesis* (practical wisdom, in particular ethics) and *techne* (skill, craftmanship, technical know-how). The famous facade of the Library of Celsus at Ephesus features statues personifying Episteme alongside Sophia (wisdom), Ennoia (thought, meditation) and Arete (virtue). The interconnections between these ideas would have resonated equally well in Neo-Confucian China, in the Abbasid Islam of Ibn Sina and in the scholastic Europe of Aquinas. They were the foundations of any integrated intellectual response to the world of life-in-nature, which had survived largely unchanged from the beginning of human history until the sixteenth century. Each of those four ideas has a rich penumbra of meaning in a classical world that was (to our eyes) a strange mixture of the rational and the magical. But what is perhaps particularly striking is the intimate nexus between virtue and knowledge. The good life followed from the nature of things; so virtue depended on understanding that nature.

Foucault uses the concept of the *episteme* to characterize such a thought world and its context. Writing about the history of European thought, he argues that 'in any given culture and at any given moment, there is always only one *episteme* that defines the conditions of possibility of all knowledge'.[16] But although Foucault writes exclusively about European thought, this clearly applies not just to European culture; the *episteme* of the pre-modern age was, in fact, universal. All societies at any time before the axial sixteenth century were fundamentally (or, as Foucault terms it, at the archaeological level) societies for which the macrocosm – all that there is, understood as a totality – provided the rational and reliable framework for the particular microcosms in which humans understood and lived out their lives. The obvious differences between theistic and non-theistic orthodoxies – between the Christian and the Islamic on the one side and the Confucian on the other – should not obscure this deeper commonality.

Foucault argues that European culture went through a two-stage change in its *episteme*. As the pre-modern *episteme* began to break down, in the sixteenth, seventeenth and early eighteenth centuries, a new *episteme* came into being, which was however still 'an unstable mixture of rational knowledge, notions derived from magical practices, and a whole cultural heritage whose power and authority had been vastly increased by the rediscovery of Greek and Roman authors'.[17] And then – as Foucault puts it – the human being began to take centre stage; rationality finally drove out magic, and the habit of analysing and classifying the world, both of nature and of human beings, based on empirical observation was established. This meant in turn that biology and botany became proper sciences for the first time, as did the objective study of human economic and social interaction, exemplified in Adam Smith's *The Wealth of Nations*. However, Foucault argues, this modern *episteme* had no way of integrating into itself any moral perspective. The old order 'was articulated on the order of the world, and by discovering the law of that ordering could deduce from it the principle of a code of wisdom'.[18] Not so any longer and, although Foucault does not spell them out, the questions posed by all this are obvious. What were to be the values of the new urban world? We will return to the human struggle with this question in Chapters 8 and 9.

The growing focus on the human being and the power of the new rationality unleashed by William of Ockham's razor are too often discussed as if this were a specifically European story. There is no doubt that during the four centuries from the sixteenth century onwards, Europe was in the ascendant; its impact on the rest of Eurasia was to be profound and irreversible. That impact is itself too often discussed as if its most important manifestation were the colonial experience. As we shall see, the impact was – and is – much deeper.

But for now, we should focus on the fact that this is not so specifically a European journey but, rather, something intrinsically connected to the development of the city. For the fact is that life in the city has always had a tendency to probe the boundaries, both social and epistemic. It may have done so from the very earliest times. We know that it has done so for at least the last two millennia. We can see how the momentum and complexity of change accelerated with mechanization and the Industrial Revolution, and has since accelerated still further under the impact of the demographic explosion and the digital wave of the last half-century. But well before that acceleration, which began in Europe, the germs of a new human era were beginning to multiply in the atmosphere of the urban milieux of the old era. Even as the great synthesizers of that period were articulating their intellectual structures based on the fundaments of their *episteme* (as Foucault would have put it), these urban germs were beginning to infect those structures and break them down.

Five masterpieces about the city

There are of course many signs of what was under way, and many milestones on the journey. In what follows, we look at five especially significant works of human creativity that reveal what was happening. They arose over a long period of time: the earliest is over three thousand years old, the most recent is from the 1950s. And they arose in very different cultures of Eurasia: from the ancient Middle East, from Europe, from China and from Japan. For all the obvious differences of time and place, they have a connecting thread. They tell the story – the poignant story – of the self-discovery of urban humanity. They are all stories, even the very first and oldest, about one story: of how human beings became detached from the natural order of things. It is, of course, an unfinished story.

It begins with one of the very oldest surviving works of literature – *The Epic of Gilgamesh*. Originating in Mesopotamia at least three thousand years ago, this story might at first blush seem to have little to say to the emerging urban consciousness of recent times. It is, in one sense, typical of the ancient stories of pre-modern cultures: it mingles gods and humans, and the humans are flawed heroes who struggle with one another and with the gods. It has obvious resonances in Greek, Indian and Chinese sagas. Its motifs occur again and again – the long journey of the hero, the titanic struggle of good and evil beings, the pursuit of the secret of immortal life. Its parallels with images and motifs of the Jewish Bible are intriguing and may well not just be coincidental: the perfect garden, the serpent, the great flood, the vanity of life's ambitions, the inevitability of death – all these are motifs of the Bible too.

But its most important feature – which is astonishing, given its antiquity – is that it is a harbinger of the human dilemma about the city. It starts and ends in the city of Uruk, of which Gilgamesh is the ruler. At the start, he is brash, self-confident, overweening; by the end he is wiser, chastened and perhaps reconciled to the human condition. He forms a close friendship with the divinely procreated Enkidu, who is a child of nature, 'eating grass in the hills with the gazelle and lurking with wild beasts at the water holes'.[19] Enkidu is brought to the city and, after struggling with Gilgamesh and telling him some home truths about his behaviour with the women of the city, becomes his companion as he sets out to conquer the power of the great cedar forest. And thus Gilgamesh participates in the ambiguous violation of nature, which is the watershed of the story; he slays the evil giant of the forest and cuts down the great cedar, which symbolizes primal nature in all its dark strength. The price mysteriously paid for this abomination is the death of his friend Enkidu. Gilgamesh then goes on a long and dangerous odyssey to find the one man who has survived the great flood and who can tell him the secret of immortal life. But there is no secret – or if there is, it remains tantalizingly out of reach, in the form of a thorny plant from the bottom of the water, which is snatched away by a serpent. Knowing himself perhaps for the first time, Gilgamesh returns to the city of Uruk, which he has already established in all its grandeur, there to die a natural death. He has achieved immortality after all, but it is an immortality through his legacy in history, not in what he has built, and not in eternity:

> There is no permanence. Do we build a house to stand for ever, do we seal a contract to hold for all time? Do brothers divide an inheritance to keep for ever, does the flood time of rivers endure?[20]

The questions behind the poetry of these questions are with us today, just as they were three thousand years ago.

We reach our second milestone on this journey over two and a half thousand years later, in the form of Europe's first modern novel, *The Ingenious Nobleman Don Quixote de La Mancha*. Hugely successful almost from the start, Cervantes' great creation became the emblem of the end of a deeply structured and integrated order of things, and of the beginning of a new era that would simultaneously enthrone and question the individual. The novel is complex and episodic, hilarious and poignant, both true and unreal, very earthy and never mystical. Cervantes creates a hero who asserts himself energetically in his 'mad' reimagining of reality. In so doing he raises a very modern – but also ancient – question about identity. Alonso Quixano is a bookworm who is so absorbed in the stories of the chivalry of the old era that he loses his grip on reality. In his mind he becomes a knight errant with the name of Don Quixote, and sallies forth on a series of preposterous adventures with the ignorant peasant Sancho Panza as his squire and companion – all of it an uproarious send-up of the old clichés of chivalric romance. He reimagines his tired old horse as a knightly steed named Rocinante. He reimagines a farm girl as Dulcinea, the heroine of the romance, who never appears and is always beyond his reach.

But this was not just parody of traditional popular storytelling based on medieval social values, storytelling in which roles were clearly defined and in which there was only very limited individualization even of the main characters. The setting is Spain as it was entering a long period of decline and failing to respond to the new spirit sweeping through Europe; but Don Quixote is a figure of far wider significance. He may be a would-be knight from a small town who wanders over the plain of La Mancha, confronting imaginary giants and armies, moving between imaginary castles that are, in fact, humdrum inns, and coming to the aid of imaginary damsels who are, in fact, serving girls either bemused or terrified by him. But it is not simply that – to use the words of his own creator in his epitaph at the end of a thousand pages of adventures – the 'absurd histories in books of chivalry' are 'thanks to the exploits of my real Don Quixote . . . even now tottering, and without any doubt will soon tumble to the ground'.[21] It was far more than that; it was symbolic of the breakdown of the old, holistic, integrated natural order of things.

For Quixote may not himself be an urban figure; but his creator was, and so was his audience. And the deeper truth – the reason why he has captured imaginations far beyond Spain, and indeed, far beyond Europe – is that he is, in reality, a quintessentially urban figure. He is individual, fractious and unsure of who he really is. And yet, for all his ridiculous imaginings, and for all the indignities heaped upon him, he somehow retains a deeper dignity. He is the first great antihero. In the end, Don Quixote regains his sanity and his real name; Alonso Quixano wakes up, as it were, in the midst of a final illness – and dies. And perhaps this reminds us of Zhuangzi's question from long before: was he dreaming he was a butterfly or was the butterfly dreaming it was him? Is Don Quixote imaginary, or is he real? And what is the true relationship between author and character? 'For me alone was Don Quixote born, and I for him; it was for him to act, for me to write; we two are as one' writes the author in the same final epitaph quoted above. Whatever the answer, it was clear that the old order of things was passing away.

But the passing of the old order has been a slow death, not a sudden end; and different cultures have been affected in different ways over the last few centuries. Our third milestone highlights the difference between Europe in the century after Cervantes – energetic and fast changing – and the contemporary China, caught in a self-satisfied stasis that amounted to a gentle, and in the end dangerous, decline. And yet, for all the differences, it points to the same fundamental shift from life-in-nature in the old order to an urban world view that is much more individuated. *Dream of the Red Chamber* is the last of the four great classical Chinese novels; it is arguably the most popular and is surely the most profoundly human. The other three, starting with the fourteenth century *The Romance of the Three Kingdoms*, followed by *The Water Margin* (the first complete edition of which is from the late sixteenth century), and *The Journey to the West* (also late-sixteenth century), are all boisterous narratives, full of interwoven plots, action-packed, often blood-soaked and based in varying degrees on historical events. Though their characters may be sharply etched, their psychology is not for the most part deeply probed. They are all of them more breathless than reflective (and they are certainly more exciting than the chivalric romances of Europe that Cervantes so despised). They belong to the external world – albeit in a guise that, particularly in the case of *The Journey to the West*, was often fantastical.

Dream of the Red Chamber is from the eighteenth century and is very different. Like the other three classics, it is long – at least double the length of *Don Quixote* – and has an enormous cast of characters. But there the similarities end. China's greatest novel is urban and domestic; and it may well have an element of autobiography in it. The core of its story is focused mainly on three young people, all just on the threshold of adulthood, in the context of two related families that have had connections in the imperial court (one of the women has been taken as a consort of the emperor) but are now falling out of favour. The young man, Jia Baoyu, is the centre of attention from his female cousins, from the maids of the household, and from his doting grandmother. He is more interested in poetry than in Confucius, to the frustration of his father. He is attracted to his slender, intelligent, sensitive, introverted and sickly cousin Lin Daiyu, but ends up marrying Xue Baochai, another cousin who is also intelligent but more conventional and socially compatible, and who inevitably has his father's approval. It becomes clear as the novel proceeds through the minutiae of the interactions of the three that disenchantment is inevitable and tragedy lies in store. The relationships among them are a subtle blend of friendship and rivalry, from which there is no escape without hurt. Daiyu dies of a broken heart and the other two go into a marriage that is destined to be distant, for all his and her obvious virtues.

But such a summary does little justice to the marvellous intricacy of this novel: its moving insight into the psychology of these and many other characters; its ability to capture social moods; its detailed observation of the life of the urban wealthy in all its claustrophobia; and its perceptive reflection of religious awareness in a society that was under the brooding influence of the Confucian order of things but also pervaded by a jumble of colourful Daoist and Buddhist beliefs and practices. This immensely rich and complex novel could not be described as bourgeois in a nineteenth-century European sense; its social setting has more in common with the Russia of Pushkin's time than with the urban Europe of traders and industrialists. The families at the centre of the novel are a long way from the bourgeois capitalists who play such a key role in the metaphysics of Marx; and their thought world belongs more to Foucault's second *episteme* than to his third – no longer the integrated world of life-in-nature but still a mixture of pre-modern beliefs alongside recognizably modern urban attitudes. But its domestic intensity, and indeed its air of melancholy and tragedy, foreshadows later masterpieces from various Eurasian cultures at times when the bourgeoisie was clearly on the rise, including, for example, Tolstoy's *Anna Karenina*, Thomas Mann's *Buddenbrooks* and Tanizaki's *The Makioka Sisters*.

The emergence of the tragic novel of the comfortable urban family is a sign that the new urban consciousness which was spreading through Eurasia – in some cultures rapidly, in others more fitfully – was far from at peace with itself. This was a long way from the ironic confidence of Don Quixote. Mao read the *Dream of the Red Chamber* several times and saw in it a study in the stultifying effects of the class system. He was not wrong, of course, but there is a much deeper point at stake. What is the worm that eats away at the apple even in a comfortable urban household?

And what then of the underclasses of urban society? Our fourth milestone on the journey from the old integrated world to the new, ruptured urban era is a novel of the nineteenth century, written about the Paris of the 1830s. By this time in Europe, industrialization was well under way and the cities were growing fast; for much of their populations they were crowded, noisy and filthy. Hardship and insecurity were rampant, and the sheer randomness of events could ruin lives with no one even noticing. *Les Misérables* is almost too well known, through the enduring popularity of the stage musical. But the novel itself – Victor Hugo's greatest masterpiece – is a highly complex and colourful portrayal of Paris, whose myriad details cannot possibly be captured in three hours on the stage. Jean Valjean is the central figure, an ex-convict who strives for a redemption that others will never quite allow him. Apart from the handful of unforgettable characters involved in the twists and turns of his life, there are dozens of other figures who feature in various subplots and even single episodes, all of which leave a general impression of the instability of fortunes and the fragility of relationships in an urban context that is rough and uncaring.

Hugo's great panorama is not, however, simply a cause for reflection on the pity of things; not for him a resigned acceptance of the destiny that misshapes our ends, rough-hew them how we will. He has a strong moral perspective on what he narrates. This is not a novel that can in any way be characterized as a programme for left-wing revolution; but Hugo is very clear about his sympathies – they lie with the downtrodden people he so unforgettably portrayed.

And he is not just clear about his sympathies. Hugo was politically engaged – on the basis of a quasi-religious conviction about the human possibilities in this new urban life. The novel is filled with essays on a variety of topics about contemporary French life, including, for example, one on the politics and personalities involved in the July revolution of 1830 and the June uprising of 1832, as well as one on the street children of Paris. But the most important such diversion is in the nineteen chapters he devotes to the Battle of Waterloo, whose site he was visiting when he finished his novel. He regards Waterloo as a pivot of history – but not because it had allowed the crowned heads of Europe to sleep in peace again. Rather, it channelled the new human spirit in a different direction: 'the day of the swordsmen was ended, the thinkers took their place. The tides of the century that Waterloo sought to stem flowed over the battlefield and still rose. That sinister victory was defeated by liberty.'[22] Hugo wrote this in 1862, well after the failure of Europe's 1848 revolutions; so he knew this remained a hope rather than the actuality. In fact, it was to take much longer before an industrializing Europe reached anything like the peaceful freedoms he yearned for. But he ends this vast novel on a poetic note of inextinguishable hope:

Should we continue to look upwards? Is the light we can see in the sky one of those which will presently be extinguished? The ideal is terrifying to behold, lost as it is in the depths, small, isolated, a pinpoint, brilliant but threatened on all sides by the dark forces that surround it: nevertheless, no more in danger than a star in the jaw of the clouds.[23]

So the cities of the nineteenth century were not only festering slums; they could also be home to small points of light that could never be extinguished. Somehow or other, it was in the cities that the new human dispensation – a new order of things – would take shape.

Yet if the hope was for a new order of things in which peace, freedom and economic well-being would prevail, would it put an end to the alienation that troubled both Smith and Marx? What would the urban life experience be then? This is the question that our fifth and final milestone on this journey into the new urban era brings into memorable and poignant focus.

Yasujiro Ozu's film *Tokyo Monogatari* (*Tokyo Story*) was made in 1953. It is his unquestioned masterpiece, regularly voted one of the best films of all time. It is technically brilliant, contemplative and insightful in its study of the various characters, all of whom are sensitively and empathetically portrayed. There is no easy emotion, no black-and-white judgmentalism, and no comforting resolution at the end. The Japanese title links it to Japan's great classical novel (and the world's oldest), *Genji Monogatari* (*The Tale of Genji*), of which all the same things can surely be said. (We shall return in Chapter 7 to this extraordinary work from a thousand years ago whose influence on all things Japanese has been so profound.)

Tokyo Story tells of an elderly couple from a remote small town who visit two of their children and a widowed daughter-in-law who are now living and working in Tokyo. In the stress of their busy lives and their small Tokyo apartments, the two children and their families find the presence of their parents an imposition. The grandchildren are bored. Only the daughter-in-law, widowed by the loss of another son in the Pacific War, gives them the time and the respect they deserve. It becomes clear that the mother has a weak heart, and later she falls seriously ill. All the family hurry to their home town; only one of their children fails to get there in time. After the funeral rites, the children depart again to get on with their lives. In the days that follow, the daughter-in-law reveals her loneliness; an unmarried sister at home reveals her bitterness towards her siblings from the big city; and the old man contemplates a lonely old age. 'Life is disappointing', he observes.

This film was at first deemed too Japanese for the international market. From the perspective of the twenty-first century, it is hard to see why. For the truth is that as we progress further into the era of the city, as we see the new society of the prosperous post-industrial city take shape, and as we see most people in developed societies come to regard themselves as middle class, this film becomes more poignant and thought-provoking than ever. The Tokyo of the 1950s is the Tokyo of today – but it is also London, Shenzhen and Dubai. There is a universality about this film's portrayal of the way urban life has changed us – and continues to do so. There is not much left of Marx's revolutionary proletariat, though certainly plenty of Hugo's underclass; but more deeply, there is not much left of the old order of things. The ugliness of the modern Tokyo is itself symbolic; what happened to the natural order that was once so important to the Japanese spirit?

We have travelled a long way from the world of *The Epic of Gilgamesh*. We have lived through the rupture of the old order. We are still in the process of urbanizing our lives, but we are everywhere becoming more used to this new order. And as we do so, we learn some timeless truths about ourselves. We learned very early on that there are no answers to be had from outside the city to some of the most basic of our questions. We learn that the city offers not only rupture but also the exuberance that comes from demolition of old norms and constraints. We learn too that no one is assured of happiness in this new era – not even the comfortable bourgeois, and certainly not the underclass. But the most important difference between the old and the new eras is that we now ask the question 'Who are we?' more insistently than before. Asking the question is not the same as finding the answer, though. In the old era, philosophers sought to relate the One and the Many in a way that underpinned the good life; now we know their syntheses do not hold. But we have nothing yet to put in their place, and we do not even know if this is possible.

Still, we might have expected the responses to the question to be increasingly similar, on the grounds that the urban experience is increasingly dominant and increasingly similar everywhere. There should surely be something culture-free not only about the question but also about our hopes – and our insecurities – as we seek to answer it. This ought to feel like a convergence of doubt, at the very least. And yet it looks as if the answers we give, rather than converging on the basis of our converging experience of the new urban life, may in fact, be *diverging* – and this at the very time in our history when we are becoming more and more conscious of shared challenges. In the next three chapters we explore those divergences, before turning in Chapter 7 to the problems we face in common during the rest of this century.

4

'What is a nation?'

Neither Adam Smith nor Karl Marx allowed much space in their thinking for the nation. The central fact they were addressing was industrialization; in both cases their attention was absorbed almost entirely by urbanization, and by the labour and capital markets. Smith lived in a culture whose universal relevance he took for granted; Marx saw culture as a superstructure whose fundaments were to be found in the economic system. For the one, the relationship between state, nation and culture was largely taken for granted; for the other, it was secondary to the real question of the nature of the economic system at its base.

For Adam Smith, nation states existed as a matter of fact, hence the title of his great work *The Wealth of Nations*, which was published in 1776, the epoch-making year when the eventual superpower of the twentieth century was born. But he does not seek to answer the question of what makes a nation; he wrote at a time when ideas about the way human social identities evolve were still in their infancy. Smith was a child of the European Enlightenment, which was simultaneously doing two things that would eventually prove incompatible. On the one hand, it was seeking to evolve an understanding of human values as both autonomous and universal; and on the other, it was energetically exploring the world around it, and in the process discovering more and more about other cultures that did not have their basis in European Christian history. Smith believed – as he argues in his other seminal work, *The Theory of Moral Sentiments* – that there are some 'principles in [human] nature' which 'interest' us in the fortunes of others, and 'render their happiness necessary' to us.[1] And it would not have occurred to him that these principles might vary from one culture to another.

Indeed, as the thought leaders of the European Enlightenment began to learn more about Asian cultures, they found evidence that seemed to confirm this universalizing view. In particular, many of them came to admire the Confucian way as an approach to the ordering of society that did not depend on the directives of a personal God, but on a humanistic understanding of virtue and order. They saw the question about identity essentially as a question about the individual and about the individual's place in a wider social order. This carried political implications, of course, and constituted a challenge to the absolutist states of that era which has reverberated down the centuries since. The existence of states as such, however, was largely treated not as a question needing investigation but as a territorial fact. Not until around the turn of the nineteenth century did the question of the difference between nations and states come into focus; only then would the idea of nationhood and the role of the nation in shaping the individual be put under the microscope.

Karl Marx developed his view of the world at a time in the nineteenth century when ideas about nationhood were rapidly evolving. But his focus was still where Smith's had been. For him, the dynamic of relations between the different economic classes of society was all-important. For him, as for Smith, nations were a fact – although for him they were a transient fact of a particular stage of historical development: 'Workers *of the world* unite; you have nothing to lose but your chains.'[2] Marx does address the obvious fact that different countries are at different stages of economic and social development, and he specifically focuses on what he terms the 'Asiatic mode of production', referring to societies in which the private ownership of land was absent, village communities were autonomous, and a despotic ruler directly appropriated the economic surplus of the territory in order to pay for his court and for the costs of defending the realm. As his thinking developed and became more systematic, he came to see this Asiatic mode of production as a stage of development that followed the primitive communism of very early human societies and preceded – or overlapped with – slavery and feudalism, which he saw as the two other pre-capitalist stages of historical importance. But the concept fades out from Marx's later writings and gets no attention in those of Engels. In essence, their thought world was of European societies that had passed beyond such pre-capitalist phases; it was these societies – which were urbanizing and industrializing fast – that would be the seed beds of revolution. Neither Marx nor Engels had any deep knowledge of Asian societies or real interest in their cultures; had they investigated them in any detail, they would have found themselves having to adapt their models substantially (in particular, Japan did not fit their mould at all neatly).

Yet, as the nineteenth century wore on, the question of nationhood was becoming more and more insistent. Europe was not only becoming urbanized; it was also becoming more and more conscious of national identity – or, rather, of its many national identities. Germany and Italy were unified into new states, not just because their components were geographically contiguous and as a result of a successful combination of politicking and military activity; they were united on the basis of an idea of nationhood. The demand for a united and independent Poland, led vocally by the hugely respected figure of the poet Adam Mickiewicz, was rooted in the same deep conviction. In all three cases, language played a decisive part in shaping the national consciousness. Conversely, the Habsburg Empire was beginning to be tormented ever more convulsively by the rising demand for separate national identities, above all from the Hungarians and then the Czechs. Britain was racked by its own centrifugal force: the Irish question. The Ottoman Empire in South Eastern Europe was falling apart, losing Greece, Serbia, Romania and Bulgaria in the course of the century. Austria–Hungary moved into the Balkan vacuum, in which Romanians, Serbs and Bulgarians were all actively staking claims. Among the major European powers, in fact, it was only France for whom the question of its own nationhood did not become a source of dangerous domestic or international tension. (But France was not at peace with itself either; instead, it went through one constitutional upheaval after another as the aftershocks of 1789 and of 1815 reverberated over the century.)

It was not only in Europe that the pressure was rising. Much of Eurasia had come under the imperial sway of aggressively competitive European powers: Germany was extending its influence in a weakened Ottoman empire; France was ensconced in Indochina; and the British in India sat at the centre of the largest empire the world has known, but had been shaken to the core by the events of 1857 – by what they called the Indian Mutiny, and what Indian nationalists were to call the Uprising. Meanwhile, Russia had moved into the central Asian vacuum and was busy exploiting the weakness of a sclerotic Persia; and in China, the Europeans were aggressively pursuing their commercial interests (including, notoriously, in the opium trade) with little or no regard for the authority or the sensitivities of the Qing government. The story of how the impact of these imperial adventures stoked the flames of nationalism is complicated, not least because of the dramatic role played by Japan. For now, it is enough to note that by the late nineteenth century, both the imperialist powers and the subject peoples (or at least their intellectual elites) were becoming ever more aware of the hopes and challenges of nationhood.

In fact, alongside the impact of urbanization, the rise of nationhood was the most striking change sweeping through the Eurasian consciousness. This was an era of unprecedentedly rapid development: industrialization was transforming the lives of people and the face of cities all over Europe; and at the same time, imperial competition throughout Eurasia (and in Africa) was at its most intense. But manifesting itself through all of this change, more and more obviously, was a new expression of identity, namely awareness of nationhood, so that within most of those same empires, there were growing nationalist demands for independence which would eventually, over the following century, tear them apart.

And if there were any illusions about the power of the urban ideas represented by Smith and by Marx to smooth over or suppress the resulting national antagonisms, those illusions were to be shattered in the summer of 1914.

Even after the assassination of Archduke Franz Ferdinand, the presiding assumption of the international capital markets was that economic rationality would prevail over geopolitical danger. Notoriously, the bond markets showed no sign of weakening in the face of impending catastrophe. Notoriously too, the Socialist International collapsed, buckling under the force of patriotic sentiment: as influential a figure as Plekhanov, father of Russian Marxism, had no doubts about the duty of the Russian motherland to defend itself; all the German socialists except Karl Liebknecht voted for the war credits; and in France, the humane and reformist Jaurès was assassinated by a nationalist fanatic, while the previously uncompromising socialist hardliner Guesde joined the French war government.

The power of nationhood

The idea of the nation has had enormous power in recent human history. But what is a nation? This was the question asked in a remarkable lecture delivered at the Sorbonne in Paris in 1882 by the French philosopher and philologist Ernest Renan. Renan's lecture was held only a few years after Germany had been united and made its appearance as the new great power on the European and world stage, and only four years after the Congress of Berlin had settled various territorial questions in South Eastern Europe in a way that left almost none of the participants satisfied, stoking geopolitical instability and national resentments that would haunt Europe all the way through to 1914. Thus, the question 'What is a nation?' was not just of academic interest. At stake were questions of identity and of international power politics that were to bedevil Europe in particular and Eurasia in general for more than a hundred years.

Renan was a figure from between the times, so to speak – an uneasy combination of attitudes from the eighteenth century with ideas that foreshadowed the darker side of the twentieth. Having rejected the traditional institutional Catholicism of his childhood, he wrote a famous and controversial *Life of Jesus* that sought at once to reveal the real historical figure by denying his divinity or miraculous powers and at the same time to strip this historical figure of his Jewishness. An idealist who admired German culture, he was deeply shaken by the conflict between Prussia and France, followed by the founding of the aggressive new German state in the ashes of the French defeat. He found it difficult to reconcile himself to the individualistic democracy that emerged in the new French Third Republic after the trauma of the defeat and the revolutionary violence of the Paris Commune. But he had no trouble arguing in support of the imperialist project on the grounds of cultural superiority. He yearned for community and disliked society (to borrow the terms popularized by the German sociologist Ferdinand Tönnies[3]). He wanted to see the nation as a community on the large scale; and out of his intellectual and emotional struggle to articulate the nature of this national community came his lecture 'What is a nation?'[4]

In this lecture, Renan argued that a sense of nationhood is not the result of either ethnic, linguistic or religious identity, and he cites some obvious, and some less obvious, examples in support of this assertion.

France, he points out, was originally a melange of different races that have gradually fused into one French consciousness; Switzerland is a unity despite not only its religious divisions but also its four different languages (and he might have added, from the vantage point of a century later, that India is a unity despite dozens of different languages); Germany is a unity despite its confessional divisions – and indeed all European countries in the modern era treat religious belief largely as a private or community affair and not as a basis for national self-definition (a position that is however now under overt attack in some European populist quarters where the growing Muslim presence is perceived as a threat to the national identity). Nor is geography decisive, even though it is clearly a major factor in some obvious cases (the fact that Britain and Japan are both islands, for example, has been a major factor in shaping their identity). Nor is it sufficient that there be a community of interest. As Renan argues, 'Communities of interest determine commercial treaties. However, nationality depends on sentiment too . . . A customs union' – of the kind Germany had been before it was formally united in 1871 – 'is never a fatherland.' No, he argues, a nation is 'body and soul at the same time' or 'a spiritual principle'. He goes on to explain more fully:

> Two things which . . . are really one and the same constitute . . . this spiritual principle. One is in the past, the other is in the present. One is the possession in common of a rich legacy of memories; the other is present consent, the desire to live together, the will to continue to assert the value of the heritage we have jointly received . . . The nation, like the individual, is the outcome of a long past of efforts, sacrifices and devotions. Of all cults, ancestor worship is the most legitimate: our ancestors have made us what we are.

Renan recognizes that this past is, to some extent, invented; he is also clear that the spirit of the nation is not guaranteed to live for ever. Indeed, he envisages that the European nation states of his time might at some point be supplanted by a form of European confederation – an argument that foreshadowed what has been happening since the end of the Second World War.

Renan is partly right and partly wrong. Some of his observations about interrelationships between European states are astonishingly prescient, and he understood how what is remembered – and forgotten – about the past shapes the 'spirit of the nation', just as it shapes the individual identity. Renan confines his examples largely to European nations; but much of what he says applies with considerable force throughout a Eurasia full of long and tangled histories. However, he does brush one point aside too easily. He argues that language does not – and should not – form a sound basis for national identity, and not only on the grounds that there are, in fact, obvious examples of flourishing nations such as Switzerland that are multilingual. He also makes a profounder point: he argues with passion that to allow language a role in the national – and the individual – identity is to constrain the human spirit:

> We must not abandon this fundamental principle: that the human being is a rational and moral being before becoming parked in this or that language, a member of this or that race, or a participant in this or that culture. Before French, German or Italian culture is the culture of humankind. Look at the great men of the Renaissance; they were neither French nor German nor Italian. They had rediscovered in the study of antiquity the secret of the true education of the human mind and they devoted themselves to it body and soul.

But this is inconsistent with his own emphasis on the importance of a shared past in forming the national identity. Does such a 'culture of humankind' really exist? And if so, how is it to be expressed? These are questions we will return to in Chapter 5 and then again in Chapter 7 (because the answers are many-layered); but for now, we should note how Renan's own answer is problematic because it is too culture-bound.

For Renan makes the assumption, which is a throwback to the Renaissance and more common in the eighteenth century than in his own day, that this culture is fully revealed by the study of classical Greek and Roman literature. Yet, as the eighteenth century unfolded, the literati of Europe were becoming more aware of other cultures: the Jesuit presence in China resulted in a growing knowledge of Chinese thought in Europe; Sir William Jones and others were at work in India, bringing to European attention the richness of the Indian past; and by the early nineteenth century, Goethe was singing the praises of the great Iranian poet Hafez, in his collection of poems, *West-östlicher Diwan* (*West-Eastern Diwan*). None of this meant that the standing of the Greek and Roman classics had been diminished; but it inevitably meant that Europeans would in time become more aware of the rich variety of sophisticated cultural traditions forming the broader Eurasian heritage. Not only that, but the nineteenth century was also busy rediscovering (and partly reinventing) elements in the European stories of the past that did not owe their origins to classical antiquity. Hence the popularity of the Arthurian legends, of *Beowulf*, of the Norse sagas, of the *Ring of the Nibelung*. In the end, as we shall see in Chapters 8 and 9 – but not for at least another century after Renan's time – the question of a 'culture of humankind' would be posed again, but this time in a radically different geopolitical context.

In any event, the shared past – whatever its content – can only be expressed through language, because the past is handed on (and remoulded) through storytelling. Renan was wrong in his belief that the great figures of the Renaissance were somehow immune from the cultural formation that their language gave them. Renan was here taking aim at the great German philosopher Johann Gottlieb Fichte, who had argued – almost eighty years earlier, in a Berlin occupied by Napoleon's troops, and at a time when the demand for German political unity was beginning to be voiced more insistently – for a German identity based on the rich culture whose vehicle was the German language.[5] But Renan's own arguments for the importance of the past, and of stories about the past, in forming the national identity meant that Fichte was right to emphasize the role of language in that identity.

What is more, the Renaissance may have resurrected the study of classical Greek and Roman literature; but it was actually the beginning of the end of a single common European language of thought; Latin was to decline into obsolescence, and the vernaculars, rather than Latin, were to become the carriers of the past. Latin remained the language of the liturgy in the Roman Catholic Church; not until the second half of the twentieth century would the mass be said in the vernacular languages of the people. But increasingly, educated discourse took place in the vernacular (with French – the language of the most powerful nation

state of Europe from the end of the Thirty Years War in 1648 until the
end of the Napoleonic era in 1815 – coming to serve as lingua franca
for international conversation). The change was gradual: Leibniz and
Newton both still wrote at least some of their work in Latin in the seventeenth century. And there is the delightful story of an encounter between
Linnaeus, the great Swedish botanist, and Sir Hans Sloane (whose
extraordinarily broad-based collection formed much of the nucleus of the
British Museum, the Natural History Museum and the British Library)
that took place in London in 1736. Sloane was a multilingual polymath but did not speak Swedish; Linnaeus could not speak any modern
European language other than Swedish. So they spoke, with some difficulty, in Latin.[6] It is one of the last examples of Latin being used as the
working language of European intellectuals.

This shift to the use of vernaculars in Europe was part of a much wider
Eurasian trend over many centuries. It is intimately related to the rise of
the idea of nationhood. The history of this shift is complex, and it takes
as many different forms as there are different cultures. In India, for example, Sanskrit (the language of the *Mahabharata*) declined as a medium
of intellectual life as Muslim rule was extended; Persian served for
many centuries as the administrative language until it was displaced by
English, but regional and local languages have always thrived as vehicles
for commerce and daily life, as well as for storytelling and poetry. Thus
the original language of India's most venerated texts is now confined to
a tiny scholarly minority; India's extraordinarily rich and vibrant poetry
has for many centuries been rooted in its vernaculars. In England for
three hundred years after the Norman conquest, French was the language of the aristocracy and of the law, and Latin was the language of
church and liturgy, while English dialects remained the language of the
people; English resurfaced in courtly life and in literature through
the pens of Langland and Chaucer in the fourteenth century, and in 1377
Richard II was the first king since William the Conqueror to be crowned
in a ceremony using English and Latin instead of French and Latin. In
each of the cultures of Eurasia there are analogous stories to be told: vernaculars take over from ancient liturgical and intellectual languages.
The specifics differ but there is an underlying trend that is common to
Chinese, Japanese, Muslim, Indian and European experience: in all these

cultural spheres, there was an intimate connection between the development of vernacular languages, the role of the city and the rise of cultural identities.

The rise of vernaculars is a trend that was well under way before the modern era, and in some cases, centuries earlier. It is in general related to the rise of popular storytelling, of secular poetry and of the novel. Thus, for example, the European chivalric poetry so derided by Cervantes was a poetry of local languages, not of Latin. In China, much poetry from the Tang Dynasty onwards was in vernacular Chinese, not in the classical language of its Confucian texts; and its four great novels substantially increased the prominence and prestige of vernacular literature (they contained both classical and vernacular Chinese, with the balance shifting to the latter, such that by the last one – *Dream of the Red Chamber* – the narrative was all in the vernacular, and only the poetry was in classical Chinese). In Japan, the tale is complicated by the role played by Chinese among the intellectual elite for many centuries: the men who administered public life until well into the Tokugawa period wrote in Chinese; and the Buddhist scholars who made up Japan's religious establishment were strongly influenced by Chinese thought, so that much of their writing was in Chinese too. Chinese thus functioned for the Japanese like a combination of the roles of French and Latin in the context of England after the Norman Conquest. But the court lady who authored *The Tale of Genji* wrote in Japanese. She as much as anyone set a direction of travel that resulted in the eventual triumph of the Japanese language – so much so, in fact, that in the aggressively nationalistic Japan of the late nineteenth century, writing in Chinese came to seem like *lèse-majesté*.

In two cases, in India and in Europe, the move away from a sacred clerical language was also given impetus by (initially) heterodox religious movements – Buddhism in the one and Protestantism in the other, both of which sought to break out from ossified religious structures hidebound by sacred texts and rituals intoned in a language only the initiated could understand. Thus, Protestant bibles played an important role in extending vernacular literacy in Germany and in Britain. In the Muslim world, Persian lost its widespread status as an administrative language as the *ummah* fragmented; but it was of course the natural language of a resurgent national Iranian polity from the time of Shah Abbas in the sixteenth century onwards. In short, vernaculars became the language of culture, and not just of the street, in much of Eurasia as the pre-modern era gave way to the urban era; and as they did so, they became the vehicles of national consciousness too.

But this journey towards a national vernacular took many twists and turns. In most cases there was no single version of the vernacular that was easily intelligible throughout the region. Rather, there was a series of dialects that were often close to being mutually unintelligible (at the time of the French Revolution, probably no more than about half the population could understand Parisian French) or even completely unrelated languages which had jostled together from time immemorial. Thus in the northern regions of the Muslim world, Iranian and Turkic languages have rubbed against one another like tectonic plates over the centuries; the languages of southern India have nothing in common with those of the north; and there are linguistic pockets all over Europe where the languages brought by ancient invaders from the steppes of Central Asia hold sway (as in Finland, Estonia and Hungary) or where what may be an even more ancient and original European language has survived into modern times (in the Basque region).

Exactly how the linguistic pattern evolved is therefore a complex story; but the general direction of travel has been the same. The rise of vernacular languages is clearly related to two other trends: the rise of dominant cities and regions (whose regional dialect thus became the basis of consolidation into a vernacular that eventually all could understand), and the development of increasing national cultural cohesiveness, which gradually turned into an increasing national consciousness. These two trends have been mutually reinforcing. Does the language create the nation? Or does the nation create the language? The answer can only be: both. But the interplay has taken very different forms in different countries and cultural spheres. China, uniquely, lived with multiple dialects and languages well into modern times, but was able to achieve literary cohesiveness through the use of a standard ideographical script; and the People's Republic has effectively forced through the use of Mandarin Chinese – the language of the north – as the common language of the whole country, such that it is now the most widely spoken mother tongue on the planet. Meanwhile, in Europe, a process of vernacularization and standardization occurred separately in one country after another. There was a shift away from the Latin of the clerics to the vernacular – and to a particular version of the vernacular, furthermore, which was that of a major urban centre. In France, the sheer power of Paris became an unstoppable centripetal force; in Germany, the role of Luther's Bible and of his pamphleteering was decisive in establishing the German of Saxony as the true 'high German'; in England, the role of London was reinforced linguistically by Chaucer and then Shakespeare, both of whom wrote in the English used in the London region in their day; in Italy, Dante's use of the Florentine dialect secured its position as the standard of pure Italian. All this took time; dialects, and particularly regional accents, remain relevant to this day (even in France, despite its being the most homogeneous country in Europe). But the broad truth is that dialectal differences have largely evaporated; and wholly separate languages – the Celtic languages of the fringes of the British Isles and of Brittany, the Sorbian of eastern Germany, and even the language of the Basque region – are marginal, and will probably survive in the longer term only with active official educational and cultural support.

Unlike China, however, Europe did not consolidate, either linguistically or politically – a profoundly important difference with consequences that extend to the present day, and to which we will return in Chapters 5 and 6. Meanwhile, the experience of the Muslim world is also of a linguistic geography that largely maps the political geography. The *ummah* is part of any Muslim's identity at some level; but not for centuries has it had any political embodiment. So although Arabic remains the sacred language of the Qur'an, it – or dialects of it – are the vernaculars only of the Arabian peninsula, of Egypt and along the coast of North Africa. For the rest of the Muslim world, its vernaculars are the bearers of separate national identities – Iranian, Turkish, Urdu (although Pakistan is far from linguistically homogeneous), and the Bahasa of Malaysia and Indonesia. All these languages became critical in the struggle to found new identities in the post-imperial era.

Meanwhile, India has pursued yet another – and unique – path. It is the only one of Eurasia's major countries that has journeyed towards national consolidation without there being an overwhelmingly dominant vernacular. Hindi, the lingua franca of northern and central

India, may now be the official language of the country (although it also 'schedules' twenty-one other languages including English, which is widespread among the educated and remains dominant in the administrative sphere). Hindi is now the third most widely spoken mother tongue in the world, but although government policy is theoretically designed to spread Hindi further and to establish it as the genuine lingua franca of India, the reality is that the country is a long way from the linguistic homogeneity that China has achieved in the last half century. It is perfectly possible to find yourself on a journey in the company of a group of Indians from different parts of the country and to discover that the only common language they have is the English that was bequeathed to them by the former imperial overlords.

The case of India reminds us to treat any easy generalizations about the basis for national identity with suspicion. It is safe to say that the sense of nationhood has been an important component of individual human identities in many cultural spheres for several centuries at least; and that nationalism in a more concrete and political sense has gained powerful momentum in human affairs during the last two centuries, under the impact of urbanization. Yet there is clearly no single catalyst – or essential ingredient – of the sense of nationhood. Language certainly plays a pervasive role, not least because it is the vehicle for the collective memory that underlies any national consciousness. But the case of India shows that a single nationwide vernacular is not necessary to national identity. The European case, however, shows how a multiplicity of well-established vernaculars, each dominant in its own territory, could facilitate a growing sense of linguistic nationhood and an evolving political nationalism that, in turn, made cultural and political cohesion at the European level more and more difficult.

Yet we can do more than simply accept that each case is unique. In particular, we need to ask where the sense of nationhood itself comes from. To answer in terms of collective memory is simply to beg further questions: why is the memory collective? How reliable is it? What is the origin and basis for this sense of collectivity? Scholars have wrestled extensively with this set of questions as they apply to particular cultures.[7] They have also sought general principles that could account for the pervasiveness of the phenomenon and thus give some insight into the human condition.

There is no agreement about whether nationalism is a product of the modern era, whether it predates it, or whether indeed it is primordial.[8] The debate is not helped by the elasticity of the terms used. But in the end, three things are clear: first, there is a real distinction between nationalism as a political concept and a sense of nationhood that is at root a cultural concept. Second, nationhood may not be primordial (since it is certainly not demonstrably universal throughout human history, and since in particular cases nationhood appears to be malleable and even completely invented); but it is clearly ancient and widespread as part of many people's identities. Third, some sense of collective, *but not universal*, belonging does appear to be a universal human instinct: the excluded Other defines the identity of the group. With origins probably going back to primeval human experience, and possibly with evolutionary significance, this need seems to be a crucial and unavoidable part of the search for identity, and in settled societies this took the form of a need to belong to the community in the territory where people were born, and where they lived and died. The rise of nationhood is on this basis more like a seamless evolution in human anthropology than a social phenomenon of the modern era that has no apparent precedent.

The individual, society and nationhood

Whether or not the sense of nationhood evolved in this way, two streams of thought came together in eighteenth-century Europe and set the context for the debate about cultural identity, nationhood and nationalism as it evolved in the eighteenth and nineteenth centuries. One was political philosophy about the roles, rights and responsibilities of human beings in society; the other was a growing interest in accurately observed social history. Both were the products of the new intellectual atmosphere of the Enlightenment, and together they had an enormous impact on the human self-understanding of the modern era.

The European debate of the eighteenth century had some features that are reminiscent of an ancient Chinese debate about the nature of human beings and the implications for the ordering of society. Two millennia earlier, the Chinese philosopher Mozi had treated human nature as malleable, but not naturally good, and had argued that a set of standards of morality should be imposed by the state on behalf of Heaven[9] – an approach that some have seen as the ancestor of the highly centralized and totalitarian system of the Emperor Qin in the third century BCE (a system known in Western commentaries on China as legalism, but meaning in effect rule *by* law, not the rule *of* law as it would be understood in a European or American context).[10] The debate about human nature continued; Mencius and Xunzi were active in roughly the same period in the early third century BCE, not long before Emperor Qin united the first Chinese empire. Mencius was the firmest proponent of the view that human nature is intrinsically good, which he saw as justifying Confucius' programme of self-cultivation.[11, 12] Xunzi, however, bluntly declared that human nature was evil,[13] a view that Emperor Qin clearly shared. Qin totalitarianism had no place for Confucius, who had stressed the importance of perfectibility and of the cultivation of virtue through wisdom; and the regime burnt his books (something that others would do repeatedly down the ages, all the way to the famous book burnings by the Nazis in 1933). But Qin rule collapsed soon after the death of the First Emperor, to be followed by the more durable Han Dynasty, which reinstated Confucian thought, though retaining (because it was in practical terms necessary) what the Chinese have always, down to the present day, known as *fazhi* or rule by law.

Thomas Hobbes, in his *Leviathan*, published in 1651, not long after the end of the terrible Thirty Years War and only two years after the execution of Charles I, argued that human lives in the state of nature were lived out in the absence of any 'common power to keep them all in awe', so that interactions were a matter of *bellum omnium contra omnes* – war of all against all; life was thus, in his famous phrase, 'solitary, poor, nasty, brutish and short'. John Locke, born in more peaceful times and a generation after Hobbes, had a view of human nature that was fundamentally different: for him, human nature was essentially and originally subject to the law of nature, which was a law of reason.[14] The state of nature was thus in effect a state of grace – a view that has an affinity to that of Confucius and still more clearly with Mencius, both of whom were strongly opposed to Mozi's essentially utilitarian argument for obedience to the will of Heaven and for the existence of the state. For them, the innate instincts of the human being gave rise both to the contents of morality and to the motivation to cultivate virtue. In China, their rhetoric inspired the neo-Confucian ethics of Zhu Xi; but the Mohist instinct was never far away from those who governed. In the European context, Locke became the father of a liberalism whose instincts were to be shared later by Adam Smith and whose individualist principles underlay the American Declaration of Independence and Bill of Rights.

Voltaire, half a century later, wrote just before the dawn of a new era that was becoming nationalist in the sense we now recognize. Unlike Locke, he was an ardent believer in the potential of the enlightened despot and kept up a rich and lively dialogue with one of Europe's most successful absolutist rulers, Frederick the Great of Prussia, as well as with Catherine the Great of Russia. His hostility to all forms of benightedness – and especially to the institutional Catholicism of his day but also to Judaism and to Islam (only Hinduism, about which he knew little, seemed benign to him) – put him in the vanguard of the secularism of the new era. He was, in short, the apostle of a new order that would enshrine a culture of moral enlightenment, in which virtue consisted in listening to the better angels of our nature. But his Ciceronian rhetoric and passion for justice went with a refusal to countenance the democratic spirit. His was an order *de haut en bas*, based on (enlightened) government of the people, for the people – but not by the people. Democracy meant to him the rule of the uneducated – the rule, in fact, of the rabble. Small wonder, then, that he was an early admirer of the Confucian order of China, which he saw as being free from the dictates of a supernatural being and based instead on the good instincts of human beings, but is elitist to its core. But his campaign for enlightened rule was inevitably doomed to disappointment, as Frederick the Great took Prussia into the Seven Years War and as Catherine the Great tightened the screws of serfdom in Russia. And this took him eventually into the pessimism that led him famously to 'cultivate his garden'.[15]

The pivotal figure whose influence was to shape ideas of nationhood throughout Eurasia over the coming centuries was not Voltaire, for all his fame and familiarity with the thoughtful despots of his day. It was his younger contemporary, whom he patronized and disliked, but who ended up as a neighbour in the Pantheon in Paris – Jean-Jacques Rousseau. His *Discourse on Inequality* – published in 1754, a generation before the French Revolution swept away the *ancien régime* – attracted vehement hostility because of its radical implications for social reorganization, but it was to become a rallying point for republican sentiment throughout Europe. And his theory of the social contract, under which individuals subordinate themselves to the general will, was to provide a completely different basis for the moral authority of sovereignty from that of Voltaire. The power of this idea came not just from the concept of the contract; it came also from the implication that humans have been on a journey from the state of nature. In that original state, human life was good because it was free – free of authority and free of the divisiveness that came with possession. The social contract became necessary at a stage in social development when ownership – originally of land – created the need for a social order and for rules of behaviour.

This is plainly utterly different from Hobbes; but it is also different from Locke. For Locke, government needs the consent of the people, who give it conditional authority in order to defend their rights to the enjoyment of their individual lives and their property. For Rousseau, the social contract permitted the emergence of a general will, which would reflect the higher selves of human beings – as distinct from their lower selves, which were motivated only by self-interest. Rousseau was not an anthropologist; he did not have a clearly articulated narrative of how the human species evolved from the noble (and apparently individual) savage to the societies and the nations of the world he knew. In particular, he never clearly disentangles the role of property from the role of family (which he believes is the most ancient and most natural form of society) in the original shift from the state of nature to the beginnings of community. This means that he has no very specific account of the reasons for, or nature of, the emerging social relationships that motivate the social contract.[16] There is also a potentially dangerous ambiguity in his conception of the general will: is this just what the citizens have decided through the democratic process or is it some higher abstraction that reflects the common good even if individuals do not recognize it?[17] Nevertheless, this theory set a morally positive tone and exuded a sense of optimism about the possibilities for the future (compared with the present he knew, if not with that idyllic past). In Chinese terms, it was more aligned with a Mohist than with a Confucian view of the world, in that Mozi had made a central feature of the universality of moral obligations, whereas Confucius had drawn careful distinctions based on family and social position. Again echoing Mozi, Rousseau was egalitarian but not individualist and he argued that it was legitimate for a strong state to enforce the general will.

His philosophy was to become more and more influential as the nineteenth century unfolded. Some historians of political ideas have contrasted two main wellsprings of nationalism as it evolved in the nineteenth century. One is seen as more political, and is associated with a line of thought in the French philosophical tradition that runs from Rousseau to Renan and emphasizes the community of common citizenship and the general will. The other is seen as more romantic. Growing on the soil of German idealism, it emphasized the importance of language, ethnicity and shared history – of the untranslatable concept of the *Volk* – in forming the national identity. In particular, the German philosopher Johann Gottfried Herder (who was a generation younger than Rousseau) became the foremost exponent of the role of language in developing the human consciousness and in shaping the human identity in community; and he in turn influenced Fichte, whose lectures were the clarion call to the German nation and had provoked Renan.

But this is arguably a misleading dualism as Rousseau and Herder shared the sense that the state of nature was a state of freedom. Rousseau saw this as a state during which no language was necessary; it was possession that was, so to speak, the snake in the garden – the original source of division and conflict, and the original trigger for the development of language. For Herder, however, language was a feature of the human consciousness even in the state of nature, and it was the role of family and tribe that led to the conflicts of society. Herder was the more insightful in his understanding of the deep history of human social development; and his influence on all subsequent theorizing about language and human identity has been profound.[18] But Rousseau too understood the importance of social cohesion, and argued for the necessity of a common culture as vital to the success of the general will in realizing itself in any state.[19] He argued that a literate high culture should be 'the pervasive and operational culture' of the whole of any society.[20] Since such a culture was inevitably language-based, and thus the bearer of a history of memories and stories, the practical implications for the national identity were more or less what Herder would recognize.

Much more important than any divergence between the heritage of Rousseau and of Herder is the difference between the paths followed in Europe under their influence and the American settlement under the aegis of Locke. America's Declaration of Independence in 1776 is one of the great watersheds of the modern era. It is beyond the scope of this book to examine in detail the very mixed motives behind the American project – a complex mixture of Puritan principles inherited from the original settlers of New England, as well as much baser motives (including the assertion of a right to repudiate treaties made by the British with Native American groups and a deliberate refusal to confront the issue of slavery). Nevertheless, the fact remains that the American self-understanding is to this day much more deeply individualist than any European culture (including that of the British), and the reasons for this lie in its distinctive history. A vital ingredient in that identity has its roots in Locke's conception that individuals hand to government only what they need to give up for the public good, and no more than that. In the history of modern Eurasia, however, it has been the spirit of Rousseau and of Herder that has flourished, rather than that of Locke – as we shall see shortly.

Less than two decades after Rousseau's death, Europe was convulsed by the French Revolution, which was the other great political watershed of the modern era as, after it, people came more and more to see themselves as citizens instead of subjects. But citizens of what polity? The national question would henceforth stalk the political stage. In France itself, the revolutionary impulse with its universalizing ambitions was degenerating into chauvinism by the turn of the nineteenth century. Nevertheless, the genie was out of the bottle; in particular, Rousseau's impact would spread ever more widely. His influence on Kant, on Hegel, on Marx and on into the twentieth century has been profound. Fichte and Renan were both responding to Rousseau as they developed their ideas of nationhood. Rousseau's ideas played a part in creating the impetus behind the unification of both Italy and Germany, as well as behind the disintegration of the Habsburg and the Ottoman empires.

To begin with, this was mainly a European conversation. By the dawn of the eighteenth century, Europe seemed irretrievably fragmented, and parts of it were moving away from the absolutism that had been the dominant form of government for centuries. The question about government and the question about the nation were inevitably intertwined, and both were becoming pressing. These questions would ultimately become pressing elsewhere in Eurasia too, of course. But not yet. This was the period when European supremacy in Eurasia was being established. In the nineteenth century, much of the rest of Eurasia came under direct European rule or under European technological, economic and military domination. It was in the various centres of power in Europe that the questions about sovereignty, government and authority were under increasingly lively discussion. In any case, neither China nor Japan had any reason to question its own nationhood, unlike the Europeans: even a weakened China knew that it was a long-standing polity with a rich cultural heritage and that its rightful place was at the centre of the world; and Japan knew that its imperial house traced an unbroken lineage all the way back to the sun god Ameratsu. India's identity is – as we shall see – altogether differently based, such that neither Fichte nor Renan offer an adequate account of its development as a nation (and neither Rousseau nor Locke can usefully be described as the parents of its polity). As for the Ottoman Empire, it was in the process of fragmenting, and would collapse in the wake of the First World War; European, Russian and American meddling would bedevil the region in the wake of the Empire's final dissolution, as would ideological struggles within Islam. The torment would last well into the twenty-first century.

In all of these cases, the need to react to the cultural and technological challenge of a modernizing and aggressive Europe became paramount. The responses were very different and varied in their effectiveness. But as nationalist figures in all of these regions became more and more vocal from the middle of the nineteenth century onwards, they found themselves, directly or indirectly, explicitly or implicitly, having to raise and answer questions posed by European thought about the relationship between the individual and the general will: 'What is the natural unit of political and social cohesion? What is the best way of establishing the general will within such a unit? When does the will of the majority become a tyranny? Are 'we the people' a collection of individuals who are thrown together by geographical happenstance? Or is there a 'people' we are part of by birth and history? Does the good society – the well-governed nation – free us to be ourselves, or does it free us to be where we belong?'

The answers have taken two main forms. One sees 'we the people' as a collection of individuals who, like the noble savages of that distant moment in the past, surrender their autonomy to the general will – but only so far as matters which affect the interest of all are concerned. The other sees peoples, rather than individuals, as the fundamental focus of attention. For the first, history matters less; for the latter, history is all-important. It is no coincidence that the first is embodied in the founding declaration of the United States of America, at a time when it was the New World to which Europeans were seeking to escape so as to make a new start, unburdened by oppressive pasts. It is also no surprise that most – though, as we shall see, not all – Eurasian nationalisms took the second form; all Eurasian cultures are laden with history they cannot escape. In cultures that yearned for a unified polity or were under threat from an aggressive and technologically superior Europe, ideas that would have been familiar to Rousseau and to Herder came to have a striking resonance. And this has helped give their nationalisms their immense power.

The rise of nationalism in Eurasia

One way or another, the nineteenth century saw the rise of nationalism virtually everywhere – and not just among those cultures yearning for independence. Among the European great powers, it became an increasingly aggressive and virulent political force that too many politicians were happy to encourage and exploit. The atmosphere darkened as the century drew to a close: imperial behaviour became more and more arrogant and cynical; anti-Semitism disfigured even the most apparently enlightened and sophisticated European societies; and military and economic competition made international relationships ever more dangerous.

Throughout Eurasia, this period saw the emergence of nationalist figures who caught the mood of the times and who articulated the new demand for nationhood and nation. The Habsburg Empire was probably doomed anyway; and the heir to its throne in 1914 knew that substantial constitutional reform was necessary if it was to survive the pressures from Czechs, Slovaks, Romanians and others. The Hungarians had essentially already won complete parity with the establishment of the Dual Monarchy of Austria–Hungary in 1867. Now the Czechs were on the same path. Urbanization was bringing them into the big cities of Bohemia and Moravia (in just one generation, Prague – which had for centuries been a German-speaking citadel – became a Czech-majority city) and they found their voice in a figure who was the very epitome of high enlightenment culture – Tomas Masaryk.

Masaryk was a philosophy professor turned politician who was in many ways the image of the ideal nationalist. He had no sympathy for extreme romanticization of the Czech identity through artificial resurrection of a medieval cultural past. Nor was he seduced by the pan-Slavism that pervaded the atmosphere in South Eastern Europe in the years running up to the First World War, with overt encouragement and support from the Russians in both Habsburg and Ottoman domains. But the language and the history of the Czechs – especially their distinctive Reformation history – were for him the essential fundaments of a national identity that could not in the end be satisfied within the imperial framework, whether or not Archduke Franz Ferdinand had succeeded in reforming it.

Masaryk's conviction that the new nation should be an independent democracy owed much to Rousseau's general will, and he saw a humanistic education policy as essential to the social cohesion this required. During the war years he drummed up support in Britain, France and – all-importantly – in America for the cause of national self-determination for a new Czechoslovakia (itself a union of two closely related but not identical linguistic groups that also had different religious histories – the Czechs had a history etched by religious dissent and turmoil, unlike the traditionally conservative Catholic culture of the Slovaks). It was a cause that prevailed at Versailles; and he went on to become President of the new country. But tragedy lay in store. The new country had a fragile identity and, in particular, included a substantial minority of German speakers – the famous Sudeten Germans. Government policy made no concessions to this separate identity within the newborn country: with immediate effect, Czech was to be the only language of public

administration and of public education. The seeds of alienation and resentment began to be sown; their poisonous fruit would be harvested all
too enthusiastically in the wake of the Great Depression in the 1930s by
the Nazis. Earlier than most, Masaryk saw the danger in Hitler's rise on
the German political stage; and he died – in honoured retirement – only
one year before his country was dismembered in 1938 at the hands of
Hitler, Chamberlain and Daladier in Munich. (Much later on, in the very
different context of the new Europe, the Czechs and the Slovaks finally
went their separate ways in the aptly named 'Velvet Revolution'.)

The nationalist wave was rolling in other Eurasian lands too. At the
other end of the land mass, another nationalism was transforming
another empire – in this case, one with an almost complete national
homogeneity and a very strong identity in no danger of breaking up – with
deeply tragic consequences. Japan, as we have seen, had been in seclusion
but was certainly not in hibernation during the Tokugawa era. The new
generation of the early nineteenth century was increasingly aware of the
threat posed by the Europeans. They were profoundly shocked by the humiliation inflicted on Qing Dynasty China through the Opium Wars. So
by the time Commodore Perry forced the opening up of Japan in 1854,
the country was ripe for revolution. The transformation that followed the
Meiji Restoration in 1868 was astonishingly radical and swift; industrialization was driven forward; education was rapidly expanded, and its
role in nurturing the national spirit explicitly articulated in an imperial
rescript (decree) of 1888; the ancient Japanese practice of Shinto was elevated into the position of national religion, while Buddhism was heavily
constrained and controlled. It was a revolution imposed from the centre,
not a popular uprising, and carried out with a ruthless and increasingly
totalitarian efficiency that would not be surpassed until the Bolshevik
Revolution in Russia. And it built on a very Japanese expression of nationalism that had, however, some obvious underlying similarities with
Rousseau's general will.

Renan's 'spirit of the nation' was expressed for the Japanese in an
almost untranslatable concept that owes its origins to ideas developed in
the middle of the Tokugawa period – *kokutai* – perhaps best translated
as 'national essence'. Japanese scholars of the eighteenth century had
already begun to suggest that the ancient myths of the Emperor's direct

descent from the sun goddess Ameratsu were the literal truth. By the nineteenth century, *kokutai* came to express the essence of Japan – the mystical unity of the Japanese people with the Emperor as its divinely descended ruler. From the start, its new national assertiveness had an unmistakable undertone of hostility to foreigners; from the start, the new Japan was driven to assert itself on the regional stage, first against a weak China in 1895, and then, more spectacularly, against Russia at the naval battle of Tsushima in 1905. There were challenges to the evolving combination of metaphysics and ideology; in particular, the respected scholar Yukichi Fukuzawa, whose face adorns the 10,000 yen bank note of today's Japan, argued, not that *kokutai* was inappropriate as an expression of the true spirit of Japan, but that it was not unique to Japan and did not depend for its validity on the myth of the divine imperial descent. In other words, Japan was neither more nor less nationalistic than – nor so fundamentally different from – its distant European rivals (or the sleeping dragon just across the sea). But Fukuzawa's views did not carry the day: Japan hurtled into the middle of the twentieth century with a carefully orchestrated quasi-religious fervour that took it over the cliff edge into catastrophe.

At a much deeper level, the great writer Natsume Soseki reacted to the upheaval with his subtle, introspective, melancholy and in the end pessimistic novel *Kokoro*,[21] published in 1914. It tells of an old man racked by guilt for having behaved in a way that precipitated the suicide of his friend, to the point where he in the end takes his own life. It is told partly in the old man's own words and partly through the eyes of a young companion narrator who himself is beginning to feel his distance from the world. The guilt and the loneliness are both an intense personal drama and also a metaphor of the national uneasiness about the revolution that was transforming Japan for ever.

China, unlike Japan, was truly an empire rather than a nation. For centuries, as we noted in Chapter 1, the emperor had claimed the 'Mandate of Heaven to rule all under heaven'. Rarely had the Chinese sought to assert this authority – and never outside its immediate neighbourhood (apart perhaps from the ultimately abortive expeditions of Zheng He in the early fifteenth century). But its all-encompassing implications did mean that the Chinese task was always seen as the assimilation of foreigners, rather than their isolation or expulsion – whether they came under imperial governance as China consolidated its territory over the centuries of expansion and contraction, or whether (like the Mongols and the Manchus) they had come as conquerors. The fact that the Han Chinese had become so large a majority of the population by the time of the late Qing Dynasty in the nineteenth century is at least in part due to this assimilative tendency. But assimilation was easier when it built on long-standing interaction with peoples from nearby, and when Chinese culture was demonstrably more sophisticated. The Europeans were another matter: all but the most blinkered Chinese intellectuals of the late nineteenth century could see that reform was needed to face the new challenge from these foreigners from distant powers with their obvious technological superiority and their metaphysics that were so incompatible with the Confucian view of the world order.

When the Guangxu Emperor took the throne at the age of three in 1875, this seemed to be a new window of opportunity; and a group of reforming nationalists gathered around him. Kang Youwei and Liang Qichao were both reformers who wanted to restate the neo-Confucianism that had largely prevailed since Zhu Xi, in a way that would open up the social order and the world of ideas, so that a more confidently progressive China could change without disintegrating. Both were steeped in the Confucian classics; both were also influenced by studies in Europe that brought them face to face with the ideas of European Enlightenment figures and nineteenth-century nationalists. Kang argued that Confucius was a figure of his times, and that his teachings stood for progress and not for a permanently static order. They argued for institutional reforms that would introduce more democratic responsiveness and allow a more rapid social and economic modernization.

It was not to be. The Empress Dowager Cixi pulled the puppet strings from behind her screen; the Emperor was effectively put under house arrest; the reforming group was broken up, and those who didn't flee the country were executed. Kang and Liang both escaped with their lives, and continued to write from exile, at first in Japan. But the hope for significant reform was lost; the foreigners continued their depredations (and in particular the Japanese menace grew more and more obvious). The Empire came to an end, followed in 1912 by an unstable new republic.

And after almost four decades of chaos and destruction, change eventually came in a very different way: China emerged in 1949 with a new Communist government and set out on a new ideological path that was, in theory – just as the empire had, in theory, been – universalist rather than nationalist. We have already seen, however, how the new universalist creed morphed into 'socialism with Chinese characteristics'.

The Middle East also saw nationalist stirrings in the nineteenth century. This region too had felt the impact of the new Europe, but there were other complications: the Ottoman Empire was crumbling. As in the case of Austria–Hungary, constitutional reform might have succeeded in providing a new framework within which national aspirations could perhaps have found durable satisfaction. But probably not; and in any case, the outbreak of the First World War put an end to any prospects of durable reform. Yet a further complication was the question of the Muslim *ummah*; was it an essential part of the popular identity or not? For if so, a modernizing nationalism would have to take on the task of theological reflection and reform.[22]

In Iran, Turkey and Egypt, nationalist thinkers emerged who sought to tackle the religious and political dimensions of the challenge of reform in different ways. All were influenced by their exposure to European thought. The leading figure who demonstrates the complexities of the challenge is the slightly mysterious Sayyid Jamal al-Din al-Afghani. Born in 1839, in either Afghanistan or Iran, he spent much of his life wandering from one Middle Eastern centre to another (but including a spell in British India as well as travels in European cities and to Russia); he died in Constantinople in 1897. In Cairo he became involved in freemasonry, and he had connections in the strange world of theosophy. He became increasingly active politically, in both Iran and in the Ottoman domains. He was convinced it was necessary to counter the Western threat through a rejuvenated Islam, true to its founding ideals and to its theology but embracing technical progress. He was no democrat, but he was a strong believer in the power of education, which he wanted to modernize and free from the traditional rote learning that had made few concessions to modernity, and become a major cause of Muslim weakness. And he wanted the intellectual elite to consider themselves free to let their curiosity roam, unfettered by the constraints of tradition.

There were certainly some who made full use of this freedom. Perhaps the most prominent was al-Afghani's disciple Muhammad Abduh in Cairo, who went on to be Grand Mufti of Egypt. He became the father of a modernism that took a liberal view of the traditions and indeed went so far as to assert the right of the thoughtful individual to a personal understanding of the Qur'an, unmediated by the clerical authorities. The faint echo of Luther is unmistakable; but his times were very different. The conservative reaction was ferocious and his position was compromised by his obvious familiarity with European ways. The Egyptian politics of the time were fraught with the tension between the British colonial masters and the Khedive who ruled under their thumb; there was no equivalent of the decisive support Luther had enjoyed as he launched his religious revolution almost four hundred years earlier. Though Abduh died in office as Egypt's most senior religious figure, his liberal modernist version of Islam did not endure.

Overall, the experience of al-Afghani, Abduh and others who sought to reform Islam demonstrates the ambivalence among intellectuals who recognized the power of the European Enlightenment as well as its metaphysical threat to the central claims of Islam – a threat more serious than Christianity had ever been. But in the end, the project to revivify the *ummah* as an effective bulwark against European ways failed, partly because of the absence of visionary political leadership among the authorities of the time in Tehran, Cairo or Constantinople, but more fundamentally because nationhood and nationalism was in the end to prove a much stronger rallying point than the *ummah*.

In Iran, the rediscovery of the ancient Iranian past was a project spearheaded by Hassan Taqizadeh, a brilliant scholar from an ultra-religious and conservative family background. He founded a highly influential journal that popularized awareness of the pre-Islamic identity of the nation and helped crystallize a distinct sense of nationhood – distinct, that is, from the Arabic-speaking world to the south. He was active in the agitation for constitutional reform in the early years of the twentieth century. But the last decades of the Qajar dynasty were a grim story of spineless leadership by the Shah in the face of blatant and cynical manipulation by the Russians, by the British and later by the Americans. In the end, the nationalist revolution of 1921 was not so much a cultural project but, rather, a military coup by Reza Pahlavi (later Shah), who then proceeded to drive through a radical modernizing and secularizing programme that continued, through ups and downs under his son, until it collapsed during the conservative counter-revolution of 1979. Iran's identity and its place in the wider world remain unfinished business.

The Turks too were on their way to rediscovering their past. Even as the Ottoman Empire was failing, reformers were pushing against deeply entrenched vested interests for modernization to counter the European threat. But what eventually won through was not the constitutional reform of Empire – which had no more chance, given its extreme cultural diversity, than it did in the Habsburg domains – but a new Turkish identity based on pride in the ancient steppe history and in its myths, a purified language (stripped of its Arabic and Persian infiltrations), and an educated society with a modernized Sunni faith. This new Turkish sense of nationhood owed its robustness to the work of two people above all – Ziya Gökalp and Kemal Atatürk. The latter is well known as the military leader who fought for, and founded, the modern Republic; the former was the intellectual godfather of the Turkish identity, a brilliant mind who was enormously influential, through his writings and political engagement, in creating the new post-Ottoman order. In particular, Gökalp was impressed by the Japanese success in distinguishing between modernization and Europeanization. His alternative to Europeanization was very clear; and at the same time his focus on the importance of education was in a clear line of descent from Rousseau.

The story of Indian nationalism is entirely different. It is in a sense too well known, and we are therefore apt to overlook what an extraordinary story it is. Indian nationalism was successful in driving out the British imperialists with very little violence, compared, for example, with the forced retreat of the French from Vietnam (the violence of the partition lies at the doors of all the parties involved, including the British; but it was not violence directed by nationalists at the occupying power). As for the national leaders themselves, the figure of Mahatma Gandhi is better known in the West than any of the nationalist figures we have just looked at in other Eurasian settings. His life story is a good deal more complex and more nuanced than his public image as the very embodiment of ascetic spirituality. But his 'Quit India' campaign did play a major role in getting the British to come to terms with realities. His nationalism was a rare blend of the spiritual, the intellectual and the practical, all underpinned by a personal commitment that took no notice of discomfort or danger.

Yet it was not Gandhi who established the new India: it was Jawaharlal Nehru who was the true father of the nation. And he is unique among the new leaders of Eurasia's major cultures outside Europe in being the only one who saw the project primarily as one of socio-economic development in a vibrant democracy, rather than as the assertion (or reassertion) of nationhood based on a defined national culture. Even for Mao, the Chinese had 'stood up' in 1949. And certainly for the Meiji and Taisho nationalists of pre-war Japan, as well as for Reza Shah in Iran and for Gökalp and Atatürk in the new Turkey, the project was about a new and purified projection of the national identity – reformed, modernized, strengthened – on the stage of history. Knowingly or otherwise, they were acting in a spirit that Rousseau, Fichte and Renan would all have recognized. For Nehru, by contrast, the secularizing, democratizing and educational principles of the Enlightenment were of fundamental importance, in a country he knew to be an astonishing cultural and linguistic kaleidoscope, with an ancient tradition of lively public debate.[23] So for Nehru, the objective could not – should not – be either a homogeneous 'general will' or a highly individualistic American-style melting pot; for him there was immense value in the ancient pluralism, which Nehru knew was of the essence of Indian-ness. The watchword of the New World of America – *e pluribus unum* or 'out of the many, one' – could never serve for India, and the new independent state would have to be a democracy with a very public square if that pluralist identity was to be properly and effectively honoured and nurtured.

By the time Nehru's hour came in 1947, nationalism had driven the European end of the Eurasian land mass into unspeakable disaster. The nationalist instincts that had become so vibrant in the nineteenth century had been infected with the bacillus of social and ethnic Darwinism and had become all too often virulently racist. The fascism of Italy in the 1920s glorified the nation state and legitimized both domestic and international violence in pursuit of its ends (in this latter respect emulating Leninist strategy, as was becoming clear from events in the

Soviet Union). The Spanish counter-revolution of the 1930s had brought the first proxy sparring of socialists and fascists, supported respectively by Russia's Communist International and by Germany and Italy. Fascist movements had appeared in various parts of Eastern Europe. And then the Third Reich had chosen to take on its totalitarian nemesis in a titanic struggle to the death, simultaneously with embarking on the complete elimination of the European Jewry that it had defined out of its warped version of the national identity.

By 1945, Europe was in ruins, both physically and morally. It has seemed to much of the European elite ever since that the very idea of nationalism is not only outmoded but also intrinsically sinister. In the seven decades that followed the war, Europe painstakingly rebuilt itself. Western Europe began to develop a new framework of economic co-operation and collaboration, designed to ensure that the catastrophe could never be repeated. It lived for forty years on the frontline of a new Cold War; it then reunified itself and stepped up the construction of a new European Union that would provide for the 'ever close union of its peoples' – to quote the phrase in the Treaty of Rome that was to become such a thorn in the flesh of British sensibilities. There are obvious questions about the future of the European project, particularly in the context of the radically changing geopolitics of a Eurasia that is becoming ever more connected – questions to which we will return later. But it is worth noting here that the European intelligentsia continues to be uncomfortable with discourse about nationhood in general and to react viscerally against nationalism in particular. The most prominent representative of this mood is Jürgen Habermas, the German philosopher, for whom any appeal to the past as a basis for identity was invalidated for ever by the whole experience of the Third Reich. For him, the only defensible loyalty is what he has called 'constitutional patriotism'[24] – to a new identity based on the humanistic values hard fought for, and learned the hard way, down European history. For him, this is the project the new Germany should devote itself to, heart and soul; and it is the basis for what Europe has to offer to the world of the twenty-first century. The irony is that, implicit in this commitment to the modern European project, there is a universalizing claim – about the value of European values: it is not at all clear that this claim is compatible with the principle of *cujus regio, ejus religio* on which Westphalian Europe was built in the seventeenth century and on which – as we shall see in more detail in Chapter 6 – the modern world of Eurasia is being built too.

But cultural nationalism has not died, even in Europe, and certainly not in the rest of Eurasia. It is striking that Japan – the other great aggressor of the Second World War – reacted to catastrophe very differently. For all that it turned its back under American tutelage on militarism and sloughed off the divinity of its emperor, it remains deeply conscious of its own nationhood and its distinctiveness. And in every other major Eurasian culture – in China, in Russia, in Turkey and, yes, even in India – there are clear signs of a resurgent cultural assertiveness that has posed a challenge to this new European ideology and, in particular, to its implicit assumption that it has the moral high ground and it has history on its side. To that new cultural assertiveness we now turn.

5

The past that is never dead

If there is one thing that all the cultures of Eurasia have in common, it is that the past weighs heavily on their shoulders. In fact, this is one of the most obvious differences between Eurasia and America.

Awareness of time passing is one of the hallmarks of humanity. No other living creature on the planet has it, and it shapes our consciousness. In all of our cultures, it is one of the most common themes of human expression. Thus, Du Fu, one of the greatest of the great Tang Dynasty poets of the eighth century, muses: 'What bright eyes and what white teeth, but where now is she?' Transience is a favourite theme of Chinese literature down the centuries since. Similarly, 'Where are the snows of last year?', the famous refrain to the medieval poem by François Villon about the great women of myth and history, came to be a trope of European culture, quoted by Swinburne, D. H. Lawrence, Ibsen, Hofmannsthal and Umberto Eco among many others. For the Japanese, the same feeling of the present that is always passing infuses the aesthetics of Zeami, who created the *Noh* dance drama around the turn of the fifteenth century, and for whom 'it is the withering of the flower that is especially attractive'.[1] The steady sotto voce tone of impermanence also underlies poems such as Buson's *haikai* from eighteenth-century Edo (Tokyo):

> Slow days build up
> The distant past.
>
> A kite
> In the place it was
> In yesterday's sky.[2]

And it haunts the famous annual rhythm of viewing the cherry blossom, described as beautifully as anywhere in Tanizaki's *The Makioka Sisters*, set in the late 1930s as Japan was heading towards the abyss:

The cherries in the Heian Shrine were left to the last because they, of all the cherries in Kyoto, were the most beautiful. Now that the great weeping cherry in Gion was dying and its blossoms were growing paler each year, what was left to stand for the Kyoto spring if not the cherries in the Heian Shrine? And so, coming back from the western suburbs on the afternoon of the second day, and picking that moment of regret when the spring sun was about to set, they would pause, a little tired, under the trailing branches, and look fondly at each tree – around the lake, by the approach to the bridge, by a bend in the path, under the eaves of the gallery. And, until the cherries came the following year, they could close their eyes and see again the colour and the line of a trailing branch.[3]

Even the effervescent Hafez in fourteenth-century Iran enjoyed wallowing in the past from time to time:

> What memories! I once lived on
> the street that you lived on.
> And to my eyes how bright the dust
> before your doorway shone! . . .
> Last night, for old times' sake, I saw
> the place where we once drank;
> A cask was lying there, its lees
> like blood . . .[4]

Different cultures have used the past differently. For the Chinese, as for the Japanese, nostalgia is a way to underscore the very real fact of transience. So nostalgia may celebrate past scenes of (inevitably evanescent) beauty and contentment, but often in an unexpectedly accepting and unsentimental mood. Thus Du Fu imagines two old men getting together in retirement and looking back on life:

Our lifelong days we, never meeting,
Move as do stars in other clusters,
Yet this evening ('and what an evening!')
We're sharing this lamp and this candlelight;
But youth and strength, how briefly it lasts
For both our heads have become grizzled
And half of those we ask about are now ghosts,
Till cries of shock pierce our very breasts;
How could we know twenty years would pass
Before I came again to your house?
Though in those days you were unmarried
Suddenly sons and daughters troop in,
'Greet merrily Papa's companion',
Ask from where it is that I come?
But such exchange remains unfinished:
You chase them off to get out the wine . . .
Now, with your 'Come, we so seldom meet',
You've charged my glass ten times in a row:
Ten times, and still I'm not quite tipsy
But filled with a sense of old acquaintance;
For tomorrow the hills divide us,
Both out of sight so far as the world is concerned.[5]

And in a mourning poem from the time of the Song Dynasty in the eleventh century, Su Shi imagines himself back in his home town, with his long-dead wife brought back to life just as she had been in all her prosaic reality – but then he realizes that she would not recognize him, now that he has grown old. For the Chinese thought world, a person's present is always passing and the past has gone.[6]

This apparently matter-of-fact Chinese perspective differs fundamentally from the Indian instinct, for which time passing is time recurring – an endlessness of which the self is, for better or worse, always a part. To look backwards is therefore always to look forwards, as hinted in one exquisite jewel from Rabindranath Tagore's *Gitanjali*, a collection of his own poems that he himself translated (loosely) into English:

I must launch out my boat. The languid hours
pass by on the shore – alas for me!
The spring has done its flowering and taken leave.
And now with the burden of faded futile
flowers I wait and linger.
The waves have become clamorous, and upon the
bank in the shady lane the yellow leaves
flutter and fall.
What emptiness do you gaze upon! Do you not
feel a thrill passing through the air with the
notes of the far away song floating from the
other shore?[7]

The often-noted absence of fundamental melancholy in so much of Indian poetry (and in the classic images of Bollywood) is surely related to this perpetual hint of the next recurrence within the pattern of the ever recurring.

The power of memory

In the European imagination, however, a distinctive note can be heard which marks it out from that of both China and India. For the European consciousness, it is not so much that the present is always passing and that the past has gone; nor is there a next recurrence at hand. Instead, the past is, for better or worse, always present to the self. In some of the unforgettable moments of European literature, the individual rebels against the past – like Dorothea in George Eliot's *Middlemarch* or like Nora in Ibsen's *The Doll's House*. But even in such dramatic moments of rejection, the past is in effect conditioning the present. With or without such rebellion, the invasion of the individual's present identity by the past – and therefore the moral connection between the past and the present – is a very European theme, first explored in depth by Augustine sixteen hundred years ago in his (then unique) *Confessions*. Memories of our past are essential to what we are; they are the building blocks of our identity. In a passage that is extraordinary for its time by the standards of any culture, he writes:

The power of memory is great, O Lord. It is awe-inspiring in its profound and incalculable complexity. Yet it is my mind: it is myself. What, then, am I, my God? What is my nature? A life that is ever varying, full of change, and of immense power. The wide plains of my memory and its innumerable caverns and hollows are full beyond compute of countless things of all kinds. Material things are there by means of their images; knowledge is there of itself; emotions are there in the form of ideas or impressions of some kind, for the memory retains them even while the mind does not experience them . . . My mind has the freedom of them all. I can glide from one to the other. I can probe deep into them and never find the end of them. This is the power of memory. This is the great force of life living in human beings, mortal though they are![8]

Augustine was not primarily interested in memory; everything he wrote was in support of his central preoccupation with the salvation of the human soul. Thus, his understanding of memory was set in the broader context of his reflections on the nature of time itself, which begins for him with the creative act of God and ends with the final judgement. He argues that our individual perception of time is of a present that is always fleeting, of a future for which we are always waiting, and of a past constituted by our memories[9] – so that without God we are perpetually subject to a sense of loss and of potential unrealized.[10] Indeed, the human condition without God is for Augustine not so far from the negativity implicit in Buddhist teaching about the nature of time (although for Buddhism this was intimately connected with a belief in the insubstantiality of the self, which Augustine would certainly never accept).

But his thoughts on memory – though subsidiary to his real interest in salvation history – set the agenda for an extended exploration of the power of memory in forming the human identity, which took European culture all the way to Freud and beyond, and is now spreading more broadly across cultures in the Eurasia of the modern era. For Augustine had seen that in a fundamental sense, memory plays an essential role in the constitution of the human self. In an influential comment, the French philosopher Paul Ricoeur has drawn attention to the ambiguity in the word *identity*, which can denote sameness but also self-awareness (whereas Latin has different words for these two meanings: *idem* and *ipse*). In French, the ambiguity is mirrored in the everyday use of the word *moi-même* (myself – a compound of the words for 'me' and 'same').[11] In English – perhaps a little baldly – the original Latin differentiation between *idem* and *ipse* could be described as highlighting two different questions: about the 'What?' – and the 'Who?' – of personal identity. Augustine was aware of the overlap between these two questions;[12] and it is hard to overestimate the influence of his reflections on European thought about subjectivity and identity ever since – as we shall see in Chapter 8 – and its implications more universally, as we shall see in Chapter 9.

Augustine's view of human subjectivity was more rationalistic than we would now accept; it would be many centuries after his time before the role of the subconscious would be probed in any depth. We now know more than he did about the capacity of the mind to suppress memories that are painful, and to transform – or even invent – the past. But he did understand the significance of the human tendency to forget as well as to remember (and of the human capacity to remember the forgotten). We recycle some memories again and again throughout our lives; we forget others until reminded involuntarily – as is the narrator of Proust's monumental *A la Recherche du Temps Perdu* (*In Search of Lost Time*) in the famous scene in which the taste of a madeleine cake dipped in tea brings memories of his childhood flooding back:

And suddenly the memory appeared to me. This taste – the taste of the little piece of madeleine that, on a Sunday morning at Combray (because that day I did not go out before it was time for Mass), when I went to her bedroom to say good morning, my aunt Léonie would give me after dipping it in her infusion of tea or lime . . . And as soon as I had recognized the taste of the piece of madeleine dipped in lime tea that my aunt gave me . . . , immediately the old grey house by the road, where her bedroom was, came like a theatre-set to attach itself to the little wing opening on to the garden – the truncated section, which had been built for my parents behind the old house, and which was all I had seen before then; and with the house, the town and the town square where I was sent before lunch, the streets where I went to do errands from morning to evening in all weathers, the paths we took if the weather was fine. And just as in that game in which the Japanese amuse themselves by filling a porcelain bowl with water and dipping in it little pieces of paper that look alike but which, the moment they are immersed in the water, stretch and shape themselves, become coloured and distinct, become flowers, houses, human figures, defined and recognizable – so now all the flowers in our garden and in M. Swann's park, and the water lilies on the Vivonne and the good folk of the village and their little cottages and the church and all Combray and its surroundings – all of this, the town and its gardens, takes on form and substance, and has emerged from my cup of tea.[13]

This is not just a piece of beautifully poetic prose; for Proust, to recover the past is to recover the person. In effect, the conception behind the title of his last volume, *Le Temps Retrouvé* (*Time Found*), is the opposite of the materialist nostalgia of Su Shi.

And, indeed, it goes further than that: in the European perception, identity comes not just from recovering the past, but from living with it. Our selves are like palimpsests – old parchments reused for a new narrative that never quite effaces the old one. The famous opening line of L. P. Hartley's novel *The Go-Between*[14] – 'the past is a foreign country; they do things differently there' – implies perhaps that the narrator has succeeded in putting a distance between himself and the traumatic past. But the whole of the rest of the novel goes on to refute that implication. Much nearer the mark is the equally famous line from an American author who is a product, not of the dominant gene of American culture, but of its melancholy southern subculture, in so many ways so European in its obsession with blood and ancestry: William Faulkner. 'The past is never dead. It's not even past.' So says the defence lawyer at the trial of a black nursemaid with a background in drug addiction and prostitution, for the murder of the baby of her white mistress, who also has a background in prostitution but who claims that her old self is now dead.[15]

What is more, the past is formative not only for the individual but also for the community (a theme, of course, that flows through the whole of Faulkner's work). The stories we tell ourselves collectively about who we are mostly look backward; they are *histories of ourselves* (even when they are obviously myths). Even Renan, who denied the necessity for nationhood to be based on a common ethnicity or a common language, knew the importance of the stories the community tells itself, and he also knew the importance of what the community chooses to forget. For him, the remembered is typically the heroic and the triumphant; what is forgotten are the failures and humiliations. He wrote, however, as a Frenchman – a citizen of a country that, like Britain, had never had much doubt about its right to pre-eminence on the world stage. In fact, however, victims remember acts of aggression much more clearly than the aggressors do. The Germany he so admired had been seething with resentment of the French for two hundred years, ever since the armies of Louis XIV had seized Strassburg (Strasbourg) and sacked the Rhineland. As would become clear in the century or so after Renan's death, many other Eurasian cultures also seethed with the anger born of humiliations remembered.

The nineteenth and twentieth centuries saw two new developments that reinforced – but also distorted – the power of community memory: the birth of states with the ambition to embody nationhood, and the emergence of an increasingly urban *demos*, the public voice that has gained more and more in legitimacy and which, in the twenty-first century, has also become increasingly strident and less structured. Each moulded the other; and the stories were fundamental to this process. The stories had origins that went far back into the pre-modern era; but they were modified – sometimes radically – as they took on their new role in modern cultural expression and nation-building.

Indeed, it is clear that many cultural traditions that are ingredients in nationhood have been extensively reshaped or even invented outright. Perhaps the most spectacular example of outright invention anywhere is the *Aeneid*. This immensely successful epic played a key role in establishing the identity of imperial Rome; but it is a work of complete fiction (albeit one that built on the foundation of the ancient Homeric legends). There have been many examples since, as was demonstrated in the highly influential collection of essays *The Invention of Tradition* by Hobsbawm and Ranger.[16] Among other cases, this book looks at the invention – largely in the eighteenth and nineteenth centuries – of the Scottish highland tradition; at the apparently venerable traditions of

123

the British monarchy, many of which emerged only in the nineteenth century as an adjunct to empire; and more generally at the mass production of traditions in Europe in the decades before the First World War. If the authors had taken a broader view of Eurasia as a whole, they might have looked also at Meiji Japan, at Atatürk's Turkey and at the *Hindutva* movement in India, not to mention Soviet myth-making before, during and after the Second World War.

Hobsbawm argues in his introductory essay that, unlike the traditions of the pre-modern era (which were specific and binding in what they required of community members), the new traditions of the modern era are typically rather ill-defined: they have filled only a small part of the psychic space left by the decline of older customs and traditions that had once structured the whole of people's lives. Nevertheless, these new traditions have surprising power: national anthems, national flags, symbolic national figureheads (Britannia for the British, Marianne for the French, Germania for the Germans), actual but quasi-sacred figureheads (the British monarch, perhaps, and certainly the Japanese emperor), all of which came to have a new sway over the newly urbanized societies of the late nineteenth century.

But while some specific traditions were indeed more or less invented, the more general point is that – whether ancient or modern – the stories were tapping into a deep root of identity. Why else were these cultural stories so important, in an era of growing urban connectivity and of the new urban classes? For Marxism, they were simply one of the tools used by the ruling classes to control the proletariat. But why *these* stories? It was because they expressed deep and long-standing identities that even Marxist–Leninist Soviet Russia discovered were better corralled and used rather than ignored or attacked. And thus, so far from the past being a foreign country, it was invaded and, where possible, reshaped. As George Orwell puts it in the terrible nightmare he conjured up in *Nineteen Eighty-Four*: 'Who controls the past controls the future: who controls the present controls the past.'[17]

Yet controlling the past is not so easy. Mahatma Gandhi once wrote: 'A nation is happy that has no history.'[18] He, of all people, knew the reason why history was to be feared in the new India. Nehru knew it too. Both offered a way for India to hold its multifarious identities together: Gandhi by his romantic vision of a craft-based rural network of communities; Nehru through the new constitution, elective democracy and active programming of economic and social development on as inclusive a basis as possible. Gandhi's vision was never realistic; Nehru's has been only partially successful. India, like every other Eurasian culture, has found that the old identities – the old subterranean roots – keep on throwing up new shoots of growth.

Continuity below the surface: India

India is the best place to begin to observe this trend that is emerging across the whole of Eurasia, because India's foundational stories are the oldest of all continuously living traditions. The oldest parts of the *Rig Veda* go back around three and a half millennia, predating the oldest parts of the Jewish Bible and the oldest Chinese and Greek texts. This vast collection includes hymns to various deities, liturgical instructions and philosophical reflection about being and origins. Also included in the Vedic texts are the *Upanishads*, which explore some of the basic ideas of what was to become the Indian mystical tradition (and became so influential among those in Europe who, from the Enlightenment onwards, were beginning to look beyond their own Christian heritage for newer inspiration).

Thereafter came the enormous epic of the *Mahabharata* – three times as long as the Bible – telling a complex story of dynastic struggles involving the whole of India from the Himalayas to Kanyakumari at the southernmost tip, and early evidence for that sense of Indian identity that has endured through all the wars and despite all the complexities of the Indian linguistic and cultural landscape. It culminates in a titanic battle, marking the beginning of the fourth and last age, the *kaliyuga* – the present era, which is seen as one of degeneration. The *Mahabharata* probably originates at roughly the same time as the *Iliad* (with which it has some clear underlying similarities), although it reached its final form significantly later; but it remains far more influential in the India of today than is the *Iliad* in modern Europe. It includes several self-contained stories – above all, the *Bhagavad Gita* (probably dating from around half a millennium after the earliest parts of the epic), which popularized the figure of Krishna and synthesized the themes of *dharma*, devotion and self-renunciation into what were to become central traits of Hindu worship and practice. The implicit focus on action in accordance with the duty required by the *dharma*, allied to an attitude of renunciation that refuses to judge outcomes, has an affinity to Kant's ethics of duty – but even more obviously to what became the Zen of the Japanese samurai (except that neither Kant nor Zen would bathe this in the devotion so characteristic of the Indian religious consciousness down to the present day).

The third main source of Hindu inspiration was the *Ramayana*, an epic that developed probably around the middle of the first millennium BCE. Like the *Mahabharata*, it is an intricate story of family intrigue among ruling clans, involving exiles, journeyings, battles, supernatural comings and goings – and all of this interspersed with philosophical and ethical reflection. Like Krishna, Rama becomes a major incarnation of Vishnu, widely worshipped as the personified ideal of a life lived to the full in conscious fulfilment of his role in the universal order of things.

Hinduism is the undertone of almost everything in India. If there is a continuity to it down the ages, it lies in three threads that have never been broken: the religious sense of oneness behind, or in, or through the many; emotional devotion – *bhakti* – to particular gods (even while recognizing that the gods are somehow a manifestation of that oneness); and the complex of duties, virtues, deeds and destiny reflected in the nexus of two untranslatable words – *dharma* and *karma* – within the endless recurrence of existence. The goal of all this is *moksha* – the blessedness of absorption into the One. At various points in Indian history, heterodoxies have emerged that sought to depart fundamentally from this broad stream of consciousness. The *Charvaka* school of philosophy, for example, was a thoroughgoing atheistic materialism, flourishing around six centuries before the Common Era. But the two best-known such heterodoxies were Jainism and Buddhism, both of which denied the authority of the Vedic traditions and emerged around the middle of the first millennium BCE. They both developed subtle and sophisticated philosophies of being, of the nature of truth and of the human soul. Much the more important historically, both in India and especially more broadly on the Eurasian stage, was Buddhism. For the Buddha, being was nothing but emptiness, and existence was nothing but suffering. Buddhist *nirvana* might be achieved in ways not so very far from the renunciatory path of the Hindu saint; but *nirvana* was oblivion, not *moksha* – not absorption into the One.

Partly in response to the implications of Buddhism for philosophy and for individual piety, the threads of Indian consciousness were woven together deftly by two figures who articulated a capacious framework for all the varieties of religious experience we now know as Hinduism: Adi Shankara and Ramanuja. There is little firm historical evidence about Adi Shankara, but he is believed to have died in his thirties in the early ninth century; Ramanuja was active in the early twelfth century. Between them they laid the philosophical and devotional foundations for that unique Hindu consciousness that can allow for almost limitless diversity of belief and worship within a fundamentally monistic framework, as well as providing the context for all the vibrant colour of Indian expression in its pilgrimages, weddings, music, films and in all its daily rituals. India in its variety defies easy categorization or compartmentalization; and yet, it has a recognizable – indeed, unmistakable – identity, the core of which is its Hinduism.

Like the Chinese, the Indians have had two important periods of foreign rule. The first Muslim incursions began around the turn of the millennium. The destructiveness of these campaigns has been the subject of some revisionist debate in recent decades; but what is not in doubt is the effect on the folk memory of India.[19] Everyone 'knows' what happened when Mahmud of Ghazni came at the end of the first millennium, just as everyone in most of Asia 'knows' what happened when the Mongols came. Later, the Delhi Sultanate established a more permanent Muslim presence; and then, in the sixteenth century the Mughals established their brilliant empire, which eventually included almost all of the subcontinent. Islam spread gradually in the wake of all this, as it had done in the ancient Christian lands around the eastern Mediterranean after the initial Arab conquests. By the twentieth century, around a quarter of the population was Muslim. By that time, the Mughals had given way to the British, the first rulers ever to control the whole of the subcontinent; they laid a thin veneer over Indian society but also – whatever else they did or did not do in a century with a very mixed record – gave

India a functioning single state (as well as a global language that enabled its elites to have a global reach). The new India might easily have been Balkanized, as it had been for most of its history; instead, it became the largest democracy on the planet.

But the struggle for identity in the new era of independence had a tragic outcome. There is rarely any point in historical what-ifs, and surely not in the case of Partition. Its inevitable effect was to make the Hindu identity even more dominant in the new India than it would otherwise have been. Muslims are still a sizeable minority; and there are other smaller minorities too: Sikhs, Christians, Jains, Buddhists. But the India that Nehru wanted to see as conscious of its Indian-ness while at the same time being inclusive, democratic, compassionate and developmental, is becoming more and more self-confidently (and self-consciously?) Hindu. In particular, the *Ramayana* took on a new and political significance in the decades after independence, as the *Hindutva* movement gathered strength and sought to fill the vacuum in the modern India's identity created by the hollowing out of democracy under Nehru's daughter, Indira Gandhi. Place names have been changed; the political rhetoric became more sectarian; and meanwhile progress in social modernization is slow trench warfare. The caste system that is deeply embedded in the Hindu view of the natural order of things may be softening, at least in urban areas (although everyone still knows which caste they belong to), but there is still a long journey ahead for minorities, for Dalits and for female equality. India faces a dilemma: the more it asserts its quintessential identity, the more it puts its modern identity at risk. Narendra Modi brought this question into its sharpest focus yet: it is a question that has still not received a definitive answer.

India exported its most important heterodoxy to the oldest continuous political identity in Eurasia: China. Buddhism reached its apogee in India in the centuries around the turn of the Common Era. No single factor accounts fully for its subsequent decline and disappearance from Indian cultural life: it had perhaps become too monastic and institutionalized, too dependent on merchant support along the trade routes into Central Asia; the depredations of the Central Asian Huns in the late fifth century wrought terrible destruction on Buddhist monasteries in the Indus basin; the Muslim incursions from the turn of the first millennium onwards did irreparable damage to its intellectual heartland, culminating in the sack of its greatest centre of learning at Nalanda by the Delhi Sultanate in around 1200; and by that time a more self-confident and intellectually articulate Hinduism was on the crest of a wave from the south. So the treasures of Buddhism in India were lost; much was destroyed and sites of extraordinary beauty, which testify to the spiritual intensity of Buddhist life in its heyday, such as the Ajanta caves, were forgotten and lost for centuries. (It is worth noting that even Ajanta shows some signs of the Hindu-izing of Buddhism – in one beautiful image the Buddha is depicted at his wedding holding the blue lotus of Vishnu, while the divine lovers Shiva and Parvati look on. No wonder the Buddha ends up in the Hindu pantheon as one of the avatars of Vishnu.)

Continuity through absorption: China

But those trade routes into Central Asia turned out to be a lifeline: Buddhism was eventually buried there too by Islam, but not before it had expanded along the silk routes into China, where it enjoyed a whole new life, evolving a long way from its early origins in the life and teachings of the Buddha. It was the first of three major foreign metaphysical systems to have a major impact in China (to be followed much later by Christianity and by Marxism). And from the first, that Chinese tendency to assimilate, which we have already noted, was at work. At a very early stage, Chinese Buddhism adopted the principle of the indestructibility of the soul. This might seem a long way from the Buddha's 'noble truth' of *anatta* (no soul). It had broader consequences: the concept of *dharma* also underwent change, becoming less a set of judgements about moral and religious behaviours that could be shared and debated (as in the *Bhagavad Gita*) and more a direct – and not fully expressible – experience of each individual. This modification allowed it to develop a typically Chinese practicality, because it avoided the tendency to devalue human experience, that had always been intrinsic to Indian Buddhist thought. Later, this evolved into the idea of the true self – or the Buddha-nature – that was present in each individual. This, in turn, provided the basis for the two main variants of Buddhism that were to survive and prosper within the Chinese thought world: the Chan school, which emphasizes sudden enlightenment available in the here-and-now (and went on to become better known in the West through its Japanese offshoot, Zen Buddhism – of which more later); and the Pure Land school, which offers rebirth in the pure land of the 'Western Paradise' to anyone who calls on the name of the Buddha Amitabha. (The Buddhism that reached China had already come to see the real Buddha not as one particular human being – the historical Siddharta Gautama – but as an eternally existing Buddha, manifested again and again through aeons of time in individual Buddhas; one of these is Amitabha, introduced in some of the most magical of all Buddhist scriptures, the Pure Land sutras, as the fount of endless love for all sentient beings and the source of light, grace and salvation.)[20]

Buddhism reached its Chinese apogee in the middle of the Tang Dynasty, before being heavily persecuted. It was always vulnerable to the charge that it was a foreign import; and as its monasteries accumulated wealth (just as European monasteries did later), so they became tempting targets for the state (again, just as in Europe). Buddhist philosophy gradually thereafter lost its intellectual leadership to a resurgent (and of course home-grown) neo-Confucianism. Neither Chan nor Pure Land Buddhism valued intricate philosophy or carefully elaborated metaphysics; so as these schools became more popular, Buddhism lost traction with the intellectual elites of China. Zhu Xi explicitly attacked traditional Buddhist metaphysics for its denial of the value of reality (even though he was in effect echoing a Buddhist idea when he argued in his great synthesis that the supreme undivided ultimate is contained within all things, alongside their own particularity). Later still, Chan Buddhism influenced Wang Yangming more than he acknowledged. But Buddhism was on its way to being assimilated at one level into China's predominantly Confucian intellectual framework, and at another level to being absorbed into its inveterately syncretistic popular array of beliefs and practices – which is where it had ended up by the time of the *Dream of the Red Chamber* in the eighteenth century.

The experience of Christianity in China is in some ways parallel. Very early contact with the Nestorian Christianity of Central Asia has left little trace (apart from the famous stele of the 'luminous religion' in Xi'an, which dates from the Tang Dynasty); and a Franciscan missionary effort around the turn of the fourteenth century came to an end after a few decades when the Mongol Yuan Dynasty was overthrown by the Chinese rebel leader who established the new Ming Dynasty. The Jesuits, however, who began arriving in China in the second half of the sixteenth century, had an altogether more significant impact. They were happy to engage intellectually with the Confucian court (even, notoriously, at the expense of downplaying or removing discordant elements – notably the crucifixion of Christ – from Matteo Ricci's catechism of 1603). Their project of assimilation eventually failed spectacularly, as their opponents in the Catholic Church accused them in effect of doing the Confucians' work for them, and they lost their treasured position of influence in the imperial court. A next wave of Christianity, this time in both Catholic and Protestant versions, washed into China in the nineteenth century as part of the influx of Westerners during China's 'century of humiliation' – which ensured that, even more clearly than Buddhism, this would be regarded as a barbarian import. And the chickens came home to roost when China fell under the aegis of yet a third metaphysical system from outside, one that threatened for a while to extirpate Buddhism, Christianity and indeed China's own Confucianism and Daoism. For the first time in more than two thousand years, the governing metaphysics of China – Marxism as interpreted by Mao – was one that was based on a dialectic of struggle, not on the ideal of harmony encouraged by all previous systems, whether indigenous or imported.

But this didn't last. In the new era of the twenty-first century, an increasingly self-confident China has rediscovered – and reasserted – its age-old instincts. Totalitarian mobilization and the subsequent chaos of the (significantly named) Cultural Revolution have given way to a mode of governance that is a blend of Qin Dynasty legalism, with its strong emphasis on directives and on right thinking, and Han Dynasty Confucianism (that is, with an emphasis on the moral social order but without the metaphysics of Zhu Xi). Marxism has not been abandoned but is being assimilated in the time-honoured Chinese way: the leadership talks explicitly of 'socialism with Chinese characteristics', meaning that Marxist metaphysics have been extensively remoulded to allow for the practicalities of China's chosen path to social and economic development. At a deeper level, this has allowed for the re-emergence of the old Confucian narratives of harmony and order. Both Buddhist and

Christian groups have found new life, and in the latter case have enjoyed spectacular growth. But the rhetoric of both is full of their role in promoting social cohesion and responsibility. The question in both cases is about whether and how they will respond over the coming decades to that assimilating urge which is not just government policy but an underlying instinct of the Chinese identity.

The capstone of that enduring Confucian identity is the Mandate of Heaven to rule all under heaven. For imperial China, it was famously both an ambition and a warning. It was an ambition because it was universal. It was a warning in that the Mandate was awarded to an emperor or dynasty on the basis of successful and virtuous governance; emperors who failed in this responsibility would have the Mandate withdrawn. The question for the rest of the twenty-first century is about its meaning in the new era of 'socialism with Chinese characteristics'. Is it now anything more than the expression of a very strong national identity, conscious of historic humiliations and convinced that its time has come?

It is certainly nothing less than that. But China has never thought of itself as just another power, or just another nation. Chinese voices often claim to represent the oldest culture in the world; that claim is contestable, especially, as we have seen, by the Indians. But China does have an arguable claim to be the oldest polity in the world; for much of its history it has also been the world's largest. Its assimilative power is also extraordinary: twice in its history it has been conquered and governed by foreigners – by the Mongols and by the Manchus. In each case, the rulers ended by being Sinicized so completely as to be effectively merged into what became the Chinese national identity. But for most of its history – up to the twentieth century – that national identity has been embodied in an empire, not just a nation. The Mandate was imperial, not national. We will return in Chapter 9 to the question of what that Mandate now means for China, and for others, as it takes its place on the world stage.

The Japanese exception, again

One relationship on that stage that China will certainly not find easy is with its island neighbour to the east. Over the centuries, China gave Japan many things: the Japanese elite spoke and wrote Chinese; they learnt Chinese science in fields such as astronomy and medicine; they planned their imperial capital at Kyoto according to the same pattern as imperial Chang'an; they studied the Chinese administrative system; and they borrowed Chinese metaphysics. But on the whole, the Japanese borrowed, and then refashioned what they borrowed for the needs of a secluded, island-based and almost entirely homogeneous nation. They borrowed Confucianism to buttress the social order, but they were not interested in the Chinese idea of the Mandate of Heaven; and they took their metaphysics largely from Buddhism rather than from Zhu Xi (whose thought was mainly mediated in Japan by Zen Buddhist teachers). The comings and goings of Buddhist scholars between China and Japan provided the main conduit for Japanese knowledge of Chinese trends; and it was such scholars who created a script for the Japanese language, which enabled it to make use of Chinese characters alongside cursive phonetic script more suited to its totally different linguistic structure. All in all, Buddhism played a much more central role in Japan than in China. The intellectual leadership that Buddhism had lost to neo-Confucianism in China from the turn of the millennium remained with Buddhism in Japan throughout the medieval period.

It was not until the eighteenth century that intellectuals began to discover in the original popular beliefs and practices of Shinto a useful alternative home-grown metaphysics (although well before that, Buddhism had become as domesticated by the Japanese power structure as had Protestant Christianity in Northern Europe). Although the Tokugawa authorities actively promoted Confucianism for the purpose of social control, the fact is that for centuries Buddhism had no rival among the educated, even if popular practice happily combined Buddhist with Shinto elements. Buddhism had been actively promoted as a unifying cultural force when the central state was being formed in the eighth century and the literature and art of the Heian era in the centuries around the turn of the millennium – including not least *The Tale of Genji* – are steeped in Buddhist sentiment and imagery.

Buddhism spread its branches, of course, just as it has done everywhere. Buddhism, like Christianity, has always had the potential to be both a pillar of society and also a revolutionary challenger of secular authority. In China it ended up being neither: as we have seen, it was both foreign and – after the Tang era – on the defensive against neo-Confucianism. But in Japan, in particular, Pure Land practice became even more intense than in China. One monk – Shinran – travelled a spiritual path in the early thirteenth century that cannot help but evoke the intense experience of overwhelming grace in Martin Luther later on. Meanwhile, another monk – Nichiren – rattled the government at the time of the threatened Mongol invasions later in the same century, to the point where he came close to execution. He was of peasant stock and preached a gospel of love without class or restriction, based on intense engagement with one of the greatest Buddhist texts of all – the Lotus Sutra. Popular in China as well, this sutra purports to be the last sermon of Gautama the Buddha: it is an extraordinary paean of praise for the cosmic Buddha and his infinite saving power; it calls for a love that has no social restrictions (a distant but interesting echo of Mozi in his contest with Confucius); and it has a parable with a striking resemblance to the famous story of the Prodigal Son from the Christian New Testament.[21]

Then there is Zen. Brought from China by, among others, the monk Dogen in the thirteenth century, Zen despised ritual and sought to discover the immanent Buddha-nature in the individual as directly as possible. In a sense, it has no philosophy: it is a discipline focused on sudden enlightenment (*satori* in Japanese) that is a spiritual, intellectual and moral release into expression and action. It does so by the meditational shock tactics that have become famous: despising reason and seeking to find unity and purpose in the most apparently mundane or even meaningless activity (in this, echoing a Christian instinct which found expression in Brother Lawrence and in the poetry of George Herbert). Its controlled focus on essentials has produced – in China but especially in Japan – some of the world's greatest art (perhaps above all in the *suiboku-ga* paintings of Sesshu); and it helped create the intensity of the best *haiku* poetry. It also underpinned the samurai code; the famed warrior class of medieval Japan absorbed Zen so deeply that it has become associated in the public mind as much with violence as with art. Zen taught a warrior to view life and death indifferently and never to look backward. One of the great generals of the period of civil war before the Tokugawa victory left the following thoughts to his retainers:

> Those who cling to life die, and those who defy death live. The essential thing is the mind. Look into this mind and firmly take hold of it, and you will understand that there is something in you which is above birth-and-death and which is neither drowned in water nor burnt by fire.[22]

As we have already seen, Japan began to modernize itself at around the same time that Europe did; the process was largely self-generated by a society that was uniquely both isolated and sophisticated. The bureaucratization of the samurai led to the domestication of Zen, which honed the tea ceremony and the art of the Japanese garden to perfection; and meanwhile the 'floating world' of Edo tapped into the introspective humanity of a more feminine culture whose tone had been set long before, by The Pillow Book of Sei Shonagon and above all by the Lady Murasaki in The Tale Of Genji, which made sensitive observation of the loves and lives of real human beings into the stuff of art.

Japan is a conundrum: the violence of the warrior code and of self-realization through action has had a Buddhist background to it; and so has the gentle mingling of pleasure and melancholy of the floating world. The chrysanthemum and the sword.[23] The dreadful aberration of the Co-Prosperity Sphere in the 1930s is a stain that the Japanese have never been able to properly expunge.

Japan has never confronted its twentieth-century past in the way Germany has, partly because there was no equivalent to the Holocaust, and partly because Hiroshima dealt it a sense of victimhood. No Japanese government minister has ever visited the memorial to the rape of Nanjing; the contrast with Willy Brandt kneeling at the Warsaw Ghetto in 1970 is telling. At one level, Japan has the strongest identity of any Eurasian culture; looked at in another way, it is one of the most vulnerable. The question for Japan will be how it does come to terms with its big and powerful neighbour, from whom it borrowed so much and to whom it did such terrible things in the last century. Both know that this past will not just die.

The *ummah*: a fractured past and open futures

A region where both the Chinese and the Japanese have much less reason to concern themselves with the past, and is of growing importance to both of them, is the Middle East – the origin and centre of gravity of another of Eurasia's great cultures. The image of the Middle East is of countries caught in a politically and socially conservative time warp. The fragility of the new Iraq, the perceived failure of the Arab Spring everywhere except perhaps in Tunisia, the impenetrable obscurity of Iran's polity, and the horrendous tragedy of Syria – all this has reinforced a perception that the region remains immune to modernization. Meanwhile, social attitudes, especially in respect of the role of women, seem still to belong to a previous era. The relative modernism and international openness of Dubai is seen as an exception that appears to prove the rule.

Yet change is afoot, even if it will take longer than the timetables of a busy world typically allow for. There is a distant echo of this in the Europe of the nineteenth century: the fact that the revolutions of 1848 failed did not mean that nothing was changing. The truth then was that the social structure was being transformed – slowly but surely – by urbanization and industrialization; this would sooner or later force open the way societies were governed. The fundaments of the twentieth-century world were being laid, whether or not the elites of the time recognized this. Urbanization and connectivity will just as surely change the Middle East in the coming decades.

There remain enormous challenges. The weakness of the literary culture in Arabic (5 per cent of the world's population produces only 1 per cent of the world's books) is all the more poignant if compared with the evidence of literary productivity in the heyday of the Abbasid empire, when a catalogue from Baghdad listed around 3,500 authors of books covering an astonishingly broad range of subjects.[24] But slowly, urbanization is spreading education, which is bringing about change. The individual creative energy this generates will gradually be felt in the burgeoning of human lives in ways that the grandparents of today's children could barely have dreamed of and will challenge the constraints of tradition. The empowerment of women will follow urbanization just as surely in the Islamic world as in all other cultures. The journey ahead may well be a long one, but the direction of travel is clear – notwithstanding the efforts of some Islamist extremists – because urbanization is impossible to reverse.

For two centuries – from Napoleon's expedition to Egypt in 1798 onwards – the region increasingly caught the attention of Europeans who were animated by a mixture of commercial, cultural, strategic and military motives. European poets and artists became fascinated by the culture of Islam; their archaeologists explored the ancient sites of Egypt, Iran and Mesopotamia; and then they discovered the oil beneath the sand. The politics of oil and the strategic rivalries of the European powers bedevilled the region until well into the post-war period: the history of British, French, American and Russian activity gives ample cause for shame. Tensions continue but the relationship is no longer a one-sided affair. For the region has found that others – not just its old colonial bullies – have an interest in what it can offer. So its connections with the rest of Eurasia are now growing fast; its geopolitical relationships are becoming more diverse and more balanced. The visible presence of the Japanese, and now the Chinese, is a clear sign of newer relationships that do not carry historical baggage.

For history matters – and not just the collective memory of subservience to Europeans, because the Middle East is not just a collection of countries with a common geography. This is a region that has a profound sense of common identity, defined by its history. It is in no way diminished by the impact of urbanization and increasing connectivity. Just as the ocean deep remains unmoved by the storms that boil the surface, so this common consciousness underlies and is undisturbed by all the rivalries and even internecine strife the world sees as tearing the region apart. The vast majority of the population of the region are Muslim, and part of the bedrock of their consciousness is membership of the commonwealth of believers. Their shared folk memory is of an *ummah* that stretched across the whole of the Middle East and well beyond – into Spain and Central Asia all the way to the gates of China.

This collective memory is of power, glory and existential threats from outside. The glittering court of Harun al-Rashid at the apogee of Abbasid power around the turn of the ninth century is the setting for several vivid

stories in *One Thousand and One Nights*. But the Caliphate's real political authority did not outlast the Abbasids. The role became increasingly
symbolic, though not empty. Its moral authority was of sufficient significance that al-Ghazali addressed the question of how caliphs should
be elected, evolving what was in effect a version of the doctrine of the
Mandate of Heaven, or better – in a more faithful reflection of the
severely monotheistic Muslim world view – the Mandate of God.
Whether it was the Chinese emperor or the Muslim caliph, the evidence
for possession of the Mandate was basically the same: the combination of
force and awe needed to compel obedience.[25]

And then there were the threats from outside: the Mongols, who fatally
weakened the Abbasid empire but whose ruling groups in the khanates
they established in the region (the Chagatai Khanate, the Ilkhanate and
the Golden Horde) were eventually absorbed by Islam; the Turks, who
eventually became the defenders of Sunni Islam against the Mongols
and the Latin Christian crusaders, who finally brought down the
Byzantine Christian Empire, and who came to see themselves as
the sword and standard bearer of Sunni Islam against all comers (including the Iranian Shiites); last – and perhaps most dangerous of all in
the end – the Europeans of the modern era, whose secularized curiosity
and internal rivalries stirred up nationalisms in the *ummah*, such that it
could never hope to reconstitute itself as any form of unified polity after
the demise of the Ottoman Empire.

And yet, the religious bond of the *ummah* gives the region a unifying
culture whose power is not dependent on a unified polity but is underpinned by the special role of the Arabic language. As the language of
the Qur'an, Arabic has a sacred significance that is hard for those with
a cultural hinterland in, say, Christendom or Buddhism, to appreciate.
For Muslims, no education is complete without study of the Qur'an in
its original Arabic. The role of Latin in European culture up until the
eighteenth century is a misleading parallel: it comes nowhere near to con-
veying the depth of the emotional and spiritual commitment to Arabic
throughout the *ummah*. For no Muslim is Arabic just another language.
It is an inalienable part of the fabric of their consciousness.

Nevertheless, language highlights differences as well as commonalities. There are three major countries of the region that do not have Arabic

as their mother tongue: Iran, Turkey and Pakistan. It is no coincidence that all these three have distinctive personas and histories. So, arguably, does Egypt, even though its own native language succumbed long ago to the invasive Arabic of its conquerors (and is now used only in the liturgy of its Coptic Christian minority). There are therefore, in effect, five major entities within the region that – though all part of the *ummah* – have distinctive identities.

There is, first, the world of the Arabian peninsula: largely Sunni, historically very conservative in the Wahhabi heartlands in the centre, while more connected and open on the Red Sea and Gulf coasts. This is the heartland of Islam, at the centre of which lie Mecca and Medina. It is not for nothing that the King of Saudi Arabia is described as the Custodian of the Two Holy Mosques. Yet oil has transformed these communities irrevocably. It is too early to tell how far and how fast Saudi Arabia will modernize itself, but any material progress in a country of such economic importance would result in Saudi Arabia becoming a more normal – and perhaps therefore more unstable and less predictable – geopolitical actor on the regional stage.

Then there is Saudi Arabia's great rival for spiritual authority in the region: Iran. This is a country that never forgets its glorious past; whether it is the legacy of Darius or of Shah Abbas, its past is alive in the present. This non-Arabic speaking Shiite citadel was never just another Muslim country, either before or after 1979. Iranians produced more of the great glories of the Islamic golden era from the ninth century onwards than any other parts of the *ummah*. The two greatest thinkers of medieval Islam – Ibn Sina and al-Ghazali – were both Iranian. Again and again, the Islamic rulers of central and southern Asia found themselves relying on Iranian bureaucrats to administer their empires, using the Persian language and thus spreading the influence of Iranian culture.[26] Even the Ottoman Turkish Empire was administered in Persian. The Iranian national epic, the *Shahnameh*, was composed by an Islamic scholar to celebrate the colourful myths of the Iranian past. In fact, the imprint of the Zoroastrian past is everywhere: the most important festival in the Iranian calendar is Nowruz, a celebration of the vernal equinox that goes all the way back to Zoroastrian times. The taxi drivers of Tehran can recite verses from Rumi and Hafez – two of the greatest poets of any culture in the world. Iran's relations with all its neighbours, as well as with the West and with Russia, are fraught with tensions and misunderstandings. An opaque interplay between theology and financial interests lies behind the struggle between modernizers and conservatives, which is not over yet. So Iran's future on the Eurasian stage remains unclear. But Iran remains a proud culture that is resource rich; it is also one of the best-educated countries in the region. It and its Sunni rivals watch one another warily.

Egypt, though geographically part of Africa, is culturally part of the Arab world; in fact, it is by far the largest Arab country. Like Iran, but for quite different reasons, it too feels that it has a special heritage. Though its pharaonic past is now a matter of museums and tourism, it is not forgotten; and it leaves Egyptians with a residual sense of ancient dignity. They may have surrendered their language, unlike Iran, and for centuries, Egypt was ruled by outsiders. But from a very early stage, those Egyptian rulers have asserted a high degree of autonomy within the *ummah*. It was Cairo that became the intellectual and theological centre of Sunni Islam (and retained this mantle even under the Ottomans from the sixteenth century onwards); Egypt wrested control of its own affairs from the Ottomans long before the peninsular Arabians did; and it was Egypt that finally humiliated the British and the French during the Suez crisis. But it has never managed to establish a stable and functioning modern polity. Nowhere else were the hopes for the Arab Spring fresher; nowhere else were they strangled so completely – first by the breathtakingly blinkered leadership of a newly elected Islamist government and then by the return of a military that proceeded to govern in the only way it knew. So the lid is now firmly on the kettle again; and the question is whether economic growth can give enough people a stake in stability quickly enough to prevent the next explosion.

Turkey faces both into and outwards from the region. It is the only Muslim country in the world with a large, diversified, sophisticated and open economy. It is the largest economy in the region. Apart from the oil-based economies of the Gulf, it is much the most prosperous Muslim state and appeared in the last century to be on a journey of secularization that was taking it towards membership of the EU. Its imperial links to the region had been cut both politically and psychologically. Some of this is now being reversed: the cultural bonds are being re-emphasized, while the journey to Europe seems to have hit the buffers. Its orientation is shifting. But the outcome of the struggle between two kinds of nationalism – the one secularist and the other assertively religious – is not yet clear; not even Erdogan has yet felt able to remove the image of Atatürk from public life. But one thing is clear, a nationalism that plays up its Turkic origins in Central Asia, together with regular references to past Ottoman glories, makes for uncomfortable relationships in a region that has not forgotten the Ottomans either.

Meanwhile, at the eastern end of the region, Pakistan has from the first been on a journey away from its Indian heritage (despite, ironically, the presence there of famous archaeological sites that were the centre of the oldest Indian civilization). The loss of its Bengali east when Bangladesh was born in 1971 left it with an orientation predominantly focused westwards and northwards, and which taps into a long history of Islamic power in the region extending back – through ups and downs – to the Umayyads in the eighth century.

Muhammad Ali Jinnah envisaged a state for Muslim Indians that would be liberalizing, democratic and modern. He died too soon to see its descent into a tussle between political venality and military domination, and a plague of religious extremism. The standoff in Kashmir and the obsession with the Indian enemy has poisoned public life. It remains a country where a well-educated and fractious elite battles with an entrenched military for leadership of a poor and badly educated majority. However, though Pakistan is not blessed with hydrocarbons, its geographic position also means that it finds itself on the route of one of the most strategically important spurs of China's great Belt and Road Initiative. The geopolitical significance of this is not lost on any of Pakistan's neighbours.

All in all, the risks are obvious: Iran, Turkey and Saudi Arabia all have problematic relationships within the region. Egypt has yet to find a stable and open form of government. For all of them, the existence of Israel has been a disturbing challenge. Pakistan lives with its endless hostility towards India; Turkey has its ambivalence about Europe. So the tensions are ramified. The futures of the Middle East remain open, and the complicated past of the *ummah* is very far from dead.

Facing two ways: the split identity of Russia

To the north of the heartland of the Muslim world lies a broad swathe of mountainous, earthquake-prone territory that extends along the north coast of the Mediterranean in one direction, runs along the Black Sea coast of Turkey, sweeps through Iran and on into the Himalayas and Tibet. This territory is the unstable area where tectonic plates rub together. South of it lie the Sunni strongholds of Turkey, Egypt and the Arabian Gulf; on it sits Iran. To its north lies a country that is geologically stable but has a harsh and cold climate and has evolved an identity shaped by suffering and hardship in a way that distinguishes it from any other major Eurasian culture: Russia. Not only geologically and geographically but also culturally, this is a different world.

Russia's relationships with its neighbours have always been uneasy at best. It is a country that has changed radically in the last hundred years; it inherits a sense of almost mystical difference from the time when it saw itself as the Third Rome, the standard bearer, after the fall of Constantinople, of Orthodoxy and the guardian of its truth. However, few Russians these days know or care much about the intellectual and political background to the original division between Greek Orthodoxy and Latin Catholicism. What is left is a divided personality. Notoriously, Russian rulers have see-sawed, not so much (as is often asserted) between West and East – although Russia began to move east across the vast and empty wastes of Siberia as early as the sixteenth century – as between the worlds of St Petersburg and Moscow.

From Peter the Great onwards, the intellectual life of the Russian elite was focused on Europe. He was the first Russian leader to travel west, using his famous sojourn in England and Holland to launch the technical modernization of the state. His new western capital city of St Petersburg became the destination of one Enlightenment celebrity after another during the eighteenth century. Tsars and Russian aristocrats accumulated treasures of European art that have made St Petersburg one of the most attractive architectural and artistic pilgrimage centres of the world. The basis was laid for the efflorescence in the nineteenth and twentieth centuries of one of the world's greatest literary, musical and artistic traditions. The Russians have not been great philosophers: there is no Russian Kant or Hegel (or Marx); and their art has been distorted by the

142

upheavals of the twentieth century (just as was German art). But their music became more and more expressive and adventurous, and this continued during the life of the Soviet Union (Shostakovich is surely the presiding genius of twentieth-century symphonic and chamber music); and from Pushkin through Dostoyevsky to Tolstoy and Chekhov, Russia produced in just one century an astonishing proportion of human history's literary masterpieces.

Yet lurking behind these treasures, which are so readily thought of as part of a rich European tradition, is the Russia whose face is the ancient kremlins of Kazan, Suzdal, Nizhny Novgorod, Tula and, above all, of Moscow. This is a country whose brutal history somehow mirrors its brutal and unforgiving climate. The fortresses are a standing reminder of a savage past spent in life and death struggles for supremacy among Russian cities, and under the menace of invaders – predominantly the Mongols, whose depredations remain the stuff of Russian folklore's nightmares. And within the kremlins the glistening onion domes and the crosses soaring above them are an assertion of eternal Orthodox truth. The art of Mother Russia is not primarily European (it is significant that the great Russian artists of the early twentieth century flourished in Western Europe): it is expressed to perfection in the work of the great icon-painter Andrei Rublev, a monk who lived in the late fourteenth century, when Moscow was establishing its supremacy over the Russian lands and facing down the Mongols. In the midst of the turbulence there is something timeless and ethereal about the still circle of completeness in his icon of the three visitors to Abraham who are also the essence of the mystery of the Holy Trinity.

The true Russia of the steppes never forgot the Mongols (even though relations were not always bad); and the Third Rome never forgot the loss of Constantinople, which demonstrated both the infidel threat of Islam as well as the duplicity of the Latins who had betrayed Byzantium. Since the time when Alexander Nevsky defeated the Swedes on the Neva and the Teutonic Knights on the frozen lake at Peipas, Russia has fought with and mistrusted everyone, especially in the west. The Europeans became her foes, one after another: the Poles in the seventeenth century; the Swedes, whom they decisively defeated early in the eighteenth century; the French armies of Napoleon, famously weakened by Russian stubbornness at Borodino and then defeated by General Winter in the early nineteenth century; the British and the French who humiliated them (and themselves, in a war that became legendary for its incompetence on all sides), this time in support of the infidel Turks in the Crimea; the Germans at Tannenberg in 1914 and then a generation later under the Nazis. In the south, Russia fought repeatedly with Safavid Persia in the eighteenth and nineteenth centuries as it moved into the central Asian domains where Iranian power was weakening, thus creating for itself a set of tensions with the Muslim world that the Russians still live with today. In the east, they fought the rising power of Japan, whose imperial ambitions conflicted with theirs – a conflict marked by the particularly humiliating catastrophe of Tsushima in 1905, which was greeted with such elation by nationalists throughout the imperial domains of Eurasia. Yet, through triumph and disaster, the Russians ended eventually by reversing even the most crushing defeats: they defeated Japan in 1939, which kept Japan out of Siberia and thus out of the European theatre of war; this in turn allowed the Russians to deploy more forces to stop the German advance into the Soviet Union; and then to overrun Germany itself in 1945 – all at an almost unimaginable cost in human lives, which it has always been willing to pay (there is a grim continuity – rarely equalled in human history anywhere else – in the Russian readiness, from Ivan the Terrible through to Lenin, Trotsky and Stalin, to use the forced mobilization of ordinary people in the service of the state).

So which is the real Russia? The elegant sadness of Pushkin and Chekhov, and the intense beauty of Tchaikovsky and Shostakovich? Or the mystery explored in the icons? Or the fascination with the east, reflected in Dostoyevsky's famous essay entitled 'What is Asia to us?'[27] Or victories pulled from the jaws of defeat at huge cost? Or empire – whether in the Tsarist or the Soviet versions? Or the endless and largely nameless tolerance of hardship among ordinary folk that is the silent backdrop to it all? The answer is, of course, all of them. And now? The modern Russia, as it leaves empire and Communism behind, is reaching back into an older identity of difference. Unlike Germany, but like Japan, it has done little to confront the brutal reality of its Leninist–Stalinist experience. But it is re-emphasizing its cultural roots in Orthodoxy as tens of thousands of churches across the land are magnificently restored. It is almost as suspicious and mistrustful of Europe and America as at any time in its history. The sudden and traumatic collapse of Communism and the end of the Soviet Union was a watershed that seemed to leave Russia morally rudderless. The new Russia is now responding to this crisis of meaning by turning to the past. The Cold War is gone but not forgotten, and Russia has developed a new – if nervous – relationship with a China, which is now the big brother, as roles have reversed since the time of Stalin and Mao. The question of Russia's role on the Eurasian stage is still open.

Russia is nervous about China, and very clear about the fault line between it and the Muslim world to its south. But Russia's identity is never put in question by either of them; Russia knows they are both alien cultures. Its relationships to its west, however, are fraught with a deep ambiguity: it has always been tempted by the siren songs of Europe, the westernmost of Eurasia's great cultures. But Europe too has been wrestling with its past. The irony is that the culture which has forced so much change in all other Eurasian cultures is now undergoing an acute identity crisis of its own.

Europe: lost empires and a heritage denied

The culture of this corner of the Eurasian land mass has in common with the Muslim *ummah* the fact that it has not for centuries been embodied in a single unified polity. Ideas of nation began to emerge in the course of Europe's interminable conflicts (thus, for example, historians have argued that the Hundred Years War between England and France was the crucible in which both countries forged their nationhood[28]). Until the Reformation, there was a single moral authority in the Roman Catholic Church. But even that began to fragment irreversibly from the sixteenth century onwards. Meanwhile, and perhaps because of the political fragmentation, Europeans – hemmed in to the east and to the south – began to set out across the oceans and to explore to an extent no one had ever done before. By the nineteenth century they had fanned out over Eurasia (and much of the rest of the world too), dominating it economically and politically, and changing it for ever.

And then Europe tore itself apart in the twentieth century. All its technical brilliance, all its philosophical musings, all the sediment of

Christian religious belief in its psyche and all its beautiful art, literature and music – yet none of this saved it from a catastrophe that is unique even by the standards of a Eurasian history, through which blood has flowed like a huge river. Its uniqueness is clear to anyone who has visited Auschwitz. The result is a tortuous relationship with the past, which means that, to this day, the European identity is deeply unsure of itself. In Germany above all, the past became for a time forbidden territory. But more generally in Western Europe, the intellectual elite has found it difficult to find a place for the past in its definition of the identity of the post-war Europe. And nationalism became a dirty word, irredeemably contaminated by its vicious results in twentieth-century history. Germany and France have been central to the project of the new Europe, both geographically, economically, politically – and philosophically. For the German elite, the project has entailed cutting off the past by confronting it, separating it out, and building a new identity solely on values, effectively those of the European Enlightenment. Neither the French nor the British have had to cut themselves off from the past in the same root-and-branch way; on the contrary, both have sought to claim a distinctive national image and to assert 'soft power' on the world stage. But both have gradually had to come to terms with their own imperial pasts, and both have had difficulties with their post-war European roles: the French still live in the shadow of earlier attempts to dominate Europe in the name of social progress, only to find that they couldn't; and the British still live with their repeated attempts to avoid European entanglements, only to discover that they couldn't. France risks having to cede leadership of the European project to a Germany that still has a neuralgic aversion to the idea that all roads lead increasingly to Berlin. Meanwhile, the British are embarking on a new chapter of their history with the notorious question about their role, having lost an empire, still unanswered.

Almost all the countries of Europe have become very rapidly secularized. The superficial sign of this is that religious observance has lost ground almost everywhere; only the pace of decline varies. But this is the exterior manifestation of something much deeper, for the European Enlightenment project has in a sense succeeded all too well, even in its own terms. Not only has much of the intellectual elite of Europe severed the link between the values of the Enlightenment and their Christian humanist background; but also they have found it increasingly difficult to defend the idea that those values themselves can be absolute or universal. The language of virtue, the good life and purpose has given ground to the language of subjectivity and autonomy, as required by the democratic principle; and cultural respect in a connected world requires what Habermas calls 'communicative rationality' – a readiness to exchange ideas and to learn, which may be enriching as well as good for intellectual humility, but leaves the question of universals hanging. So what *does* Europe stand for? Are the values it aspires to universal – or not? We return to these questions in Chapters 8 and 9.

Meanwhile, Central and Eastern Europe – newly freed from the Soviet empire and rejoining the European cultural mainstream for the first time since the Second World War – is much clearer, at least about what it is not (having escaped from Soviet overlordship in recent memory and, more distantly, from Turkish overlordship). The result of all of this is that Europe's identity is strangely fragile. Europe may be unified and at peace for the first time ever; it may have the largest economy and, after Japan, be on average the most prosperous of all Eurasia's cultures; but it remains vulnerable to fracture along many fault lines. Perhaps the most dangerous of those fault lines is the one that has opened up between the intellectual elite and a public square filled with noisy protestors who feel the world is changing about them without their having voted for it. Very few of these voices see themselves as primarily European. Indeed, the vast majority of Europeans have never seen Europe as their primary identity.

The European intellectual debate is very focused on its internal difficulties: its cumbersome, opaque governance; its centrifugal tendencies; tension between west and east, between north and south; how to integrate migrants; and its strategic vulnerability to its southern neighbourhood. It is uncertain how to deal with its suspicious eastern neighbour, or with an America it senses is losing interest in it, or with a China it perceives is inevitably going to dominate Eurasia. And its engagement with the Muslim world is fraught with ambiguity: on the one hand, its elite is deeply committed to an open society with a clear separation between the public and private domains; on the other hand, many in the public square fear a community that seems to blur those distinctions, to grow in numbers and to harbour extremists who challenge those core values

147

right at their very heart. Europe's intellectuals debate the challenges; meanwhile, in the public square, its nationalisms are far from dead, and its European-ness is only embryonic. All in all, like the other cultures of Eurasia, but for its own very particular reasons, Europe's identity is a perpetual struggle with its past.

So from one end of Eurasia to the other, we see its major cultures – for all their differences – grappling in one way or another with the past that is intrinsic to their identity. Urbanization is changing all these cultures radically; but although it has dissolved older structures, it has strengthened the hold of the past and nurtured their sense of nationhood. And we have seen that the nationalism that became an ogre in the European mind in the wake of its twentieth-century nightmares is still a pervasive impulse throughout every single one of them. Just at the very time in human history when some of the most critical challenges they all face are ones that require a shared commitment in response – climate change and environmental degradation, for example – assertive cultural nationalism is on the rise everywhere. China has the most confident cultural identity; while Europe is the most uncertain of itself. Japan has the most homogeneous identity of them all, but one that feels strangely vulnerable to itself and faces a significant geostrategic dilemma directly related to its difficulty in coping with its past. India has two versions of itself – a constitutional one and a Hinduizing one – and it is not clear which will, in the end, prevail or what the implications will be for the country's identity. Russia in its vastness bestrides Europe and Asia, knowing it is different, smarting from recent humiliations and determined to assert its regional position and cultural identity. Meanwhile, the futures of the various peoples of the *ummah* are open: of all the cultures of Eurasia, this is the one that has found the challenge of modernity most difficult.

The question for the next chapter is, what does this all mean for today's Eurasian order, which is, as we have already noted in Chapter 1, effectively a Westphalian system? We need next to look at its prospects, given this growing intrusiveness into the present of the pasts that are never dead.

6

Westphalian Eurasia?

In the north of Germany lie the two cities of Münster and Osnabrück, both of them former members of the Hanseatic League, both set in the region of Westphalia, both with old medieval centres heavily damaged in the Second World War but carefully reconstructed in the 1950s, and both with imposing cathedrals and beautiful city halls that date back to the fourteenth and fifteenth centuries.

In the seventeenth century, these two city halls were the setting for a diplomatic achievement that, at that time, was unique in human history. A group of envoys from sixteen European states, dozens of member states of the Holy Roman Empire and many other interest groups had been labouring for months to bring an end to a war that had gone on far longer than anyone expected, causing unprecedented devastation across a wide area of Europe and causing the most catastrophic loss of life since the Black Death. The Thirty Years War had begun in 1618: the precarious balance of confessional power between Catholic and Protestant states in the centre of Europe had been upset by the decision of one of the Protestant prince electors of the Holy Roman Empire to accept the crown of Bohemia at the invitation of its Protestant nobility. This crown had always previously been held by a Catholic and also carried an electoral vote. With a Protestant king on the throne, this meant that the Protestant voice would have a majority in the election of the Holy Roman Emperor. The response of the existing Emperor and of the Catholic electors was immediate: imperial armies invaded Bohemia and ejected the new king. War spread fast and soon engulfed much of Europe. One state after another within the Holy Roman Empire got involved; then Sweden intervened in the Protestant cause – as did France when the balance seemed to be tipping in favour of its arch enemy the Habsburg Emperor.

The war became notorious for an endless series of battles that could never bring it to an end; for the depredations of marauding soldiers, often under nobody's effective control; for totemic horrors such as the burning to the ground of the city of Magdeburg; and in general for an increasing sense of weariness and pointlessness. It was a dreadful forerunner of the First World War. It even produced its own war literature, just as its twentieth-century follower did, in the shape of some heart-rending poetry and, perhaps above all, of *Simplicissimus*. This picaresque novel by Hans Jakob Christoffel von Grimmelshausen, who himself saw military life in the war, is a masterpiece that displays the human survival instinct in all its determination and ingenuity, in an unforgettably fast-paced narrative (in which the influence of the literary world created by Cervantes is unmistakable).

Like the First World War, this war also ushered in the end of an era. The second half of the seventeenth century was to see religious fervour give way to a new enthusiasm for enlightenment. The war had begun with the intoxication of religious passion – just as the later cataclysm began in an orgy of feverish nationalism. By the end, in both cases, the enthusiasm had been stifled by the pain. But whereas the aftermath of the First World War was to be a further series of mistakes and disasters leading to a second great conflagration, the story in the case of the Thirty Years War was different. Painstaking negotiations over many months gradually achieved a detailed settlement: Sweden gained territory along the north German coast; the French gained much of Alsace and Lorraine; Bavaria and Brandenburg-Prussia both gained weight in the Empire; Switzerland's independence from the Empire was formally recognized; and the Dutch Republic was recognized as an independent state, after decades of struggle against Spain. The treaties that embodied all this (and other smaller territorial adjustments) were signed in the city halls of Münster and Osnabrück in the epochal year of 1648.

Far more important for Eurasian history than these specific changes, however, were the principles enshrined in the Westphalian Peace treaties. Westphalia established a precedent for settling disputes between sovereign powers through diplomatic congress. It also reconfirmed and strengthened the principle that religion was a matter for each ruler to decide, not a universal order to be determined by either Empire or Pope. This principle had, in effect, already been established at the Peace of

Augsburg, which brought the religious wars of the sixteenth century to an end. The Westphalian arrangements effectively confirmed the Peace of Augsburg (except that they recognized the presence of Calvinism alongside Lutheran Protestantism for the first time). For precisely this reason, the reigning Pope Innocent X launched a virulent attack on the whole settlement – although without effect: the principle *cujus regio, ejus religio* (the ruler of a region determines its religion) had come to stay as the watchword of interstate relationships in Europe in the new era.

This recognition of the religious sovereignty of the ruler was of enormous significance; Pope Innocent X was right to see it as such. It was fundamental to a modern understanding of sovereignty and of nationhood. For, as the centuries went by, its implications became ever broader: the ruler changed from being the absolute ruler into the government answerable (one way or another) to the voice of the people. The *regio* became the nation state, not just a region whose borders were defined by dynastic rights of inheritance; and the *religio* evolved from being the official institutional religion supported by the government, into the broader culture that gave the nation its identity. Meanwhile, religion in the strict sense was gradually confined to the private sphere. All of these changes occurred over long periods; only hesitantly for example, and with plenty of reversals, did rulers come to understand the effect of the voice of the people on their roles. But even Louis XIV – he who is famously reported to have said 'L'état, c'est moi' – saw his role as embodying the glory of France. And Frederick the Great of Prussia, though he was an uncompromising absolutist, equally famously described himself as the first servant of the state. But these were just milestones on the journey towards Rousseau, Herder and Fichte, and beyond – a journey that would end in the enthronement of the sovereign nation state with its defined national culture and identity.

The new Westphalian approach to international relations evolved in the early nineteenth century into a new balance of power among sovereign nation states, embodied in the institutional framework of the Concert of Europe. Russia had been drawn into Europe by the defeat of Napoleon (as it would be again by the defeat of Hitler) and so the Concert initially comprised the four major powers that had defeated Napoleon – Austria, Prussia, Russia and Britain – but soon came to include France itself under the restored Bourbon monarchy. This formal framework did not last for long, however, not least because the British were reluctant to be drawn into an arrangement that provided a platform for dominance by the arch-conservative Austrian and Russian leaderships. But on the European stage the great powers formed and reformed alliances and sought to order the affairs of smaller states. Half a century after the Congress of Vienna had settled European affairs in the wake of the fall of Napoleon, another great Congress was convened – which not even the British felt they could ignore – in Berlin, capital now not just of Prussia but also of a recently united German Empire. Its overt purpose was to resolve the instability of South Eastern Europe, in a way that balanced the interests of Austria and of a Russia determined to sponsor the emergence of its Orthodox brothers and sisters from under the Ottoman yoke. Its deeper purpose was to demonstrate that Germany had arrived on the European stage as its newest and most energetic great power.

The Congress of Berlin was not a global congress; it was not even a gathering of Eurasian powers. Neither the resurgent Japanese nor the sclerotic Chinese governments were involved; India was of course at that time a British possession; and America – despite the rhetoric of its founding principles – was focused, in the same sort of way as other great powers have been before and since, on extending its own territory westwards to the Pacific and on keeping European powers out of Latin America. Not until the Versailles negotiations at the end of the First World War did emerging Eurasian realities begin to be reflected. This time America was there – and indeed, in the dominant role, reflecting its emergence on to the Eurasian stage, having joined the war against Germany in 1917. But perhaps because Versailles focused on the Old World and not on America's national interests on its own continent and in the Pacific, Woodrow Wilson was able to put all his moral authority behind the principle of national self-determination as the new underpinning of the international order. The Habsburgs, the Ottomans and the Romanovs were all gone. New states were formed in Central and Eastern Europe and in the Middle East, but inevitably these mostly represented messy compromises between the principle of national self-determination, the realities of mixed populations and the strategic interests of the great powers. Meanwhile, the new Russian government stayed away from Versailles, and the Bolshevik Red Army set about snuffing out any aspirations former Russian colonies might have had of achieving independence. The Japanese came to Versailles as the new Asian great power, with a large delegation determined to ensure delivery on a promise made by its Western allies during the war that it would be awarded the German holdings in Asia – especially the concession at Qingdao in the Chinese province of Shandong. The new republican government of China was also there, claiming national sovereignty over the same territory on the basis of the American principles of self-determination. Shandong, as the Chinese delegation reminded everyone, was the birthplace of Confucius. This conflict too was resolved messily: Japan prevailed because of British support; but Britain then vetoed Japan's other cherished proposal, for a racial equality clause in the convention establishing the new League of Nations. Meanwhile, the Chinese refused to sign the Versailles Treaty, in protest at the decision in favour of the Japanese. That decision provoked riots in China and was later overturned through American mediation. But the Japanese retained effective economic dominance in Shandong and continued to control the transport system.

All in all, resentment was stored up on all sides. A century later, the failings of the whole Versailles process are well understood. But it was nevertheless a milestone on a journey whose direction is a lot clearer now than it was at that time. America had already compromised its ideological hostility to colonial ventures when it seized the Philippines from Spain in 1898. Even before that it found itself using force to protect its citizens and its commercial interests in China; and it had forced the opening of Japan in order to promote trade and open the door to a Christian presence. Now, in a war that was still – despite its name – a largely European affair rather than a global one, it had finally intervened after the provocation of German U-boat activity in the Atlantic. That intervention was decisive, but what followed was catastrophic. The Versailles settlement humiliated Germany (in stark contrast to the far wiser approach of the Congress of Vienna in the wake of the fall of Napoleonic France in 1815); the Americans (with the schizophrenia about international entanglements that has always been a hallmark of their identity) turned their backs on the fragile new League of Nations; both the Germans and the Japanese eventually walked out of it; fascism fed on economic depression and on the Bolshevik menace from Russia; and the course was set for another war – this time still not truly global, but certainly Eurasian in its scale. America was sucked in once again, and in the wake of the war found itself entrenched at both ends of the Eurasian land mass. It would never be able to leave it again.

The new Eurasian stage

In the decades following the Second World War, the other Eurasian empires – the Japanese, the British, the French, the Dutch, the Portuguese and finally the Soviet Russian empires – were all dissolved in their turn. And by the turn of the millennium, it had finally become clear what the new Eurasian great power configuration of the twenty-first century would look like. China, India, Russia and Japan are all present on that stage. So is America. But how were the other two great cultures of Eurasia to be represented? What of Europe? What of the Muslim world? We will return to both these questions later. But before we do, it is worth noting three points about this new Eurasian stage.

First, it is no concert in any formalized sense like the Concert of Europe in the early nineteenth century. But all the powers have particular Eurasian hinterlands that are a matter of significant national interest to them (in America's case, this national interest is primarily in the east); all have economic muscle and most are well armed (several with nuclear weapons).

Second, though the language of great powers and of major cultures inevitably leads to a focus on six major countries or regions of Eurasia, with the addition of America as a special case, there are of course other countries that play important roles in Eurasian international relations. Some of these countries have less impact than their demographic weight would suggest. Indonesia, for example, which is not only Eurasia's third-largest country but also the world's largest Muslim country, was, in the first two decades of its independence, a leader – together with India – in the world's non-aligned movement, but it now spends most of its governmental energy coping with the massive tasks entailed by its own social and economic development. The Philippines and Vietnam are also examples: the one is the only majority Christian country in the east, the other was the centre of the world's attention for two decades as America was drawn into a war where it learned – even more clearly than in the case of the Korean War in the early 1950s – the limits of hard power. Both these countries think of themselves as small (because they have a very large neighbour with whom they must cope); but both would be much the largest in their region if they were in Europe. However, they are both now preoccupied with the internal challenges of social and economic development.

By contrast, there are other countries that have an impact out of all proportion to their demographic weight: Singapore, the world's most vocal proponent of the merits of the Confucian order; the two Koreas, one of which is one of the world's most successful economies, while the other is one of its least successful but also one of the world's most dangerous and unpredictable rogue states; the Ukraine, because a fault line between the European and Russian cultural worlds runs through it; and the United Arab Emirates, the energetic and outward-looking beacon of the Middle East that hosts the largest international airport in the world.

Third, we need to reflect on the special case of America. Samuel Huntington, in *The Clash of Civilizations*,[1] treated 'the West' as a single culture or civilization, of which America and Europe were parts (alongside Canada, Australia and New Zealand). In this he was following a well-trodden pathway. But this classification is misleading: it tends to be used by American commentators who then proceed – as Huntington does – to view international relationships in general, and Eurasian relationships in particular, through an American prism, with the tacit or even explicit assumption that the European perspective is essentially similar. Both Henry Kissinger[2] and Zbigniew Brzezinski[3] also do so – not because they are unaware of the cultural and attitudinal differences between Europe and America (how could they be since both were by birth Europeans?), but because they see international relations fundamentally in terms of strategies for maintaining a balance of power calculated on the basis of relative economic, technological, military and demographic strength, and political willpower.

However, the centre of gravity of the American identity is, in fact, very different from that of Europe. We have seen how history weighs on the shoulders of all Eurasian cultures and certainly not least on the shoulders of the Europeans. America is different: it may no longer be young enough to claim innocence, and it treasures its own past with a care that condescending Eurasians find amusing because it is so recent. But it is still in an important sense the New World that left the old behind. Even now, America is a country of immense space, with a population density much lower than in the crowded heartlands of Eurasia. And somehow, that space still translates into a sense of potential: the individual can always move on. The myths of America are onward-looking and forward-looking. Alexis de Tocqueville, the highly perceptive French aristocrat who visited the country in 1831, noticed a special sense of purpose, even calling. As Henry Kissinger noted, Tocqueville traces a distinctive American identity to what he called its point of departure – the Puritanism of New England. Tocqueville wrote that this 'was not just a religious doctrine: in many respects it shared the most absolute democratic and republican theories' as a result of 'two perfectly distinct elements which elsewhere have often been at war with one another but which in America it was somehow possible to incorporate with one another, forming a marvellous combination. I mean the *Spirit of Religion* and the *Spirit of Freedom*.'[4] This New World is older than it was, and has known the pain of civil war, the shame of slavery and traumatic failure in Vietnam, as well as a gnawing sense of dissatisfaction with more recent unhappy excursions in the Middle East. It sees its strategic interests as threatened by the rise of China and is gradually coming to recognize that its time as the world's only superpower has drawn to a close. And yet, America is still not a country whose national psyche is overburdened by loss, guilt or shame. America and Europe are different, not only because their geopolitical position and interests are different but also because their history is different; and this means their identities are different.

Europeans share much with America, of course. At one level, both Europeans and Americans are inheritors of Christendom and of the Enlightenment. They share the values that are common to democracies (values all too often taken for granted by those who have never had to live without them and never had to fight for them). But at another level there are obvious and profound differences in values and priorities. Americans are typically more individualistic than Europeans (even while also being more patriotic). This is the legacy of Locke, of that Puritanism which Tocqueville remarked on, and of the millions of Eurasian immigrants who arrived in the nineteenth and twentieth centuries, whose energy and determination was certainly not captured by the image of the tired, the poor and the huddled masses yearning to be free (from the lines by Emma Lazarus quoted on the Statue of Liberty). It has a flexibility and a dynamism that manifest themselves in an economy that is constantly reinventing itself in unexpected ways. It may not be the world's only superpower any longer, but it remains an immensely sophisticated and powerful presence on the world stage. And it is much clearer about its identity than are the Europeans. It has had no absolutist or totalitarian past to haunt its nightmares. It also had no pre-Enlightenment past of its own to react against (and, ironically perhaps, nurtures more pre-Enlightenment thought patterns – notably, for example, the widespread pre-scientific attitude towards evolution and human origins).

So the differences are many and profound: between the degree of geographical and social mobility; between European and American assumptions about the right of privacy, or about the right way to provide health care in society, or on such matters as capital punishment or gun control; and in the extent of religious conviction and of religious observance. Some of this is changing in the twenty-first century, but it is all a reminder that the centre of gravity of American attitudes is very different from that of a much more thoroughly secularized Europe. (It is also a reminder to the British, who are more apt than other Europeans to overlook these differences, that they have far more in common with their continental neighbours and less with their transatlantic friends than they often recognize.) In short, America is indeed a special case, and an analysis of twenty-first-century international relationships in Eurasia is not helped by treating America and Europe as a homogeneous 'West'.

What is true is that the Europeans and the Americans have both had a profound impact on all the rest of Eurasia over the last two centuries. That impact has been many-layered: technological, commercial, imperial, and – not least – cultural. Indeed, that same intellectual curiosity and thirst to explore, which was the engine of Europe's enlightenment and the basis of its energy and economic power, also led the Europeans to explore and interpret the cultures of Eurasia. So the eighteenth and nineteenth centuries saw Europeans fanning out all over the land mass to dig, to observe, and to categorize and classify. And this has produced a strident debate, associated particularly with the name of Edward Said, a Palestinian-born American professor (and close friend of Daniel Barenboim, with whom he co-founded the famous West-Eastern Divan Orchestra). His revolutionary book, *Orientalism*, was first published in 1978, a time when the Middle East had been pushed centre stage by the politics of oil and by the fraught relationship between Israel and its neighbours.[5] Said mounted a passionate critique of the way European scholarly narratives about the East in general and the Middle East in particular had been instrumental in equipping colonial administrations with an 'understanding' of the peoples being ruled, as well as infused by a less-acknowledged and deeper desire for affirmation of the rulers' cultural superiority. Indeed, he argued that, from a very early stage, Europeans had defined Asia as the 'other' and that this fundamental sense of the alien and/or the sinister is reflected in Aeschylus (in *The Persians*) and in Euripides (in *The Bacchae*, in which the Asiatic origins of Dionysus are explicit) and continued to inform the medieval world view, as reflected in Dante. Then, from the early eighteenth century onwards, a newly inquisitive European interest in the East was accompanied by a rush of romanticism, before being followed by a disillusionment that was as distorting as the first flush of excitement.

Said has had his equally vocal critics, who have accused him of an emotional lack of objectivity and of making elementary mistakes in his analysis.[6] But the essential point has stuck: that it is necessary to see the cultural and political relationships that have characterized Eurasia through the eyes of those who were subject to the political imperialism of the Europeans and the cultural and economic imperialism of the Americans. Said's most profound point is that 'pure' academic objectivity, freed of all cultural bias, is unattainable. The best that can be hoped for is 'spiritual detachment and generosity' of the kind called for by the medieval English scholar Hugh of St Victor, who is quoted with approval by Said:

> The man who finds his homeland sweet is still a tender beginner; he to whom every soil is as his native one is already strong; but he is perfect to whom the entire world is as a foreign land.[7]

Samuel Huntington, writing almost twenty years later, took this essential point. In *The Clash of Civilizations* he argued that the West was losing its historically overwhelming superiority as other cultures surged ahead economically and technically, and as a result the new era would be multipolar and multicivilizational. In such a world, he argued,

> societies sharing cultural affinities cooperate with each other; efforts to shift societies from one civilization to another are unsuccessful; and countries group themselves around the lead or core state of their civilization. In this new world the most pervasive, important and dangerous conflicts will not be between social classes, rich and poor, or other economically defined groups, but between peoples belonging to different cultural entities.[8]

Huntington's book is in some ways dated: he spends many pages on the break-up of Yugoslavia and its civilizational background; though much of what he says is not wrong, it seems less central from the vantage point of the new millennium than it did at the time. He clearly overemphasizes some cultural bonds and their potential political significance (the bonds of Orthodoxy, for example, will not cause either Romania or Bulgaria – now both embedded in the EU and in NATO – to listen to siren songs from Russia, and have not prevented the Ukrainian Orthodox Church from breaking away from the Moscow patriarchate in the context of the Ukraine's struggle to escape from the Russian sphere of influence). He was also writing before it became clear just how prominent China would become on the Eurasian stage.

But his central proposition – for which he was attacked again and again by the left and by liberals, both of whose world views he challenged – was uncannily prescient. Some have found it easy to accuse him of precisely the sort of orientalism Said had berated. But that is a slipshod response. He writes through an American lens and as a passionate believer in the values of American civilization, for sure (and thus fails to recognize some of the deeper issues facing the Europeans). But he understands the power of culture in determining identity. Amartya Sen, one of India's greatest modern intellectuals, sought to downplay this cultural impact on the individual, arguing that we do not 'discover' but, rather, we 'determine' our identity.[9] But recent years – in India as much as anywhere – have done nothing but confirm the force of Huntington's insight. He may not have given the role of collective memory – particularly of colonial rule – enough of a part in the determination of particular civilizational identities, but he was certainly aware of the dangers of a pushback against the West by newly self-confident cultures; indeed, he could be accused of overemphasizing this as a generic tendency and of underestimating older rivalries and tensions on the Eurasian stage that have subsequently become more obvious.

Huntington's core point – that the world in general and Eurasia in particular are multicultural – is a reminder that the new Eurasian great power configuration is essentially a new Westphalian order. Just before the collapse of the Soviet Union, in 1989, Francis Fukuyama wrote his famous essay 'The end of history?'[10] Often forgotten is the fact that this title ends with a question mark. But it was widely influential in the heady days when the liberal democratic order seemed to carry everything before it. Since then we have seen a global financial and economic crisis, the emergence of Islamist fundamentalism, the failures of the Arab Spring, the rise and fall of American neo-conservative international policy, the rise and rise of China, and extensive questioning of the post-war international order on almost all sides. The assumption that the liberal democratic order would prevail has been buried – at least for now. The beneficiary has not been its main ideological rival of the post-war era (and fellow European export from the thought world of the nineteenth century), international communism. It too seems to have had its day. What has emerged instead is cultural nationalism. As the Japanese philosopher Takeshi Umehara suggested soon after the demise of the Soviet Union:

> the total failure of Marxism . . . and the dramatic break-up of the Soviet Union are only the precursors to the collapse of Western liberalism, the main current of modernity. Far from being the alternative to Marxism and the reigning ideology at the end of history, liberalism will be the next domino to fall.[11]

Significantly, Umehara's life work had sought to re-establish an authentically Japanese approach, one that is not derivative of European or American thought patterns, to Japanese cultural and philosophical studies.

Cujus regio, ejus religio on the Eurasian stage

We will return to the question of the end of history in Chapter 9. But for now, we should note how universalist ideology has given way to the multiculturalism of a multipolar world. *Cujus regio, ejus religio*. The Eurasian order of the twenty-first century at its deep structural level looks remarkably like the European world of 1648. And we saw how Europe gradually succumbed to the nationalist rivalries of the sovereign states that emerged in the Westphalian era. None of those states (except the France of the revolutionary years) even pretended to have universalist aims. They promoted their own interests, through trade, through diplomacy, through competitive colonialism, and where necessary, through aggression. This was international relations conducted on lines favoured long ago by Kautilya, the Indian minister from the fourth century BCE whose theory of statecraft is set out in a (rather un-Indian) text known as the *Arthashastra* (the science of government). This remarkable work is a comprehensive analysis of what it takes for a state to survive and prosper in relentless competition with its neighbours. It is analogous to the approach made famous centuries later by Machiavelli and by Richelieu (who was happy to take Catholic France into the Thirty Years War on the Protestant side against the Habsburg Emperor on the principle that my enemy's enemy is my friend).

Westphalia was no guarantee of peace. The wars that disfigured Europe from then until the First World War were not religious wars in the narrow sense. The Napoleonic wars were ideological, and Waterloo was arguably not just the defeat of France but also of the modernizing and universalizing impetus of the French Revolution – as Victor Hugo understood so clearly in those reflections in *Les Misérables* as we noted in Chapter 3. Napoleon had in effect laid down a direct challenge to the principle of *cujus regio, ejus religio*. Not for another hundred years would such a universalist challenge confront any power in Eurasia. Instead, European wars gradually morphed into nationalist wars. Then came the Bolshevik Revolution and the zeal of the Comintern, which was certainly a very direct challenge to *cujus regio, ejus religio* and ushered in what now looks like an interlude of major ideological conflict. But from the vantage point of the new century, we can see how this has now given way to an older and more familiar pattern – the new Eurasia looks Westphalian again. Each of this century's great powers has a geographically defined area that it regards as its natural sphere of influence or as an area of vital national interest. And in each case, there are areas of overlap, and therefore of actual or potential friction. There are also areas that have no clearly dominant regional power (or as Huntington termed it, a core state), which creates an obvious risk of conflict. Truly horrific would be what eventually did happen when the First World War broke out: a conflict between two or more of the great powers. In the twenty-first century, the prevalence of nuclear weapons makes this less likely to happen than it was then – but more unspeakably terrible if it did.

Thus, for example, China clearly has its regional red lines: Taiwan, Tibet, Xinjiang, the South China Sea. It also expects to have influence over the future development of the Korean Peninsula; and following an ancient Chinese instinct, it seeks to extend its influence westwards, just as it did in the era of the Tang Dynasty. It expects Mongolia to be pliant to its interests; and it expects certain South East Asian nations – notably Cambodia and perhaps Myanmar – to be pliant beneficiaries of its support. All in all, China has a clearly delineated view of its own inalienable territorial reach, as well as a regional hinterland in which it expects to be the senior partner. History matters for China as for others: the painful memory of the Japanese Co-Prosperity Sphere; the long and largely unsuccessful history of its attempts to dominate Vietnam; the fluid and tense relationship with Russia from Tsarist times onwards across the empty spaces of Siberia; the interaction with Islam along the silk routes, part of which became incorporated into China as Xinjiang Province. One way and another, down the centuries China has tussled geopolitically with every other great Eurasian culture – and these encounters remain sources of actual or potential tension to this day. And now there is America, whose Pacific commitments constitute another tectonic plate nudging against its regional sphere of influence.

Russia is equally clear about its view of its natural sphere of influence: the Ukraine, Byelorussia, Georgia and Armenia (Russia has made it abundantly clear that any attempt to incorporate any of these into the EU would be a major provocation and that it might even regard their joining NATO as a *casus belli*). It grits its teeth over the Baltic states of Estonia, Latvia and Lithuania, which were once part of the Soviet Union and, before that, of the Tsarist empire – although it recognizes the fait accompli of their EU and NATO membership, and will confine itself to occasionally testing NATO's alertness and resolve. Furthermore, it regards the Crimea as an inalienable part of Russia (as well as being strategically vital because of the importance of Sevastopol as a deep-water port for its naval presence in the Black Sea and the Mediterranean). Russia's stage management of the Crimea's secession from the Ukraine was not just opportunist, and it has no intention of ever disgorging it. (Was this a breach of the Westphalian principle that sovereignty is sacrosanct? Or was it the rectification of a past administrative nonsense, perpetrated in Soviet times, in a way that confirms the power of culture in determining sovereignty?) In Central Asia, Russia intends to maintain significant security links with, and thus influence in, the former members of the Soviet Union; and Turkey is a country with which it has had a long history of enmity and tension, but will work with when there is a shared enemy to confront in the Middle East. Russia is building a closer relationship with China, despite its nervousness about the long-term effects of Chinese commercial involvement in Siberia. It does so partly in order to diversify its energy business away from a Europe that it sees as potentially interfering in its own backyard, and partly in a sort of coalition of the willing against the perceived universalism of America. For it resents what it sees as the triumphalism of America, even as it senses America's waning enthusiasm for its European commitments.

India is less strategic and more defensive about its neighbourhood: its main concern since independence has been with the intentions of Pakistan and the stalemate in Kashmir; this has not gone away but is being increasingly overshadowed by a fear of encirclement fed by China's growing presence in Pakistan, in the Persian Gulf, in Sri Lanka and in South East Asia. India's long border with China is possibly the tensest between two great powers anywhere in the world. Meanwhile, India's liberal and business establishment looks more and more to America – and less and less to its former imperial overlord – as a source of inspiration.

Japan is, like India, less visibly assertive and more defensive in its interests: both distant and recent history have left it with an inferiority complex in relation to China; it is highly nervous about the Korean Peninsula; it would like its northern islands back from Russia, a claim it will never give up but it will never assert abrasively; and it will use its still considerable economic clout to protect its markets and its energy security in the face of a China whose footprint now seems to be everywhere. Geopolitically, Japan is less entangled with the rest of Eurasia's great powers than any of the others are (although it has extensive commercial relations with all of them). It has only two strategic geopolitical relationships that matter (possibly existentially) to it: America and China. Above all, Japan does not want to have to choose between these two behemoths it has had to live with ever since the disaster and humiliation of war; and it fears that this poses an increasingly difficult long-term strategic dilemma.

Meanwhile, the Europeans feel under siege; their deep history from Roman times onwards is of invaders from the east; much more recent experience has left them with a fear and suspicion of the great bear, which is at the same time locked in an economic embrace with Europe by the gas pipelines that make Russia and Europe tensely dependent on one another. And on its south-eastern flank, Europe is exposed to the turmoil in the Middle East; recently it has been the tragedy of Syria, tomorrow who knows where (Egypt?); that same turmoil means that it has to deal with a Turkey it increasingly mistrusts. More than ever, Europe is schizophrenic about America; it senses the waning commitment of America to the security of Europe, now that the Cold War with the Soviet Union is over. And above all, along its southern flank, it fears the demographic challenge of Africa. All in all, this stirs nightmares: from the time when the Vandals swept through North Africa and cut off the grain supplies to Rome; from the time when the Mongols ransacked the plains of Central Europe; or when the Muslims poured into Spain and later into south-eastern and central Europe, all the way to the gates of Vienna. In one form or another, down to and including the present, the Europeans fear the barbarians at the gate. They recognize the growing power of China, and are nervous about Chinese strategic involvement in their own backyard (the Sixteen plus One initiative of the Chinese brings together all the eastern members of the EU as well as all the would-be members in the Balkans, encouraged by the promise of investment as part of China's extended Belt and Road Initiative). Like Japan, the Europeans are not prepared generally to be assertive about their strategic interests. Also like Japan, they face a dilemma about America: what if it were to withdraw its shield and go home, as it has done before in its long love–hate relationship with the devious, hidebound, ungrateful Old World it left behind more than two centuries ago? For the Europeans, in fact, this is a higher risk than it is for Japan, where the Americans have greater strategic interests, now that the European Cold War is over.

Finally, there is the Muslim world; like Europe it lacks clear leadership by a core state; unlike Europe, it does not even have a dominant bloc with the potential jointly to provide political direction (such as the combination of Germany and France gives to the European project); and unlike all the other major cultures and regions of Eurasia, the *ummah* is riven with its own internal hatreds and strife. Syria has brought all the resulting problems into very sharp focus; proxy or direct involvement by Iran, Saudi Arabia, Turkey and Russia turned this tragedy into something much more like a pre-Westphalian battlefield free-for-all than a post-Westphalian sovereign entity. *Cujus regio, ejus religio* would ring very hollow in the Syria of the early twenty-first century. America has made no serious efforts and taken few risks to influence the outcome; the Europeans have been even more reluctant but have had to wrestle with the resulting human tragedy of vast numbers of fleeing asylum seekers; and meanwhile, the Chinese have kept their heads down.

So what of America? For it, the most obvious fact of this century is the shift in its definition of its prime rival. For half a century this was the Soviet Union. When it collapsed in 1991, America's triumphalist tone was hard to miss: the subliminal – and sometimes even the overt – message was 'we've won', not 'you've been freed'. Not only has this left a sour taste in many Russian mouths to this day, but also the triumphalism was in any case to be short-lived. As late as 1997, Brzezinski was still more focused on the implications of the end of the Soviet Union for the grand chess game than he was on the new China. But by the turn of the millennium, it was increasingly obvious that the economic opening up of China was going to have the profoundest of geostrategic implications.

Unlike the Europeans, America believes that the relationship with China is indeed with a rival. America is involved in Eurasia against its deepest instincts: its appetite for and interest in the minutiae of regional and local cultural politics is limited; ever since the Korean War, its experience in deploying its military strength in open conflict in Eurasia has been very mixed; its public has become less and less ready to tolerate the sacrifice of American lives in such conflicts, so that its involvement is increasingly limited to airborne activity and to behind-the-scenes technical support. At the same time, the combination of a nuclear age and borderless terrorism has brought home to Americans that there is no such thing as a conflict that is far from home. That dawning awareness increases the desire to turn their back on it all, but also makes it impossible to do so. The danger America sees is of its Chinese rival gaining support from a Russia that neither trusts nor is trusted by it; of that rival happily increasing its influence in a Middle East the problems of which remain intractable; of an incohesive and internally obsessed Europe that regularly abuses America but expects it to provide its main security umbrella; and of a Japan which it doesn't expect (and probably doesn't want) to increase its geopolitical punch. And even as it builds closer links with India, America is aware of that new Indian cultural assertiveness which reminds it that India is hardly a natural soulmate.

One part of the American psyche is universalist and uncomfortable with the Westphalian order; but the other is uncomfortable with the implications of global superpower status and is happy to settle for such an order, so long as it is stable and in balance. Yet at a regional level, as Huntington noted, peace and balance may be incompatible: peace may require the acceptance of dominance by a regional great power; balance may require confrontation. The universalist part of America's psyche is uncomfortable with the realpolitik implied in countenancing such regional domination; in fact, it is uncomfortable with the acceptance of tyranny within a sovereign state. It is uncomfortable, in short, with the Westphalian principle. But, to borrow a famous phrase from Goethe's Faust, two souls live in America's breast.[12] One soul wants to put the world right; the other soul wants to go back home to its own simpler world.

But it cannot go home. Not only would its universalist soul not rest if it did so, but also the realpolitik (which accepts, for example, the continued abuse of the North Korean people by its bizarre and secretive elite) knows that the Westphalian balance cannot be relied on to preserve itself without active engagement. Yet it is decreasingly willing to pay the cost – and certainly not when another major power is involved. What happens, though, when it is two great powers that confront one another? Indeed, for the next century of Eurasia's history – and therefore of world history – there is one overwhelmingly important geopolitical question: how will America and China deal with one another? There is also a second question, almost as important for the future of the continent: how will its two behemoths, China and India, deal with one another? The answer to these two questions will be crucial to the long-term duration of the new Westphalian order. But neither question is just about geopolitics, as we shall see shortly.

There are more than a few similarities between this new order and the world of Europe before the First World War. Both then and now, as we have noted, many wanted to believe that economic interrelationships create vested interests in peace. Then and now, a newly emerged great power comes on the stage and changes the balance (then it was Germany, now it is China). Both then and now, one of the players – on some measures, at least, the most powerful one – is offshore but has an interest in preventing the emergence of any hegemonic power among the rest; then that role was played by Britain, now by America. And as if those parallels weren't enough, Germany set about challenging the most important means by which Britain projected its power globally – its naval supremacy; now China's growing navy is doing exactly the same to America. Finally, the Korean Peninsula is an uncomfortable parallel to the Balkans. (In both regions, long memories matter: the Balkans had been an unstable three-way cultural fault line between Orthodoxy, Islam and Catholic Central Europe for hundreds of years; for the Chinese and the Japanese, Korea has over the same long timeframe been an unstable cockpit of competing kingdoms that were rarely united, and an important conduit not only for ideas but also for invading armies.)

None of this is to argue that a catastrophe on the scale of the First World War is about to bring down the new Eurasian Westphalia. But there are two fundamental challenges that the new Westphalian Eurasia will face over the rest of this century. They are very different from the challenges that faced the old world of Europe. How the major protagonists face them will determine the future of the continent – and therefore of the world.

The problem of the commons

The first challenge becomes more obvious and more urgent with every passing year. The problem of the commons is created by the interaction of sociology, economics and the environment. At its core lies the simple point that what is rational for the individual may not be rational for the community. If an asset is freely available but its supply is not unlimited, it will be overused. The classic example from agricultural societies is common land, which was always at risk of overgrazing; but the problem lurks within human history and experience in all sorts of ways. Underlying the recurrent westward movements of steppe peoples through much of Eurasian history, there is in effect a problem of the commons: the search for new lands for the nomadic way of life, the depredation of agricultural communities, and even the sacking of cities for their booty were ways of seizing assets freely available at little cost to the successful warrior, as demonstrated above all by the Mongols and the Turks. The same problem of the commons underlies the rapid and uncontrolled urbanization we have already noted throughout Eurasia: the opportunities of city life, both economic and social, compared with the economically unproductive and socially restrictive countryside are, seemingly at least, freely available to the individual; so newcomers pour in, and the resulting impact on the city's infrastructure is a burden borne by all.

Thomas Malthus' famous counter to the optimism of the eighteenth century was in effect addressing the problem of the commons. His pessimistic theory, set out just before the turn of the nineteenth century – not long before the global human population began its rapid and remorseless rise – held that populations always tended to expand to use up the available resources, such that no improvement in living standards would be possible. Malthus was an Anglican clergyman who followed his logic through to some unattractive conclusions – such as his opposition to the Poor Laws – and who argued that the only possible alternative to misery, given this dynamic, was 'moral restraint'. Over the two hundred years since he wrote his *Essay on the Principle of Population* he has been shown to be wrong: he did not foresee the substantial growth in living standards, which has, in fact, accompanied population growth and itself has been much larger than he could have imagined. (Nor did he envisage birth rates falling as they have done throughout Eurasia – and he certainly would not have countenanced the contraception that has facilitated this.) For technological progress has given humanity a remarkable ability to maximize yields, to find new reserves of resources that are becoming scarce, and to develop alternatives to particular resources. So doomsayers about limits to growth have repeatedly found themselves embarrassed by their predictions.

And yet, was he so wrong? What if the entire planetary system itself is disturbed, and on such a scale that biodiversity is seriously under threat and the conditions of living are degraded? For that is the version of the problem of the commons that confronts us over the rest of this century. The problem has now become everyone's problem, because the total impact on the planet of the urban demographic explosion has created a catastrophe in the making. We now live in the Anthropocene era – the era of overwhelming human impact on planetary life – and have done so for the last century or more. What is more, we are still in the early stages of its outworkings. The whole planetary environment is the commons of the new connected, urbanized era. Some parts of that environment are pure examples of commons – that is, assets available to all falling under no sovereignty or any form of private ownership, such as the oceans, Antarctica, the Arctic ice cap, the stratosphere into which we pump carbon. These are all available to all human societies on an entirely unrestricted basis – unless we choose collectively to restrict access. And where we don't, the full force of the problem of the commons is becoming clear. Thus, for example, climate change is warming the northern oceans so that the Arctic ice cap is melting, to the point where the Chinese Belt and Road Initiative can contemplate opening up northern shipping lanes into the Atlantic world, and to the point where the future of the polar bear is in grave danger.

One way or the other, the world at large – and the great powers of Eurasia in particular – face the challenge of cooperation in the face of the mounting threats to the global commons. There is some evidence of its ability to rise to this challenge in certain specific areas. Thus, in 1961, the Antarctic Treaty came into force, setting the continent aside as a scientific preserve and banning military activity; subsequent protocols have banned waste disposal and exploration of mineral resources (other than for research purposes). Similarly, the International Whaling Commission regulates whaling to ensure effective conservation and development of whale stocks; it has not been without controversy, but it was the first example in human history of a collective decision to intervene to protect an animal species. By the time it began work in the 1950s, the number of blue whales – the largest creature that has ever existed on the planet – had plummeted to just hundreds. Since then, the world has seen numbers of these majestic animals climb to several tens of thousands; they are back from the edge of extinction. We have also seen rising awareness in the last decade of the dangers to the oceans both of overfishing and of plastic pollution. There is a long way to go on the journey towards robust international action to limit further damage; but the longest journey begins with a single step – and that first step is to recognize the problem. Finally, and despite some uncomfortable bumps on the road, the world is moving towards decarbonizing its economic growth, through international agreements in which all the major Eurasian countries have played a role (and even if America has suffered a spasm of irresponsible non-cooperation in recent years, it seems unlikely to play the sulking child for long). However, the climate and the environment are not yet unambiguously the most urgent priorities of any country (even in Europe), and it is too soon to tell whether any of this will be enough to prevent or even significantly limit damage to the environment over the rest of this century.

The planetary environment also has assets that are not commons in the strict sense, because they are under sovereign control and, in some cases, in private ownership as well, and yet they are, so to speak, gifts to the whole of humanity. The irony is that a Westphalian order enthroning national sovereignty may make it even harder to achieve progress in the case of goods under sovereign control than in the case of goods that are pure commons. The tropical rainforests are the most obvious example because of their importance in the carbon cycle (as well as their significant potential in pharmaceutical research). Of the three main areas of tropical rainforest in the world, one is in Eurasia; the other two are in Africa and Latin America. In the absence of effective controls on forest clearance in any of the main countries concerned, they are disappearing as fast as the Arctic ice cap; and the effects on the world's climate and environment are as serious.

Meanwhile, the world's fresh water supplies are under growing stress, particularly in some of the most populated regions of Eurasia. Asia has less fresh water per inhabitant than any other region of the world. And the facts of geography have ensured that the resulting challenges are cross-border threats to the Westphalian order. The high Tibetan plateau with its bountiful sources of glacial water is the source of no less than ten of Asia's major rivers. As many as eighteen other countries depend on one or more of these rivers for fresh water. Dam construction, as well as industrial and agricultural pollution, are serious sources of tension, affecting, in particular, the Brahmaputra and Mekong rivers in Bangladesh and in South East Asia. In Central Asia, the Aral Sea, which straddles the frontier between Uzbekistan and Kazakhstan, used to be the fourth-largest lake in the world. Irrigation projects in Soviet times drained its feeder rivers and it is now less than ten per cent of its original size and badly salinated, resulting in the almost complete destruction of its fish stocks. Lake Balkhash in Kazakhstan is now at risk of the same fate; it is being drained by the growing offtake of water from its feeder rivers in China's neighbouring Xinjiang Province. As urbanization, economic development and demographic pressure continue, the demand for water will continue to rise. It would not be hard to envisage this becoming one of the most dangerous flashpoints of international relationships in the twenty-first century, particularly in Central, South and South East Asia. At the same time, the biodiversity of fresh water is degrading rapidly: more than half of all freshwater species are on the endangered list of the International Union for Nature Conservation.

The end of the post-war order?

The second great challenge facing today's Westphalian Eurasia is that the architecture and defining principles of post-war international relations are being questioned by some of its major powers. The post-war order was determined during and after the Second World War, largely on the initiative of America. Britain played a supporting role and the Soviet Union paid lip service, while ensuring that it was not in practice constrained in any sphere that was important to it. Some of its key components function in a way that suits the new great powers well. In particular, the UN was equipped with a Security Council on which all three of the allies of convenience – together with France and China – were given veto powers. The structure suits China and continues to suit Russia – and indeed all the other veto-wielding powers – perfectly. The fact that it is out of kilter with the political landscape of the modern Eurasia (Why are there two European vetoes? Why does India not have a permanent seat and a veto?) generates little international excitement. The structure all but guarantees that the UN cannot act, or authorize action, against any great power or in any area in which any great power has a material interest. The one and only time this happened was in Korea, and all those involved paid a heavy strategic price: China lost any possibility of unifying Taiwan for a century (because the mess in Korea led America to give unqualified commitment to the Nationalist government in Taiwan);[13] the Soviet Union lost the respect and trust of the Chinese because it encouraged the original decision to invade the South but then refused to engage its own military, thus pulling China into a costly and distracting conflict; and the Americans lost their aura of invincibility.[14] The Korean experience is never likely to be repeated. There have been over thirty UN peacekeeping missions in Eurasia since 1945, doing useful but mostly low-key work in conflict avoidance and resolution, a role that underpins the balance of power but in no way constrains the sovereignty of the great powers themselves.

But none of this means that the great powers are entirely content with the international architecture and its workings, for there are two significant areas of actual or potential friction among the major countries of Eurasia. First, while the UN itself may be structured to the satisfaction of all, the economic and financial institutions of Bretton Woods are not, and nor is the US dollar-based international payments system (with all the scope this gives for America to enforce economic sanctions as part of its geopolitical objectives). America has refused over decades to come to terms with the implications of the changing economic weight of members for their voting shares in the World Bank and the International Monetary Fund; and China has led the way in creating what may become a parallel architecture of development finance institutions. It has also actively promoted its own currency as a trading mechanism; its share in global trade and as an international reserve currency is rising, even if it is a long way from pushing the dollar off its perch. (There are others – notably the Japanese and the Indians – who fear that this strategy will in the long run simply redistribute economic and financial power between the two giants rather than produce a more open system less subject to geopolitics.)

Second, and more subtly – but perhaps, in the end, even more significant – it remains the case that the foundational texts of the UN sit uneasily with Westphalian geopolitics. It is not simply that they enshrine a principle of self-determination for all peoples. This principle was accepted through gritted teeth as early as 1941 by an imperial Britain desperate for America to join the war in Europe; and it was subsequently incorporated in the Charter of the UN. Stalin blithely ignored it, just as Lenin had done earlier when reconstituting the Russian Empire as the Soviet Union; and following the close of the Soviet era, the principle of self-determination is now assumed to have been implemented (or in some cases conveniently ignored, depending on which groups of people the great powers count as peoples) throughout Eurasia.

However, the issue is about more than just self-determination. For in 1948, the UN adopted the Universal Declaration of Human Rights. This was in effect an elaboration of principles embodied in the UN Charter – principles that committed all member states to 'universal respect for, and observance of, human rights and fundamental freedoms for all without distinction as to race, sex, language or religion'. The Declaration was drafted by a committee appointed by the UN and chaired by Eleanor Roosevelt, widow of America's longest-serving president. It was a Canadian legal scholar, John Peters Humphrey, who did most of the drafting work. Its thirty articles cover a broad range of themes: equality and dignity of all; condemnation of slavery and cruelty in punishment; the right to justice on principles we are all familiar with (the presumption of innocence, the right to a fair and impartial trial, and so on); the right to freedom of movement within the country of residence and the right to return to it; the right of asylum; equal rights in marriage; the right to own property and the right to intellectual property; freedom of thought, conscience and belief; and the right to democracy.

This list is remarkable enough, but there are also other articles that define economic and social rights: the right to work; the right to 'just and favourable remuneration' and to holidays with pay; the right to social security; and the right to education, which should be free and compulsory 'at least in the elementary and fundamental stages'. Finally, there is an assertion that 'everyone has the right freely to participate in the cultural life of the community, to enjoy the arts and to share in scientific advancement and its benefits'.[15] All in all, this is by any standards a remarkable, inspiring – and demanding – manifesto. Hardly a single UN member, and certainly not its leading proponent in 1948, has complied with all its requirements.

At the time there were fifty-eight members of the UN. Of these, forty-eight voted in favour, none against, and there were ten that abstained or didn't vote. Perhaps predictably, all the eight Soviet bloc members abstained (though it is noteworthy that they did not vote against it, and instead merely ignored its key provisions); significantly, Saudi Arabia abstained on the grounds that its stipulations about the freedom of religious belief and about marriage were not compatible with sharia law. The Declaration has never been amended, but there are certainly Islamic scholars and commentators who take the view that it would never have been adopted in later times less dominated by America.[16] Half a century after its adoption, at the turn of the millennium, the Organisation of Islamic Cooperation adopted an alternative declaration, which had been produced at a conference of member states in Cairo. It stipulates a freedom and right to a dignified life 'without any discrimination on the grounds of race, colour, language, sex, religious belief, political affiliation, social status or other considerations'. But it also states that 'all the rights and freedoms stipulated in this Declaration are subject to the Islamic Shari'ah'.[17]

Meanwhile, a conference of Asian states preparing for the World Conference on Human Rights in 1993 issued the Bangkok Declaration, which – among carefully crafted resolutions, using the sort of baroque language UN diplomacy has grown used to – included the following revealing assertion that:

> While human rights are universal in nature, they must be considered in the context of a dynamic and evolving process of international norm-setting, bearing in mind the significance of national and regional particularities and various historical, cultural and religious backgrounds.[18]

This is significant. It would be inaccurate and too cynical to conclude that realism had triumphed over idealism, even if it is obvious that many states and many leaders have barely paid even lip service to the principles or the specifics of the Universal Declaration. This is not the realist voice of Kautilya or of Machiavelli asserting the right of each state to define its own interests and to act accordingly. Unlike the Cairo Declaration, which is essentially a reassertion (albeit as a rearguard action) of the Westphalian principle of *cujus regio, ejus religio*, this is something more profound: it accepts that there are universals, but asserts that *we do not yet know what they are in their final form* and that *the journey of discovery has to explore people's cultural heritages*.

This goes much deeper than Article 27 of the Universal Declaration itself, with its call for people to be able freely to participate in the cultural life of their community. For it is clear that there is one unresolved issue in particular that has yet to be fully explored. It is striking that the Universal Declaration has just one clause relating to individual duties to society: Article 29 asserts that 'everyone has duties to the community in which alone the free and full development of his personality is possible'. This certainly mirrors the Confucian (as well as an Aristotelian and a Catholic) perspective. But it is hard to deny that if the Universal Declaration were being crafted in the early twenty-first century, there would have been a strong and indeed very widespread demand that it should include certain more specific duties of the individual – particularly towards those with whom they have a relationship of responsibility, but surely also towards the planet and to future generations.

One increasingly clear voice in this debate is that of Confucianism, with its strong sense that there are social obligations arising from the natural order of things and not simply from the liberal principle of acting in a way that does no harm to others.[19] The Singaporeans in particular have been vocal about the need for balance between rights and obligations: they have become the voice of a Chinese view of the world that is, in essence, Confucian. Thus, for example, Lee Kwan Yew argued that 'the values that East Asian culture upholds, such as the primacy of group interests over individual interests, support the total group effort necessary to develop rapidly.'[20] There is no doubt that this perspective has a resonance not merely among the leadership of China itself, but perhaps even among many in Europe and America too, as they confront the anomic behaviour of their prosperous modern societies.

All this means that it would be wrong to see the challenge to Eurasia's Westphalian order simply in terms of maintaining a balance of power. Yes, the biggest geopolitical question facing the world over the next century will be posed by the relationship between China and America in Eurasia. And yes, the handling of the relationship between China and India will be the second most important geopolitical challenge. But the deeper threats are posed by the problem of the commons. And the deepest challenge of all is posed by this question of universals and values. This is not just the age-old clash between idealism and realism; and it cannot be settled just by wise statecraft. For it is the tension between two perspectives on what is good for human beings. The question is how that tension is to be resolved. We could take the view that these two perspectives are irreconcilable, in which case, we face a bleak prospect: either one of the two prevails, almost certainly at considerable human cost, or we live with the stasis and fragility of the Westphalian principle for the rest of history. It would mean the end of a human journey of exploration, yet without really having arrived. It might even mean that Thucydides – who believed that when a rising power challenges an existing power, sooner or later war is inevitable – is shown to be right for our times as well as for his.[21]

If, however, we are to refuse the conclusion that these two perspectives are irreconcilable; if we refuse to accept that the deep American commitment to the individual and the Confucian sense of order in human relationships are incompatible; and if we refuse to accept that because they are both universal claims they cannot both be right, then we have

176

to explore how the journey of human self-discovery can continue in the spirit of that subtly worded Bangkok Declaration: we have to continue a 'dynamic and evolving process' that takes into account the various 'historical, cultural and religious backgrounds'; and we have to hope that we have not yet reached either a permanent Westphalian stasis or the end of history.

And the next stage on that journey of the human spirit is to search out the *commonalities* of human experience across all those major cultures of Eurasia. That is the task we begin in the next chapter.

7

Not lost in translation

From the ice age onwards, humans have expressed themselves in art. We can surmise that carved figures of animals had some association with spirit worship; some figures with obviously female features were almost certainly fertility symbols; but what the handprints on cave walls meant we will probably never know. Their world was probably filled with spirits – perhaps of their ancestors, perhaps of the animals they fought with and hunted. We have no idea whether the humans of the ice age worshipped in dance and music, let alone what utterances accompanied the rhythms of movement. All that is left is their art, which has a mysterious beauty about it. We recognize the hand of our ancestors, a thousand or more generations back, twenty thousand years or more ago.

As the millennia rolled by, our ancestors began to leave more and more evidence of how they expressed themselves in dance and song, in stories and drama, and in architecture. Gradually, all this became the expression not just of worship but of human life itself. In fact, human expression in art gradually took on a life of its own. It was a very long, slow journey of separation from its probable original function as a medium of worship. Who knows whether the Harappan dancing girl of four thousand years ago had any kind of religious significance? But what is clear is that the last two or three millennia have seen more and more human artistic endeavour devoted to the celebration of life in community, to the glorification of power, to the expression of beauty for itself, and to the external expression of inner experience.

This journey has taken human beings through different landscapes in the great cultures of Eurasia. The sheer variety of it all is itself a testament to the richness of the human genius. The art of Eurasia has an enormously large register. From China's majestic epics and its naturalist poetry, to India's glorious myths and its mystical hymns of worship, to the intricate patterns and geometry of Muslim design, to the intense simplified this-ness of Japanese painting and poetry, to a Russia that is both Rublev and Chekhov, and to a Europe that is both Bach and Beethoven, both Raphael and Cezanne – the result of all this, and so much more, is a treasure trove too big to explore, even in a whole lifetime. From the expansive to the intricate, from the heroic to the intimate, from the patterned to the explosive, humans have found ways of expressing their deepest selves in every medium available to the senses.

The differences in artistic expression among the cultures of Eurasia are obvious, and these differences are clearly related to the different world views their histories have given them. At least as interesting, however, are the cross-cultural echoes and resonances, for these are the direct signs of a common humanity. The great German literary colossus of the period around the turn of the nineteenth century, Goethe, saw the emergence of what he called *Weltliteratur* (world literature) as being the future of human expression. He read the Chinese novels that were becoming available in translation and, famously, he discovered the glories of the poetry of Hafez, again in a new translation. His last great work, published when he was seventy, was a cycle of poems he called the *West-Eastern Diwan* (a diwan is a collection of poetry), in which he responded to the stimulus of the Muslim Persian world that his reading had opened up for him. The excitement of the old man is itself captivating: it reminds us that much we now take for granted was then new and revelatory. As he predicted to his young admirer Johann Peter Eckermann: 'I am more and more convinced that poetry is the universal possession of humankind, revealing itself everywhere and at all times to people in their hundreds.'[1] And he would of course have expected the emergence, not only of a *Weltliteratur* but also of a *Weltkunst* (world art) and a *Weltmusik* (world music). Indeed, the next century saw Monet discover Japanese woodblock prints and Puccini incorporate the pentatonic tones of East Asian music into two of his greatest operas.

Was Goethe right to expect the emergence of a world literature (and by implication a world art and a world music)? It is a question that has been a starting point for considerable philosophical and scholarly reflection in the increasingly globalized world of the centuries after his death. Marx, for instance, had a point of view on this that derived from his broader metaphysical position. For him, the rise of the bourgeoisie as a new global class meant the rise of a world culture determined by bourgeois tastes. Particularly from the twentieth century onwards, world literature has become the focus of increasingly specialist academic analysis. Thus, for example, the sheer volume of world literature – given the geometric growth in population and the progress made in education – has now reached the point where no one person has any chance of reading more than a small proportion of the human creative output of even just one of the world's major cultures. So scholars have sought to draw distinctions, particularly between three kinds of work that might be classed as world literature: world masterpieces that are widely acknowledged as such beyond their home cultures; other works that are, so to speak, important windows into other cultures; and what is sometimes rather dismissively called 'shopping mall culture'.[2]

But this does not, of course, mean that the world's masterpieces are somehow culture-free, unlike other literature, or that they can be up-rooted from their historical contexts. What Goethe meant was that *all* great literature is a window into another culture, *and* that this window enables us to look both ways: the more we study the masterpieces of other cultures in their context, the more we learn about our own. Those who know nothing of foreign languages, he said, know nothing of their own.[3] For Goethe, to know a language was to engage with its culture. If you know nothing of other cultures, then you do not know your own. But the force of this point is stronger than possibly even Goethe would have appreciated. For him, as for many of his contemporary Europeans, there remained, in effect, one real standard of cultural validity: the Classical Greek and Latin tradition. But the disorientating truth that follows from his own exploration – and celebration – of the glories of other cultures is that there is no fixed Archimedean point from which the poet can measure or move the world. Context matters for all human creativity: everything we create is a creature of the particular culture we belong to. There is no universal culture.

And cultural context matters – more for literature than it does for the visual arts; and more for the visual arts than for music. Literature is enclosed in a linguistic shell, whereas music is not. Culture has an enor-mous influence on the development of music, of course; so the listener who studies its cultural background will be deeply rewarded. But music can move without words, and even when it is song, the sound of the words can move even those who don't understand them. Visual art sits between music and literature: it translates more easily than literature and less easily than music. The content of visual art can speak without words, yet the content and style clearly have their fullest meaning in the idiom of a particular culture; so the viewer who studies that culture will uncover depths of meaning in the images it displays. (Both Chan Buddhist Chinese painting and European medieval paintings of biblical and Christian motifs are obvious examples of this point.) And what is true of visual art is true above all of literature: to communicate, it has to cross the linguistic barrier. But translation across languages always comes at the cost of transformation.

Translation across culture

That linguistic barrier can have one or both of two dimensions: it can be a barrier between different cultures; and it can be a barrier across time. Goethe was focused on the former. His was the enthusiasm of a fresh, new encounter with the glories of Iranian Muslim poetry in translation. But translation across time is as subtle a challenge as translation across cultures. The fact that today's Japanese would find it difficult to read the Japanese of *The Tale of Genji*, that fewer and fewer modern Chinese can read the language of the great classics, that very few Indians can read the Sanskrit of their sacred texts, or that most Europeans would struggle to read the vernacular literature of their medieval literary heritage – all of this is a reminder that translation across time within a cultural tradition can be as much a challenge as crossing the linguistic borders of today.

Furthermore, translation in either of these two dimensions is about so much more than just linguistics. It is not just a question of finding the equivalent word or phrase; it is a matter of recognizing what a text means or meant in its own cultural context *and what it means in the new context*. Goethe was therefore right: great literature enables us to see both ways, and good translation across the barriers of time and culture can add immensely to the riches of the original. Something is always lost in translation: puns and allusions, poetic rhymes and rhythms that can only be retained (or at least imitated) by moulding the meaning of the words. Yet some things are not lost, and whole new layers of meaning can be gained. But we need to recognize what is new about such layers of meaning and why they are different. Thus, when we look at the great culturally formative texts of the pre-modern era (of which there are arguably no more than a dozen or so), we find that the more we can glimpse how they spoke in their original context, the more we recognize how they have been interpreted, both over time and as they have been appropriated across cultures. And the more clearly we recognize this, the more powerful they become for us.

Thus, for example, the *Iliad* and the *Odyssey* arose in a world where the gods were on stage and where they determined events; for the human actors in the drama, destiny and fate were the dominant themes. Europeans of the Enlightenment came to resonate less with these themes and more with the sense that the tragedies involved result from the weaknesses of the great heroes, which in the end bring them down. Achilles' famous heel (which, in fact, is not in Homer but a later addition to the tradition) is not a sign of the working of fate so much as a metaphor for pride and recklessness. This search for the character flaw or the tragic error of judgement is not new. It is there in Aristotle's philosophy of tragedy and has been deeply influential in European literature ever since it entered the Renaissance thought world (from Spain, like so much else that medieval Europe owes to Islamic scholarship). So the tragic human hero with the flawed character takes centre stage in Shakespeare, Racine and Schiller. Nor does the journey of interpretation stop there; by the twentieth century, the ancient Greek heroic prototype becomes inverted as the antihero who is the plaything of forces, or of a system, that cannot be controlled. So fate and destiny are in a sense back, as tormentors of ordinary people (whom Aristotle would not have seen as dignified subjects for tragedy at all) – as we can see, perhaps above all, in James Joyce's *Ulysses*.

All those developments took place within what is arguably a continuous cultural inheritance from classical Greece to the modern European consciousness. When the transition is across cultures as well as across the ages, the transformation wrought by translation is all the greater. A spectacular example of this process is the journey of *One Thousand and*

One Nights from its origins as an Arabic collection of stories (some of which had Persian and Indian roots), loosely connected by the framework story of Scheherazade, into a global treasure store of memorable characters – thanks, first, to its translation by the French orientalist Antoine Galland at the turn of the eighteenth century and, second, to Disney in the twentieth century. In this case, the evolution has been so creative that some of the best-known figures – Aladdin and Sinbad the Sailor, for instance – were not in the original Arabic collection at all. The colourful and rumbustious bawdiness of some of the stories caused problems for nineteenth-century European translators; and to this day, the 'Nights' has less standing in conservative parts of the Muslim world than it came to have in the West. Translation was its passport to global heritage status.

The translation of *The Tale of Genji* has a different and altogether subtler story to it. This thousand-year-old novel was written by a court lady of the Heian period in early medieval Japan. We know little about Lady Murasaki Shikibu other than that she was a lady-in-waiting at the imperial court in Kyoto. The story of Genji, the son of an emperor and a concubine, and of his loves has no overarching narrative or theme. But the psychological observation of the central characters as they grow old is nothing short of extraordinary. There is no climax, and the story stops without an ending (giving rise to unresolvable scholarly debate about the author's intentions). The 'Tale' quite rapidly became foundational for Japanese literature and also for Japanese visual arts. Reflecting the courtly habits of its time, the story is laced with poetry, some of which included quotations from existing poems that would have been well known to her readers. To a modern European reader, much of this seems like unnecessary verbal flourishes, and the classic 1920s English translation by Arthur Waley simply leaves most of it out. But for the Japanese, the poems have always been central and, indeed, they often only read excerpts from the complex narrative to set the context for particularly well-loved poems. Already in the twelfth century, the poet Fujiwara no Shunzei argued that the Tale was essential reading for any would-be poet,[4] and at about the same time, a pictorial scroll was produced to illustrate the events and themes of the Tale; this scroll was to be highly influential in Japanese painting (much of the scroll has been lost, but the surviving parts are now in various Japanese museums). Incidents from the Tale feature in Japanese paintings and in woodblock prints regularly in subsequent centuries – in a way that faintly echoes the prevalence of biblical imagery in European art at the same time.

Yet what brought the Tale recognition outside Japan as one of the greatest literary masterpieces of any culture is its humane, gentle and perceptive observation of relationships. The world of the Heian court was small and confined; and yet we resonate with the emotions and reactions, described so shrewdly by Murasaki. They glow with life because, for all the immense gulf between their world and ours, they are also universally human. So, just to take one example from the hundreds with which the Tale is dotted, Genji takes the ten-year-old Murasaki (who is possibly an autobiographical figure) into his household. Rumours abound of a new concubine and his wife is not amused. Genji reflects on his rather distant relationship with his wife in terms that sound as true today in modern Europe as they did in medieval Japan:

> If she had complained to him openly, he might have told her everything, and no doubt eased her jealousy. It was her arbitrary judgments that sent him wandering. She had no specific faults, no vices or blemishes which he could point to. She had been the first lady in his life, and in an abstract way he admired and treasured her. Her feelings would change, he felt sure, once she was more familiar with his own. She was a perceptive woman, and the change was certain to come. She still occupied first place among his ladies.[5]

Discovering what we have in common

In a different context, those words could have been written by Jane Austen. And this reminds us that down the ages and across cultures, we see again and again how the universally human finds expression in literature all across the cultures of Eurasia. For all the differences in life experience, human beings have always – all through recorded history, it seems – known the excitement of joy; the vulnerability of love; the grief of loss; the awareness of mortality; the sense of fate and tragedy, sometimes infused with moments of melancholy acceptance; and perhaps also the sense of being on a lifetime's journey to an uncertain end. There are other human commonalities too, of course: pleasure, pain, anger, hatred, fear and mistrust. But it is those deeper moments of awareness – of reflective self-awareness – that have given rise to the most poignant consciousness of what we share, and to much of the greatest and most enduring human creativity.

Thus, for example, Hafez writes of joy with a subtlety that comes, perhaps, from recognizing its fragility:

> The orchard charms our hearts, and chatter when
> our dearest friends appear – is sweet;
> God bless the time of roses! To drink our wine
> among the roses here – is sweet!
> Our souls' scent sweetens with each breeze; ah yes,
> the sighs that lovers hear – are sweet;
> Sing, nightingale! Rosebuds, unopened yet
> will leave you, and your fear – is sweet;
> Dear singer of the night, for those in love
> your sad lament is clear – and sweet.
> The world's bazaar contains no joy, except
> the libertines; good cheer – is sweet!
> I heard the lilies say 'The world is old;
> to take things lightly here – is sweet' . . .[6]

And joy bubbles up in so many other cultural contexts too – each distinctive and yet so basically similar. The world of the English Catholic priest and poet Gerard Manley Hopkins is a long way from Hafez, but he is just as spellbound by the beauty of all around him and his love of life is just as transparent:

> Glory be to God for dappled things –
> For skies of couple-colour as a brinded cow;
> For rose-moles all in stipple upon trout that swim;
> Fresh-firecoal chestnut-falls; finches' wings;
> Landscape plotted and pieced – fold, fallow and plough;
> And all trades, their gear and tackle and trim.

All things counter, original, spare, strange;
Whatever is fickle, freckled (who knows how?)
With swift, slow; sweet, sour; adazzle, dim;
He fathers forth whose beauty is past change:
Praise Him.[7]

Ode to Joy ('Freude, schöner Götterfunken, Tochter aus Elysium'), by the great German poet and playwright Friedrich Schiller, is usually heard in combination with the exhilarating brilliance of Beethoven, which has given it a global resonance: it never loses its power to excite. Nor – in a modern and very different Indian context – does the irrepressible vibrancy of Bollywood.

Then there are the endless joys and travails, the highs and the lows, unions and separations, hopes and fears – of love. The compulsion and vulnerability of love have been the inspiration again and again for some of the greatest masterpieces in every human culture: from the Indian playwright Kalidasa, to *Dream of the Red Chamber* from China, to Pushkin's novel in poetry *Eugene Onegin*, to Wagner's *Tristan und Isolde*, to Monzaemon Chikamatsu's *Love Suicides of Amijima*, to the delightful love ghazals of the female poet Jahan Malek Khatun who lived in the royal court of Shiraz in the fourteenth century. Two writers from very different cultures – India and Japan – on the subtle irresistibility of love beautifully demonstrate the universality of this theme. Kalidasa's play *The Recognition of Shakuntala* is India's best-known dramatic master-piece (written probably sometime in the third or fourth century CE); here is the voice of the king enthralled by the loveliness of the girl:

> Seeing rare beauty
> hearing lovely sounds,
> even a happy man
> becomes strangely uneasy . . .
> perhaps he remembers,
> without knowing why,
> loves of another life
> buried deep in his being.[8]

Kalidasa also produced one of India's greatest love songs: 'The Cloud Messenger'. This short but exquisite poem imagines a *yaksa* – a sort of faery – who has been banished to a remote hillside and pines for his lovely wife. Seeing a cloud heading north for his true home, he charges it with carrying his message to her, in a rich evocation of the beauty of the natural world over which the cloud will travel, almost as a sort of mirror in which she can see herself:

> I see your body in the sinuous creeper, your gaze
>   in the startled eyes of the deer,
> your cheek in the moon, your hair in the plumage
>   of the peacocks,
> and in the tiny ripples of the river I see your side-
>   long glances,
> but alas, my dearest, nowhere do I see your whole
>   likeness![9]

And then from the Japanese female poet, Lady Otomo no Sakanoue, writing in the eighth century in a very different mood, we have this short and psychologically acute song of the waiting lover who knows she risks disappointment – and yet she waits:

> Even if you say, 'I come',
> at times you will not come.
> Now you say, 'I will not come.'
> Why should I look for your coming –
> when you say you will not come![10]

Like love – and indeed related to it – is the pervasive experience of the grief of loss, perhaps especially when it is loss out of time, out of the natural rhythm of things, such as when a parent is grieving for the loss of a child. From Cicero's mourning for the loss of his beloved daughter Tullia, to a haunting Indian bas-relief of a grieving woman from the second century (now in the National Museum in New Delhi), to Chekhov's grief at the death of his three-month-old daughter, the story is repeated down the ages. From our vantage point in the developed world of the

twenty-first century, we risk making the assumption that people in earlier times accepted all this with resignation because it was so common.
They didn't. Here is the Japanese *haiku* composer Issa Kobayashi from
the early nineteenth century, subtly rejecting condolences on the death of
a baby daughter, which had been expressed as a Buddhist platitude about
the transience and unreality of all things:

> The world of dew
> Is the world of dew
> And yet, and yet.[11]

And from a thousand years earlier, here is the Tang Dynasty poet Bai
Juyi, who lived at the turn of the ninth century CE and was one of the
most popular and prolific writers anywhere from so long ago, on
the death of his only daughter:

> Having a daughter is truly a burden,
> But without a son, how can one help becoming attached
>   to her?
> It was scarcely ten days that she was ill,
> And we had already nourished her for three years . . .
> Her old clothes still hang from the rack,
> What's left of her medicine yet at the head of her bed.
> I went with the coffin far into the village lanes,
> Saw the mound of her little grave in the fields.
> Don't say she's only a mile or so away –
> She and I are separated by eternity![12]

Somehow, the context in which girls were less important than boys
simply heightens the poignancy of a poem that could have otherwise
been written yesterday. Its intimacy is telling: we even know the little
girl's name – Jinluan, meaning 'golden bell'. The death of a small child
may indeed have been all too commonplace; but the human in all of us
can never pass by unmoved.

More generally, the sense of mortality knocking on the door has been
a cause sometimes for defiance and sometimes for sombre reflection, in

every age and virtually everywhere. The Roman poet Horace spoke for the many who have sought immortality in the legacy of their own work, in one of his most famous *Odes*:

> I have raised a monument more lasting than
>   bronze
> and higher than the regal pyramids,
> which neither the weathering rains nor the wild
>   north wind
> nor the countless years that pass and the time that
>   flies can destroy . . .[13]

In the next line comes the telltale phrase: *non omnis moriar* or 'I shall not wholly die'. For his poetry will live on, and thus a great part of him will escape the grave. This was the voice of someone who knew that he was exceptional and had been deft in making his way in the corridors of Roman power and influence, but who could also never quite forget his humble origins. No one was ever going to forget *him*. But such a legacy is given to very few; it can also be fragile (the sketch of Horace drawn by the historian Suetonius is less than wholly flattering); and to what extent will recognition for his poems survive the now very sparse knowledge of Latin?

From a much older work, which we have already looked at, comes a far subtler, surely more honest – and surely also more universally human – confrontation with the fact of death. The intense poetry of *The Epic of Gilgamesh* reminds us both that life is fleeting, and that death is immanent even in the midst of it:

> It is only the nymph of the dragonfly who sheds her larva and sees the sun in his glory. From the days of old there is no permanence. The sleeping and the dead, how alike they are . . .[14]

From the Japanese Buddhist monk Yoshida Kenko, writing in the early fourteenth century in his *Tsurezuregusa* (*Essays in Idleness*), comes a strikingly matter-of-fact picture of death and of the psychology of bereavement that has the ring of truth for anyone who has ever stood in a graveyard and wondered about tombstones so weathered the names on them can no longer be read:

There is no such mournful time as follows on a death . . . A crowd of people go up to some mountain village . . . and there they busily perform the offices for the dead . . . The last day is pitiless indeed; for in silence they gather together their possessions, each for himself, and go their several ways. Only when they have returned to their own homes will they begin to feel exceedingly sad.

Months and years pass by, and still they do not forget, though, as the saying goes, the departed grows more distant every day. However that may be, they seem not to feel so deeply as at the time of death, for now they chatter and laugh together. The body is laid to rest on some lonely mountainside, where the mourners come on rare appointed days; soon the tablet is overgrown with moss, covered with fallen leaves, and looks in time as if none came to visit there save storms and the nocturnal moon.

There may be some who will recall the dead and think of him with grief. But soon they themselves must pass away. Then how can later generations grieve, who know him only by repute? After a time they no longer go to his tomb, and people do not even know his name or who he was. True, some feeling folk may gaze with pity on what is now but the growth of grasses in succeeding springs. At last there comes a day when even the pine trees that groaned in the storms, not lasting out their thousand years of life, are split for fuel; and the ancient grave, dug up and turned into rice field, leaves not a trace behind.[15]

In classical Indian literature, by contrast, the theme of mortality is not prominent. This is the reflection of a culture steeped in the cycle of reincarnation and in which death for the individual self pales into insignificance beside its identification with the joyful essence of Brahman. So, as is often noted,[16] this is not a culture in which the sense of tragedy flourishes; the happenstances and injustices of life are all under the influence of the pervasive workings of *karma* and become less significant in the context of the aeons of time. For Indian classical culture, therefore,

the purpose of drama is to entertain, first and foremost; it is not a vehicle for moral education. Thus, for example, Kalidasa's *The Recognition
of Shakuntala* has its twists and turns, from love at first sight between
the king and the young girl raised in a secluded hermitage, through the
king's forgetfulness and his rejection of her under a curse he is unaware
of, to reconnection through lucky chance and thence to renewed union.
This is the Indian equivalent of Shakespeare's Forest of Arden.[17] Seven
acts of beautiful and often poignant poetry all end happily ever after.
Even the one character who is nearest to a conventional villain turns out
to be nothing more sinister than an angry man who invokes the curse
but nevertheless offers a way out. It is certainly not tragedy, either in the
classical Greek sense in which moral agents face insoluble moral dilemmas and great people are brought down by their flaws, or in the more
general sense of reflecting the pity of things.

But Indian culture has produced tragic art nevertheless. At the in-
stigation of Rabindranath Tagore, his friend Prabhat Mukhopadhyay
wrote a short story called 'Devi' (Goddess) that was then filmed by one
of the twentieth century's greatest directors, Satyajit Ray. The story is of a
young and dutiful wife of a nineteenth-century Bengali landowner, who
looks after her father-in-law while her husband is away on business. The
old man has a dream that she is the avatar of the goddess Kali; soon
the entire village is worshipping her – the more so when she seems to
heal the grandson of an old beggar. But then tragedy strikes after she fails
to heal her brother-in-law's small son, whom she adores. She is blamed
for his death and loses her mind, finally fleeing towards the river, pre-
sumably to drown herself. The specifics of this powerful and moving
film are very Indian; but its theme is at the same time universal in its
human, tragic (and anti-heroic) story of this gentle and guileless woman
who comes to believe – or at least partly believe – the credulity of others.

It is often noted that Chinese drama doesn't know tragedy either – if
for rather different reasons.[18] China has a lively theatrical and operatic
tradition; but the Confucian world view sets humans in the context of a
cosmic order that is fundamentally good and appropriate. The heroes of
the great Yuan and Ming Dynasty plays are not typically tormented by
unresolvable moral or existential dilemmas. One of the most striking,
Snow in Midsummer by the thirteenth-century dramatist Guan Hang-

qing, is almost an exception that proves the rule. A young widow re-fuses the attentions of a boorish man, who then accuses her of killing his father. She stands trial rather than marry him; but when the judge calls for her mother-in-law to be tortured, she confesses to the crime she did not commit. She then inveighs against heaven in terms that would have suited the Greeks perfectly, before calling down disaster on the vil-lage as evidence of her innocence and as punishment for the injustice of her death. Finally, her father – who abandoned her as a child – re-appears to wreak punishment on those who wronged her and brought about her death. This is not the same as conjuring up a happy ending as in *Shakuntala*, or as in Nahum Tate's notorious seventeenth-century reconstruction of *King Lear*. But it does allow a moral closure of a kind that takes some of the sting from the tragedy. Somehow, the Confucian order of things resists loose ends.

Yet classical Chinese literature does also know of real, unresolved loss and failure. Perhaps the best example is its most famous novel, which we have already discussed, *Dream of the Red Chamber* – a novel that is, however, intrinsically Buddhist rather than Confucian in outlook. The enduring Confucian instinct, which has been the dominant gene of Chinese culture, is as antithetical to tragedy as are Hindu metaphysics – and this despite the extraordinary extent of suffering that the various convulsions of Chinese history have inflicted on the Chinese people and their consciousness. (There is a striking contrast between this instinct and the very different response of Russian culture to a similarly sus-tained collective memory of suffering.)

But it is also clear that the metaphysics of European Christianity and Sunni Islam are similarly antithetical to tragedy, just as are those of Confucian China and of Hindu India. The reasons differ radically in all four cases, but all have biases that sit uneasily with the drama of failure and the morally unresolved: Confucianism invokes the benign nat-ural order under Heaven; Hinduism sees the joyful essence of Brahman in every individual self; Christianity centres on a salvation story whose climax is not tragedy but redemption; and Islam looks to a Day of Reckoning when justice will be done to all.

Islam – unlike China, Japan and Europe – had a relatively undeveloped and unformalized performative tradition until modern times (when its public culture came under the influence, for better or worse, of European traditions). Its overwhelmingly dominant vehicle for human expression in literature has been poetry. It is often noted that the Muslim intellectuals of the Abbasid heyday, who were busy translating much of the corpus of Greek learning into Arabic, did not show any interest in Greek theatre and tragedy, but only in Greek philosophy, science and medicine. What is less often noted is one of the reasons for this. By that time, Greek drama was centuries past its zenith and sat uneasily with the theology of the Byzantine world, so that part of the reason for the lack of Muslim interest in it was the lack of Christian interest at that time. But Arabic poetry (going back indeed all the way to pre-Islamic times) shows a keen sense of the impact of destiny in human affairs and an introspetive awareness of the complexity of the human condition. And the Shiite tradition of re-enacting the killing of Husayn ibn Ali at Karbala is a close emotional parallel to the sense of shame and guilt conjured up by Christian passion plays and oratorios.[19]

However, in both cases, these re-enactments sit in the context of a theology and eschatology in which the good triumphs over what is evil, at least in the end. Perhaps only the very different Japanese cultural psyche, with its deeper sediment of Buddhist life-denial and self-denial, was more naturally attuned to a melancholy recognition of the pervasiveness of suffering and death. *Mono no aware* is the phrase the Japanese themselves use to describe this mood – a sense of the pity of things. (And that leaves us with a question: why *did* European Christendom in the end develop such a powerful tradition of tragedy, despite its ruling Christian cultural norms – moulded so durably by Augustine[20] – such that to this day, the works of Shakespeare, Racine and Schiller, as well as Aeschylus, Sophocles and Euripides, continue to fill European theatres? The answer lies in the gradual disintegration of the Christian metaphysical synthesis on the journey from the Renaissance and the Reformation through to the Enlightenment and beyond – a journey we will explore in Chapter 8.)

Yet in all of these cultures, not just in Japan, we see evidence sooner or later of that sense of the pity of things that we have already noted. One way or another, elements of deep sadness as an unavoidable element in the human condition find expression in the plays, poetry and

novels of all the major Eurasian cultures. In what is probably the most
famous verse in the whole of the *Aeneid*, when Aeneas sees murals in a
Carthaginian temple depicting the battles of the Trojan War from which
he has escaped and in which he sees portrayals of his lost friends, he is
moved by an overwhelming sense that his new hosts are compassionate
people who also know what loss and sorrow are. He cries out: *sunt lach-
rymae rerum et mentem mortalia tangunt* ('there are the tears of things,
and what is mortal touches the heart'). It is the Latin equivalent of *mono
no aware.* Here indeed is a universal: in the tale spun by Virgil, Aeneas'
descendants become the mortal enemies of Carthage; this episode serves
as a poignant reminder to the Romans that their enemies were human.
All cultures, however different from one another, have been touched by
tragedy and know about the tears of things.

And all cultures know not only about tragedy and the tears of things
but also of wrong – and guilt. It is sometimes argued that East Asian cultures, in contrast to those with a Christian heritage (the Europeans and
the Russians), know more of shame than of guilt. Ruth Benedict asserts
this in particular about Japan.[21] Conversely, European culture, both in
its Catholic and in its Protestant variants, can express itself in morbidly
guilt-laden form (satirized mischievously and brilliantly by James Joyce
in *A Portrait of the Artist as a Young Man*[22]). But as Benedict acknowledged, the distinction is not binary. In fact, differing ways of talking
about wrongs done should not delude us into assuming that wrong is not
recognized for what it is – as many individual Japanese reactions to the
misdeeds of their grandparents make clear.[23] And Soseki's great novel
Kokoro comes to its sad conclusion with the following reflection by a
man about to commit suicide:

> From around this time, a horrible darkness would occasionally
> overwhelm me . . . What this feeling produced was, quite simply,
> a keen awareness of the nature of human sin. That is what sent me
> back each month to K's grave. It is also what lay behind the nurs-
> ing of my dying mother-in-law, and what bade me treat my wife so
> tenderly. There were even times when I longed for some stranger
> to come along and flog me as I deserved. At some stage this trans-
> formed into a conviction that it should be I who hurt myself. And

then the thought struck me that I should not just hurt myself but kill myself. At all events, I resolved that I must live my life as if I were already dead.[24]

The burden of guilt, as this brilliant novel shows, is not just a Christian invention.

The universal human journey

We learn all this through journeying, which is yet another universal motif in the literature of Eurasian cultures. The journey of discovery and of self-discovery seems always to have been invested with deep human significance. The earliest known such journey is undertaken by Gilgamesh, as we have already seen in Chapter 3. Journeying into the unknown is also the background to the formative stories of the Jewish Bible ('my father was a wandering Aramean'[25]). The *Odyssey* has imprinted itself so deeply on European culture that the word itself has become a common noun for the complex and risky journey of personal discovery. The Qur'an extends the wanderings of Abraham to a sojourn at Mecca, and the journey of the Hajj is a central goal of the fulfilled Muslim life. For the Chinese, *The Journey to the West*, the great classical novel that tells the story of the travels to India of the Buddhist monk Xuanzang (known in the novel as Tan Sanzang), is as full of drama and fantasy as is the *Odyssey* – and has as many layers of meaning. While for Indians, the *Ramayana* is at least in part yet another such journey, as Rama goes on his expedition to rescue Sita from the evil Ravana with the support of the supernatural monkey figure Hanuman (an authoritative, superhuman figure, unlike the equally fantastical monkey figure Sun Wukong who accompanies Tan Sanzang in *Journey to the West*).

Human beings from all Eurasian cultures have written about many journeys, some of them apparently matter-of-fact travel records of extraordinary adventures into the unknown (such as those of Xuanzang, Ibn Battuta and Marco Polo). But the much more overwhelming power of the great epics of Greece, China and India does not depend on their having any literal or historical core. Nor does it typically depend on there being much in the way of character development: it would be hard, for example, to detect any significant learning – either about himself or about Sita – on the part of Rama. Nor is there much philosophizing in the *Odyssey*. These are not in any sense the kind of story that nineteenth-century Europe came to call a *Bildungsroman* (novels about the formation into mature adulthood of the young person). Rather, their power depends on fast-moving and vivid storytelling – and on the interpretation (and endless reinterpretations) given to them by generation after generation over the centuries. Typically, the narrative itself offers little in the way of deeper meaning or reflection; that work is left to the listener or reader. They are in that sense exterior – rather than interior – journeys (even if much or all of their content is imaginary and fantastical).

But from the first, such journeys have often also had an interior, as well as an exterior, dimension, as illustrated clearly in *The Epic of Gilgamesh*, in which the adventures of Gilgamesh have an explicitly interior dynamic of self-discovery. In fact, long before the modern era, the interior journey of the traveller becomes the real point. This is particularly obvious in the mystical and devotional works of Islam and Christianity. In the substantial literature from the Muslim Sufi tradition, for example, the journey is often seen as significant, partly because of the Sufi's own itinerant lifestyle and partly for its inner spiritual meaning. According to a saying attributed to an early Sufi mystic of the ninth century:

> I have made three journeys. From the first journey I brought back knowledge that both the common folk and the elite can understand. From the second journey I brought back knowledge that only the elite can understand. From the third journey I brought back knowledge that neither the elite nor the common folk can understand.

This was in all probability meant both literally (of journeys he made to be with three different teachers) and mystically.[26]

Christian expression too has often seen the spiritual life of the human being as an interior journey. Dante's *Divine Comedy* is a complex allegorical journey through hell, purgatory and heaven that is in a sense the poetic embodiment of Thomas Aquinas' great theory of everything, which we have already looked at in Chapter 3. A very different, but also very remarkable, literary testimony to the intensity of the Christian absorption in the journey is the book that for around three centuries was the most widely read Christian text in the Protestant world after the Bible itself: John Bunyan's *Pilgrim's Progress*. Dante's work is the epitome of the medieval Catholic metaphysical system; Bunyan's is steeped in that very individualistic Protestant yearning for salvation that was so pervasive – and so revolutionary – in the England (and America) of the seventeenth century. Both are interior journeys; both are presented as dreams that bring their creators face to face with a reality beyond their senses.

Even Japan has its famous journey, despite its long seclusion under the Tokugawa regime – in this case a real physical journey on foot, albeit a domestic one through the countryside of the Japan of the seventeenth century. But it was far from being just a physical journey. The poet Basho knew great success in his own lifetime, in a culture that has always valued the skills of poetry and knew a genius when it encountered one. His pre-eminence has never been seriously challenged, and he now enjoys worldwide fame as the greatest haiku composer of them all. But he seems never to have been at ease with social and literary success, and more than once he retreated on journeys by foot through the countryside. One of these resulted in the remarkable *Oku no Hosomichi*, usually translated as *The Narrow Road to the Deep North*. A combination of prose and poetry, this is at once a travel diary and a poetic reflection on places and experience that shows the effect of the Zen meditation he used to seek calm of spirit. In a very different way from the Sufis and the Christian mystics, he too was taking a journey into his own soul – a journey in the way of Japanese Buddhism, with all its concentration on the 'this-ness' of things, with all the intense simplicity that was the secret of his haikai. Yet for all its Japanese distinctiveness, his introductory sentences seem to have a universal human resonance; wandering is in some way in our genes:

The months and days are the travellers of eternity. The years that come and go are also voyagers. Those who float away their lives on ships or who grow old leading horses are forever journeying, and their homes are wherever their travels take them. Many of . . . old died on the road, and I too for years past have been stirred by the sight of a solitary cloud drifting with the wind to ceaseless thoughts of roaming.[27]

Gradually, as the centuries go by, the interiority of the journey becomes more and more significant – to the point where James Joyce can use the metaphor of *Ulysses* for a narrative that never moves from Dublin. Gradually, too, there was in the European context a growing sense that the end of the journey is unclear, or cannot be framed in terms of culturally received teaching about the purpose of life or the meaning of history. This new sense of unresolved openness is a long way from Dante or Bunyan, or from the Muslim Sufis, or from Hindu mystics in search of *moksha*. It is also different from Basho, for whom the journey itself was the purpose and the 'this-ness' was all. Thus, even for a relatively orthodox Anglican Christian such as T. S. Eliot, there is a disturbing feeling that old nostrums have become empty husks and the interior journey really is into the unknown. Eliot wrote *The Waste Land* in the years after the First World War, when he was still in his thirties. The poem's very title seemed to sum up both the blasted landscape of the trenches and the state of mind of a traumatized Europe. Old certainties were gone – irretrievably. But like Joyce's masterpiece, Eliot's poem is rich in literary allusions – to the Greek and Latin classics, to Augustine and to Dante, but also to the Upanishads and to the Fire Sermon of the Buddha. And this was a sign that whatever was new in the human spirit would have to be found in the old, which was both timeless and universal.

Two decades later, in the midst of another terrible war, Eliot wrote the last of his *Four Quartets*, 'Little Gidding'. It was his last significant poem. By this time, he was clear that the journey of self-discovery had to continue, even if we couldn't know the purpose before reaching some kind of destination; even if we might never know it at all. What we imagine to be the purpose changes as we approach it. Eliot ends this poem with a passage that has become famous for a sense of mystical resolution that itself harks back to the 'shewings' of the medieval Christian anchorite Mother Julian of Norwich, who sensed that, in the end, all shall be well. So Eliot reaches a point of resolution and does so within the broad Christian tradition. But the passage begins with lines that have a more universal resonance, as the questioning journey of the poem becomes the interior journey of self-discovery. Somehow, like Proust conjuring up Combray from his cup of tea, Eliot comes back to where he began – and knows it 'for the first time'.[28]

These words could serve as the preface to resolution in any of Eurasia's cultures. History has given those cultures different starting points and their metaphysics have given them different premises about the human condition; but human experience has given them so many commonalities – as we have seen – and therefore so many touch points. Furthermore, urbanization will multiply those touch points, while also changing them. So the question is: what are the implications for the journey forwards in the twenty-first century? That is the question for the remaining chapters of this book.

But first, we need to note the ways in which human beings – sometimes collectively and sometimes individually – have sought to find sense in and to master their life experiences. For the attempt to do this, rather than simply live from one impression and one action to the next, is another commonality we share across cultures. Humans are, as we have earlier discussed, 'language animals', but they could equally well be described as religious animals – or at least as animals that are metaphysically aware.

For much of history, humans in every culture have believed that the world of the senses was only part of their world, which was also inhabited by a vast crowd of gods, spirits and demons of various sorts. Some cultures gravitated towards a monistic theism of some kind, notably in the Middle East, where all the world's great monotheisms emerged during the course of the last three millennia. Monotheists – Jewish, Christian and Muslim – have assumed down the ages that the journey towards spiritual maturity is a journey away from a world full of spirits towards monotheism. But there is nothing inevitable about this: their own cultures have not journeyed away from the world of spirits as far as their intellectual leaderships would like to believe. Furthermore, neither Chinese nor Japanese culture has journeyed towards monotheism (unless Pure Land Buddhism is viewed as, in essence, a theism). And although Hindu worship can be seen as the outward expression of a deeper monism, its most obvious characteristic is the plethora of divinities that are its objects.

European post-Enlightenment thought, however, sits uneasily with any sense that human beings are naturally religious animals, and has sought to be more radical in exorcising gods and spirits out of human experience. Whether the journey has been from the spirits and the gods to one god (the journey to monotheism), or whether it is a journey towards recognition of the One revealed in the Many (the journey of monism), the Enlightenment has wanted to see this as being just one stage on a greater journey towards secularization on the basis of a scientific theory of everything. Indeed, for many Europeans of the nineteenth and twentieth centuries, as we shall see in the next chapter, one of the most exciting facts about modernity is precisely that the gods have finally departed from the stage.

Yet such a view is as much metaphysical – in the sense that it is looking for a theory of everything – as any of the traditional theologies it rejects. Scientific materialism based on nuclear physics and Darwin is metaphysical; so is Marx's economic materialism; and so is the brilliant anti-Christian invective of Nietzsche (whom we shall come back to in the next chapter). In other words, the truth is that while humans may not be religious animals in any narrow meaning, in a broader sense they are precisely that, because neither collectively nor individually can they avoid the metaphysical questions. This seems to be part of the very nature of humans. It does not of course mean that they always adopt a clear metaphysical view, let alone a specific theology. But it does mean, to put it at its most basic, that they cannot avoid searching – either explicitly or implicitly, either by cultural inheritance or by individual choice, either clearly and articulately or by habit and intuition – for some sort of theory of everything that sets a framework for their decisions and actions. This is just as much a universal as are the experiences of joy, love, loss and journeying we have looked at in the expression of all the cultures of Eurasia. Thus, to take just one instance recorded in twenty-first century China:

> Mr Liu laughed but was not in a jesting mood. The alcohol had done nothing but delayed the questions. 'Tell me, foreigner, why are we here? . . . isn't it so we can eat and drink and have fun?' . . .
> He sank lower into his chair and kept asking me why, and I knew he meant it all: the big questions and the small, the death of his father, and the injustice of having had to stay behind to tend the family farm while his siblings had moved to cities to earn money . . .[29]

The specific context of this is a rapidly modernizing China; but its sentiment could almost certainly have been replicated in any society anywhere. The question is essentially universal.

Controlling the unknown and uncontrollable

Humanity has shown a huge range of different responses to the experience of living, much of it about controlling the unknown and uncontrollable; and the sheer variety has provided rich material for anthropologists. But some instincts manifest themselves again and again across cultures and down the ages.

The first is the sense that the world is enchanted, that it is the home of spirits – a sense that was never wholly eliminated even by the strongly monotheistic religions that spread out from the Middle East in the last two millennia. Even today, in Europe, in the Orthodox world of Russia, and in the Muslim world, there is ample evidence of continued enchantment in one form or another – of ordinary people looking for healing, for exorcism, for material help or other forms of relief from saints and shamans, from fortune-tellers and from various kinds of talisman.

In the case of India, the only significant difference is that the spirits of enchantment readily become gods. Hinduism may be fundamentally monistic but it is not a strict personal monotheism and has no tendency at all to disenchant the world. Buddhism in its earlier phases might have worked to at least dampen the enchantment, rather as Christianity and Islam have done. But it began to expand, even as it was gradually fading from Indian life during the first millennium of the Common Era, into the so-called 'Great Vehicle' of Mahayana Buddhism (in which form it migrated into Central Asia and China), which certainly did not seek to disenchant the world. Meanwhile, Jainism – the other great heterodoxy that emerged at roughly the same time as Buddhism – maintained (unlike Buddhism) a thoroughgoing atheistic metaphysics; but although it has had a continuous presence in India, it has always been of marginal significance. The result is a Hindu world in which gods and goddesses proliferate – and continue to do so. Santoshi Mata – mother of satisfaction – emerged as a subject of veneration (especially by women) as late as the 1960s. A 1970s Bollywood film gave her iconic status (and a parentage, as the daughter of the widely revered elephant-headed god Ganesha); she is the giver of favours to women who perform a series of ritual fasts on consecutive Fridays. (The echo of the widespread Catholic practice of the novena is hard to miss.)

Furthermore, enchantment was certainly never eliminated – or even significantly diminished – as Mahayana Buddhism spread into China. At the core of original Buddhist teaching is an ontology that has no obvious place for a realm of spirits to be honoured by the individual on the journey to *nirvana*. But we have already noted the radical transformations that Buddhism underwent as it moved into China and then into Japan. In China, where Buddhism never gained uncontested intellectual supremacy, it mingled more and more with Daoism and with traditional religious practices. It is not that it lost its identity, and there is to this day a difference of focus: Daoist rituals are typically used for the exorcism of ghosts, while Buddhist rituals are popular for the deliverance of the souls of the dead. Sacred mountains – some traditionally Daoist and some Buddhist – are still a feature of the Chinese spiritual landscape. Feng shui (with its Daoist roots) has an impact on the design and location even of buildings constructed in the twenty-first century. And Guanyin – the most popular deity in the Chinese thought world – is originally the Buddhist bodhisattva Avalokitesvara, whose name in Sanskrit reveals that he is the one who hears the cries of the suffering of the world. There are beautiful frescoes of Avalokitesvara at the Ajanta caves in India, and sculptures of the same figure appear in the caves at Yungang in China. In Chinese popular religion, Avalokitesvara becomes the female Guanyin, who bestows blessings (particularly of fertility) on women. In fact, there is an unmistakable similarity between Guanyin and the role of the Virgin Mary in Catholic piety, so much so that, in Vietnam, where both Buddhism and Catholicism are widely spread, the statues of these two figures can look almost interchangeable. Thus, the traditional customs of China have identifiable Daoist and Buddhist elements; and, in the absence of any emotionally powerful alternative for those who were not members of the Confucian intellectual elite, such customs have kept the enchanted world alive and well in the popular imagination, right down to the twenty-first century.[30]

In Japan, the ancient sense of enchantment continued unabated throughout the era of Buddhist intellectual dominance, through the creation of State Shinto in the Meiji era, and into the post-war period. As in China, the relationship between the ancient customs and Buddhism is a complex interaction that has evolved over many centuries. In its heyday, Buddhism might have ended by absorbing – or 'baptizing' – the old traditions, as it did in Tibet, Sri Lanka and South East Asia (and as Christianity did in Europe and Russia). But from the ninth century onwards, imperial court ritual procedures were organized so as to protect the ancient traditions and myths. And gradually the *kami* – the local deities of Japan – came to symbolize a distinctive sense of Japan's uniqueness, even at a cosmic level (by the thirteenth century, the Mountain God Sanno was identified in texts associated with Hie – the Shinto shrine complex in Tokyo – as the Japanese manifestation of Shakyamuni the Buddha himself, and, at the same time, not only as the greatest among the *kami* of Japan but also as supreme in the cosmos). The trajectory from this to State Shinto as it began to emerge in the Tokugawa era is an essential part of the story of the development of Japan's modern national identity; but it was always a superstructure set over a cultural landscape of local *kami*. Vast crowds still visit the major Shinto shrines on ceremonial occasions (notably at the New Year); many leave their fortune-telling *omikuji* papers tied to trees there; and many still use Shinto rites to celebrate marriages, and at other important life moments.[31]

It is too soon to tell how the experience of urbanization will affect the enchanted world. Sociologists from the nineteenth century onwards assumed that the spread of knowledge about, and control over, the natural world would lead to the decline of enchantment – a word first used in this sense by Max Weber in his classic study *The Sociology of Religion*.[32] Weber himself was ambivalent about the development of the modern secular and technocratic urban society; but he nevertheless saw it as inevitable. But little scholarly attention was given to the distinction between structured institutional religion and popular beliefs and practices; anything that might be considered non-scientific was non-rational and would therefore give way to the new order.

An important breakthrough to a more sophisticated understanding was the publication of Keith Thomas's influential *Religion and the Decline of Magic* in 1971. This detailed a very different relationship between institutional religious observance and the magical practices of the enchanted world. He focused on one particular context – that of Protestant England from the sixteenth century onwards into the era of the Enlightenment.[33] The differentiation between religion and magic – or perhaps better, between institutional religion and enchantment – provides a firmer basis for understanding human responses cross-culturally. Thus, for example, the thesis that institutional religion gradually got the better of magic because it was more effective at adapting itself to the new world – to Foucault's new *episteme* – is arguably too Eurocentric. In a sense, the experience of modern China and particularly of modern Japan is the opposite: enchantment has by no means disappeared, while organized religious activity has plenty of ritual but much of it has very little clear metaphysical content. Furthermore, to draw too sharp a dichotomy between institutional religion and popular beliefs is to risk ignoring the way in which religion has *enchanted* the world in a broader sense, by transforming the whole artistic and representational life of all the major cultures of Eurasia – as vividly shown in respect of Christianity by Jörg Lauster's masterful cultural history of Christendom, whose German title *Die Verzauberung der Welt* (*The Enchantment of the World*) is a deliberate riposte to Weber.[34]

If enchantment is universal, one of the ways it has always manifested itself is in ritual. Ceremonies to please, or placate, the gods and the spirits (sometimes of ancestors) are legion in their variety; as are rituals around key moments in life – birth, marriage and death above all. Calendrical practices, such as at the Chinese lunar year festival, Eid, Diwali, Yom Kippur, Christmas and Thanksgiving, are now major features of modern social experience, since urbanization and connectivity have made all of them more and more familiar to all of us. Pilgrimages remain as popular as they were in medieval times; in Japan, China, India, in the Muslim world and even in a secularized Europe (note, for example, the extraordinary popularity of the Camino de Santiago, with its ethos of self-discovery and its obviously invented rituals). Anthropologists have debated the origins and purposes of ritual: does it function as a means of social ordering and control? Is it, alternatively, just the outward sign of the way society works? Does it serve a socio-psychological purpose by providing assurance and a sense of security? Does the Dionysian element in some festivals function as an outlet for rebellion against the natural order? Does it, alternatively, reinforce the psychology of community?

The phenomenon is too complex to permit simple answers. But one thing is clear: ritual is an element in much religious activity, both structured and informal, both public and private, in all cultures. Whether at a Japanese shrine or a Chinese temple, an Indian temple, a mosque or a church, in any of these (even in the most austere Protestant assembly), ritual is an obvious feature of the religious life of those whose needs they serve. In all these cases, a religious faith that can be articulated as a sophisticated metaphysical system is also expressed in rituals and symbols that are on the face of it simple. How will such ritual fare under the impact of urbanization? Will it decline, just as Weber and others expected the world to become disenchanted? In fact, the answer appears to be that it will not. All the signs are that ritual will remain an important part of people's lives because it is such an obvious token of identity. We go on creating new rituals. Witness, for example, the widespread – but relatively recent – practice of leaving bunches of flowers at a roadside where someone has died in an accident. We assert something about who we are through our various rituals; in particular we acknowledge through them that we are not alone. Thus the real question is not about the durability of ritual; it is about whether *particular* rituals will survive if they lose their religious dimension and, if not, what will replace them.

The other religious phenomenon that has been widespread over the millennia, manifesting itself again in every Eurasian culture, is mysticism. This too is a phenomenon that is very diverse and has given rise to extensive scholarly debate – starting with the question of its definition. Is it a strong personal epiphany or a more continuous orientation? Does it always involve an altered state of consciousness, and if so, can neurological phenomena be connected with it in some way that accounts for it? And what is its relationship to institutional religious doctrine and practice? There is often a streak of the esoteric about mystical experience, various groups in several religious cultures having presented it as a special knowledge (*gnosis*, to use the Greek term) that gives the practitioner access to the secret bliss of ultimate reality, beyond what the normal rituals of public worship can offer. Jewish Kabbalah is a clear example, as is tantra (with the difference that the goals of tantric practice may

not only be spiritual but also remarkably material). Some mystic traditions are essentially individualistic (early Christian desert mysticism or
much of Hindu mysticism, for example). Others (such as Muslim Sufi
practice) are often more communal and even develop their own institutional structures. Mysticism generates poetry that often has obvious
resonances across quite different cultures. Thus, to take just one example,
a southern-Indian *bhakti* poet sings a song to Shiva, whom he addresses
as the 'lord of the meeting rivers', in terms that are reminiscent of some
of the most emotive and devotional chapters of the book of Isaiah or the
book of Psalms:

> As a mother runs
> Close behind her child
> With his hand on a cobra
> Or a fire,
> The lord of the meeting rivers
> Stays with me
> Every step of the way
> And looks after me.[35]

Some seem to draw nourishment happily from quite separate institutional traditions; thus, in particular, the remarkable Indian
fifteenth-century mystic poet Kabir – born a Muslim but in the Hindu
holy city of Varanasi – speaks a language that would resonate with any
Hindu holy man or any Muslim Sufi. And the great thirteenth-century
Iranian Sufi poet Rumi could write in a way that would not sound wholly
strange to the mystical traditions either of India or of Chinese Daoism:

> I died as a mineral and became a plant,
> I died as a plant and rose to animal,
> I died as animal and I was Man.
> What should I fear? When was I less by dying?
> Yet once more I shall die as Man, to soar
> With angels blest; but even from angelhood
> I must pass on: all except God must perish.
> I shall become what no mind ever conceived.

O let me not exist! For non-existence
Proclaims in organ tones, To Him we shall return.[36]

Perhaps the most fundamental distinction is between mystical experience that is of a union with the Absolute and that which is the awareness of emptiness or nothingness. But there is no neat compartmentalization to be had. Monotheistic traditions have produced both sorts of experience, even though monotheistic belief would seem hard to reconcile with emptiness. Conversely, Buddhism has also produced both sorts of experience, even though its core teaching of *anatta* (no soul) seems hardly compatible with anything else than emptiness. In the Indian tradition, characteristically, the variety of mystical experience is so great as to defy any attempt at categorization. For example, the classic Indian objective for the holy life is *moksha*, which (as we have seen in Chapter 5) is union, not emptiness, and the contrast of this with the classic Buddhist objective of *nirvana* – the escape from all reality into oblivion – accounts for much about the cultural history of India. Japan, equally characteristically, evolved something rather different. It was not so much a mystical tradition of the kind that would be recognizable from parallels in the monotheistic worlds of Christianity and Islam; nor one which would be familiar to the monistic world of Hindu thought. Instead, the influence of Zen Buddhism produced the intense focus on the 'this-ness' of things, which we have already noted. Thus Dogen, the deeply influential Zen master of the thirteenth century, wrote in his classic essay *Genjokoan* ('Actualizing the Fundamental Point') that:

To study the Buddha way is to study the self. To study the self is to forget the self. To forget the self is to be actualized by myriad things. When actualized by myriad things, your body and mind as well as the bodies and minds of others drop away. No trace of realization remains, and this no-trace continues endlessly.[37]

Mysticism is virtually never part of the mainstream experience of any culture, unlike religious ritual. In general, the life of mysticism is far more demanding. Like monasticism (which has often been the setting for mystical experiences in both Christian and Buddhist cultures in particular), it has therefore always been a calling for the few, not the many. Its disturbing intensity is hard to combine with the routines of a normal life in the world. But mysticism has always been able to call on the sacred texts of institutional religion in all the main cultural traditions for its imagery and its inspiration. Thus, to take just a few examples, the *Upanishads* have numerous accounts of the experiences of early Indian mystics; Paul talks of his mystical experiences in the New Testament;[38] the Pure Land sutras describe the land of Sukhavati (ultimate bliss) in great detail; and the Prophet Muhammad's mystical experiences are recorded in the Qur'an.[39] Furthermore, some of the greatest figures in the cultural history of Christianity, Islam, Buddhism and Hinduism have undergone mystical experiences that have marked their lives and infused their legacies. Saint Francis, al-Ghazali, Dogen and Ramanuja are only a few of the most prominent figures from the pre-modern era whose mystical experience has inspired countless followers in their respective traditions.

Nevertheless, mysticism has always been prone to antinomianism – to drive behaviour that is socially disruptive and even revolutionary. Its claim to special insight into the ultimate is easily seen as a challenge by the guardians of religious orthodoxy, and when it generates visions of a new social or political order, it represents an obvious challenge to the secular order too. The history of Eurasia is strewn with examples of the disturbances caused by mysticism, and it is therefore no surprise that religious and secular authorities everywhere have so often regarded it with suspicion.

Will mysticism continue to flourish in the urbanizing world of the modern era? There will always be some – either within mainstream religious traditions, or outside them – who feel drawn to a more intense journey of spiritual experience. There will always be those who retreat from the swirl of urban life in search of stillness. There will certainly be those who gain spiritual enrichment from the writings of the great mystics of the past. However, these have always been a minority; and secularization may mean that many people, who in previous generations might have found inspiration in mysticism, will increasingly find their consolation instead in the practice of meditation without the trappings of any explicit metaphysics. But the instinct to look within and beyond – within our own beings and beyond (or through) the mundane –

will always be there, in all cultures. It is another universal of the human condition.

The metaphysics of Eurasia are shot through with differences that have their impact on cultural identities evolved over the centuries. Some are based on the essentially Indian concept of transmigration (reincarnation) of the human soul; others are based on the view that each soul has only one mortal existence. Some posit a single, personal deity; others set the human order under an impersonal heaven. But no distinction in the realm of metaphysics is clear cut: Buddhism inherited from its Indian origins the assumption of transmigration, which was, however, in logical terms, inconsistent with its own theory of the nature of being; Hindu expression can often sound not merely monistic but monotheistic – as in passages where the *Upanishads* describe the ultimate more as a personal god than as being or essence:

> He enriches all things, radiant and bodiless,
> unharmed and untouched by evil,
> all-seeing, all-wise, all-present, self-existent,
> he has made all things well for ever and ever.[40]

These words could have been those of a Christian or Muslim philosopher or mystic. Similarly, the idea of divine incarnation to save the world from evil – so central to Christianity – is familiar to Indian metaphysics too. In the *Bhagavad Gita*, Krishna reveals himself as Vishnu incarnate:

> Whenever the Sacred Law fails, and evil raises its head,
> I take embodied birth,
> to guard the righteous, to root out sinners,
> and to establish the Sacred Law,
> I am born from age to age.[41]

And the opening lines of the famous and beautiful hymn of creation from the *Rig Veda* ('then even nothingness was not, nor existence . . . the One breathed but there was no wind and it was self-sustaining; there was that One then, and there was no other'[42]) have obvious echoes in the Daoist song of Zhuangzi: 'in the great beginning there was non-being; it had neither being nor name. The One originated from it; it has oneness but not yet physical form.'[43]

The conclusion from all these cross-cultural echoes is not that there are no deep differences between them. The incarnation of Vishnu in the *Bhagavad Gita* and the incarnation of Christ in the New Testament may have similarities at one level, but they are profoundly different in what they mean in their respective contexts. And Zhuangzi may echo the *Rig Veda* in its opening vision of the origin of being; but the differences soon become obvious (not least because of the surprising agnosticism of the Indian text).

But over the last few centuries – and particularly in the nineteenth and early twentieth centuries – there have been writers in Europe and in America, as well as in India, who have argued for a fundamental identity of the religious instinct in all human traditions. Thus, to take just one example that was well known and influential in its time, Aldous Huxley published *The Perennial Philosophy* in 1946, in which he 'recognizes a divine reality substantial to the world of things and lives and minds' and an ethic that 'places man's final end in the knowledge of the immanent and transcendent ground of all being'. He speaks of a 'highest common factor' that can be found in both the 'traditional lore' and the 'higher religions' of every era. From the vantage point of a new century, this now looks naive – both from the perspective of a much more secularized Europe and also in the light of the growth of more assertive cultural identities on the geopolitical stage. In any case, at the level of philosophical metaphysics there are obvious differences that should be explored, not ignored or explained away. For these differences pose significant issues about the nature of reality and the implications for the individual and for society. And they are, in any case, part of the specific stories and histories of each culture, which we ignore both to our impoverishment and at our peril.

And yet the evidence, both of the human expression of responses to ordinary experiences down the ages, as well as of human religious responses to what is beyond our senses – to the unknown or the uncontrollable – is that there are indeed commonalities which shine through the written testimonies of all the cultures of Eurasia. They are not lost in translation. They remind us that we are on the same journey of discovery and self-discovery; they remind us of the value of continuing on that journey, even if it takes us across rough ground. They remind us why settling for the human implications of a Westphalian Eurasia would be a council of dangerous despair.

We need, therefore, to understand more clearly what that human odyssey of discovery and of self-discovery involves. In particular, we need to look at the growing awareness of the self – at the rise of individuality – down human history and across the cultures of Eurasia. We need to ask the question, what does this mean for the journey going forwards, both individually and collectively? That is the question for the next chapter.

8

First person singular

So many changes came together in Europe, in the short space of about three hundred years, that it is fruitless to pick out one of them as somehow fundamental to all the others. Foucault, as we have seen in Chapter 3, saw this period as the shift to a new *episteme*. In his influential book *After Virtue*, Alasdair MacIntyre describes it as the time when the 'distinctively modern self was invented'.[1] Certainly, the changes were interlocking, wide-ranging and mutually reinforcing. They hugely expanded the wealth of human knowledge about the cosmos and about the planet. Science broadened its horizons, opening new perspectives on everything from the molecular world to the stars. Voyages of discovery opened new vistas on the planet and provided the source data for the modern earth and life sciences. Technology both helped and was helped by the new science: printing was a technology that revolutionized the dissemination of scientific knowledge; and the marine chronometer made great ocean voyages over long distances and across latitudes easier and more reliable.

But why Europe? Knowledge was certainly not a European monopoly. Perhaps the single most important technical invention – printing – had been developed by the Chinese several centuries earlier. In fact, China had been in advance of Europe in a whole range of technologies: paper-making, gunpowder, clocks, the compass and porcelain all started life in China (Europeans only worked out how to make porcelain as late as in the eighteenth century). Indian mathematicians were using decimals and zeros long before Europe – which, in the end, absorbed Indian mathematics, just as it absorbed so much else from the more sophisticated cultures to the east from Muslim sources. Politically, in the fifteenth century, Europe was still of little account. Ming Dynasty China was larger, more sophisticated and more prosperous. Mughal India was not as prosperous as China; but it was cultured, sophisticated and increasingly magnificent. The Sunni Muslim world in the Middle East was well past its Abbasid zenith by then; but the great glories of Iran under the early Safavids were still to come; and when the Ottomans finally seized Constantinople, they established an empire that was for more than two centuries the most cosmopolitan on the planet.

And yet there were straws in the west wind. Within forty years of the demise of Byzantine Constantinople, the last bastion of Muslim Spain fell as the resurgent Christian armies took Granada – in the same year that Columbus sailed towards the New World. Soon after that, the Portuguese sailed into the Indian Ocean and then the Portuguese explorer Ferdinand Magellan led a Spanish expedition westwards round the world all the way to the Philippines. Within forty years of Gutenberg's invention of a printing press based on moveable metal type, there were printing presses in more than a hundred cities throughout Europe and already by 1500 there were over twenty million printed books in circulation. By contrast, it was to be over two hundred years after that before a printing house began to publish books in Arabic in the Ottoman Empire, and even then, the output was minuscule until well into the nineteenth century. In India, too, it was not until the late eighteenth century that printed material became widely available; Mughal India had reached its cultural apogee in the sixteenth century but had gone into a slow decline thereafter. Meanwhile China had entered a long period of ossification. The Wan Li Emperor reigned for almost half a century over the turn of the seventeenth century, in a country that seemed to spurn all its most energetic and creative talents. The brightest and best succumbed to frustration and despair – whether they were public officials who wanted to root out inefficiency and corruption; or military generals who saw the rising threat from the Manchus and wanted to modernize the country's defences; or philosophers who wanted to challenge the comfortable complacency of the suffocating neo-Confucian orthodoxy.[2] Europe's effervescent curiosity and energy was, in short, all the more striking by contrast with the torpor that was increasingly in evidence in much of the rest of Eurasia from the seventeenth century onwards.

One reason lies in the unique cultural and political conditions of pre-modern Europe.[3] The successful spread of Latin Christianity through most of western Europe had substantially weakened older social structures based on extended family and kinship; and at the apex of society, the distinctive voice and moral authority of the institutional Church (to which there was no parallel in the Chinese, Indian or Muslim worlds – nor in the eastern Christianity of Byzantium or Russia) meant that secular power could never be total.[4] Concepts of property and of independent law could therefore evolve more easily in an atmosphere that transcended the constraints of clan and kin as well as calling into question the claims of secular power. The result was a degree of individuality at an early stage – particularly within the family and affecting decisions involving marriage and property – which was measurably different from anywhere else at that stage of human history. And that individuality within the familial context was accompanied, as we have noted in Chapter 2, by the all-important autonomy of so many cities that were becoming centres of trade and exchangers of knowledge.

The hunger for knowledge was thus stoked by social change. But something else was in the atmosphere too: changes in belief systems were altering people's views of their place in the world. The integrated metaphysics of Catholic Christendom had broken down, as the nominalism pioneered by William of Ockham gradually ate away at the fabric of the Thomist 'theory of everything'. This cleared the way for a new interest in studying the world as it actually is. Meanwhile, a renewed focus on Greek and Latin thought helped give birth to the new humanism of the Renaissance – to an emphasis on the dignity, beauty and potential of the human being.

Then came the Protestant reformations. Protestantism was something of a Hydra, but whatever else it became, its original impetus was to underscore the eternal significance of the individual's decision before God. Luther probably never said 'Here I stand; I can do no other.' But, as Diarmaid MacCulloch puts it, 'this can stand for the motto of all Protestants – ultimately perhaps of all western civilisation'.[5] Weber attributed to Protestantism – particularly in its Calvinist form, with its pronounced stress on predestination – an immense but subtle influence on the rise of capitalism. In his seminal 1905 book *The Protestant Ethic and the Spirit of Capitalism*, he argued that this doctrine of predestination created a psychological need to see in worldly economic success a sign of eternal salvation, and that this drove the desire to succeed in commerce. R. H. Tawney's famous and influential *Religion and the Rise of Capitalism*, published in 1926, broadly accepted the linkage; but he emphasized the contribution of the individualism and the frugality of the Protestant lifestyle rather than the theology. Historians, sociologists and economists have argued the toss in the subsequent decades, on the basis of conflicting evidence and counter-examples (notably the Italian Renaissance cities). Some have suggested that the relationship between Protestantism and capitalism is real, but the cause is neither theology nor ethics but the strong focus of Protestantism on literacy (which, in turn, gave the printing revolution its huge social traction).[6]

The point is not to overemphasize any one of these phenomena, or to fix on a single underlying cause. Nor is it to argue for a Marxist or a Foucauldian or any other particular perspective on what is 'fundamental' and what is 'superstructure' (to use Marxist terms). Weber himself finishes his book with a direct rebuttal of such perspectives as he writes in his last paragraph that 'it is not my aim to substitute for a one-sided materialistic causal interpretation of culture and history an equally one-sided spiritualistic one'.[7] The point, rather, is to acknowledge the radical and broad-based changes in the metaphysics of the European cultural world – having impacts on both Catholic and Protestant thought streams – that accompanied the huge growth in knowledge.

It is not the case that there had been no stirrings of a new spirit of enquiry anywhere else in Eurasia during the same period: the great Mughal Emperor Akbar fostered a remarkable culture of intellectual curiosity, artistic creativity and religious broadmindedness in India during the very decades when Europe was tearing itself apart through its religious wars. And yet the European experience was different. India under Akbar's great grandson Aurangzeb saw its humanistic and pluralistic instincts stifled as this long-lived monarch sought to impose a much more conservative religious policy on the country. (One of the perennial what-ifs of history asks what would have happened to India if Aurangzeb had lost the war of succession to the throne and his elder brother Dara Shikoh – an intellectual and religious liberal in the tradition of Akbar – had won.) Aurangzeb died in 1707 at the age of eighty-nine and was buried in an ostentatiously simple grave in a little village near Aurangabad. By that time, he had brought the Mughal empire to its zenith of size; but he had overstretched it financially, and under a series of weak successors it went into terminal decline. Europe, however, had survived its religious wars, established its new Westphalian peace and was already becoming the hothouse of intellectual life that spawned the Enlightenment.

This European Enlightenment was one of the most extraordinary phenomena of human history. Throughout the eighteenth century, enquiring minds explored and debated a vast range of issues: from the workings of the mind itself to the physics of the planet; the principles of causality; the nature of trade and exchange; the way species of plants and animals were formed and developed; the rights and responsibilities of individuals and of government; the necessity of God; and the principles of history. The Enlightenment was never a single body of ideas, a single coherent philosophical system or a single programme. Nor was it an age with a defined beginning and end – although its outer boundaries are arguably in the early seventeenth century on the one hand (marked by the work of Descartes) and at around the turn of the nineteenth century on the other (marked by the death of Kant). None of its key themes was wholly new: its ancestors could be found in ideas traceable more or less clearly in the medieval scholastics, in the classics of Greece and Rome and in the Renaissance. Nor did it ever reach stasis: in the last half of the eighteenth century there was an almost unquestioning confidence in the power of human reason to conquer all before it, although this was already giving way to recognition of a much more uncertain balance between rationality and feeling. This change manifested itself in the Romantic movement and in a newer and more elevated view of aesthetics that came to see the artist as a sort of priest of human expression. Meanwhile, the scientific journeys of the Enlightenment continued on into the nineteenth century and beyond: Humboldt, Darwin, Einstein, Crick and others were all heirs of the great Enlightenment figures who changed the way humans think about their world for ever.

A very European question: who are we?

But all this scientific progress continued without reaching a resolution to a dilemma that underlay the whole Enlightenment experience. For the more the philosophers put the world under the microscope, the more they seemed to face an uncomfortable choice between the random and the determined – between scepticism (not just about 'revealed' religious belief but about 'providence' and the 'laws' of nature) on the one hand and, on the other hand, a determinism that sat uneasily with their belief in the autonomy of the rational individual. The French physicist La Mettrie opted for a sort of determinism that exposed the dilemma. Nature, he writes, operating under 'certain laws of motion', unthinkingly makes the human being as a 'machine which thinks':

> Granted the existence of certain laws of motion, they formed eyes which saw, ears which heard, nerves which felt, a tongue sometimes capable of speech . . . At last they produced the organ of thought. Nature constructed, within the machine of the human being, another machine which proved suitable for retaining ideas and for producing new ones . . . Having made, without sight, eyes which see, it made, without thinking, a machine which thinks.[8]

Diderot, the great encyclopaedist, agonized about the determinist implications of causality in a moving prayer that is to be found at the end of his *Pensées sur L'Interprétation de la Nature* (*On the Interpretation of Nature*):

> O God, I do not know if you exist . . . I ask nothing in this world, for the course of events is determined by its own necessity if you do not exist, or by your decree if you do . . . Here I stand, as I am, a necessarily organized part of eternal and necessary matter – or perhaps your own creation . . .[9]

Meanwhile, David Hume – the most rigorous sceptic of them all – denied flatly that there is any principle of causality beyond the evidence of consistent correlation, demolished the claims of natural law and of Providence, and rejected outright the existence of any personal God. He also denied the existence of a stable and durable self (Locke's 'consciousness') as such. But as he noted, the result left him in an uncomfortable position:

The whole is a riddle, an enigma, an inexplicable mystery. Doubt, uncertainty and suspense of judgment appear the only result of our most accurate scrutiny . . .[10]

All these three sceptics wrote within ten years of one another in the middle of the eighteenth century. All had agonized about causality and the ability to reach sure knowledge of the workings of the material world. But the dilemma was also – as is clear from La Mettrie's 'machine which thinks' – *about the nature of the human consciousness itself.* It was, in other words, both an exterior and an interior dilemma. And the two dimensions were inevitably linked: if the world of nature operated in accordance with 'certain laws of motion' (which La Mettrie acknowledged we might not fully understand – as he put it, 'causes hidden within nature itself may have produced everything'), then a question arose to which he had no answer: what precisely is this machine which thinks? Is it subject to those same laws? What exactly, in short, is human self-consciousness? And if Hume's radical scepticism was justified, then the question posed itself in an even more radical form: is there a thinking machine at all? Is human self-consciousness an illusion? And if, one way or another, it was deemed possible to establish, or at least accept, the existence of the rational self, then a secondary question – which was, in fact, an old chestnut of European debate – arose. This was the long-standing 'epistemological' question: how can this human mind know anything for certain about the real world that is outside the self?

This European debate about the self as subject represents a challenge to all the cultures of Eurasia, partly because Europe came to have such a profound impact on the whole of the rest of Eurasia, but partly also because it is not just a European question. Long before, as we have noted in Chapter 3, Zhuangzi hinted at the double dilemma of the self and the perception of reality; in India, Jayanta, a philosopher writing around the turn of the tenth century, argued that 'the notion of the ego is within us; some kinds of notion of the ego are in close connection with the body . . . and some kinds are in close connection with the knowing agent, such as "I know" or "I remember".'[11] Then a century after Jayanta, Ibn Sina had conducted his famous 'floating man' experiment to convince himself of the real existence of the immaterial human self.

Yet this European exploration was different. For one thing, Zhuangzi's musings did not become the mainstream of Chinese thought: in China, the prevailing classical wisdom understood the relation of the human mind to the external world as being one in which both the mind and that external reality were ordered structurally by the same overall organic system. There was therefore a *correspondence* between the cosmic and the human mental structure – not, as in European thought, a fundamental *cleavage* between the self and the external other. The basic task was therefore to understand those correspondences, and this gave the classic Confucian orthodoxy a strongly pragmatic cast that did not need to wrestle with doubts about the nature of the self or with epistemological scepticism. This perspective did not go unchallenged, though: Mozi drew a distinction between things as they are and things as they appear in a way that would have been familiar to any European philosopher. This epistemological scepticism is, furthermore, part of a general Mohist outlook that – as we have already noted in Chapter 4 – took a view of human nature which had many resonances in the emerging European thought world. But Mohism never gained the upper hand in China. From Confucius through to Mao and beyond into contemporary China, there is a deep continuity that sees the human mind as related structurally to the wider reality it inhabits. In Confucian China, the Enlightenment could not have taken the form it did in Europe.

And it could not have done so in the Muslim world either. After al-Ghazali's onslaught on Ibn Sina, there was relatively little analytical reasoning about revealed religion or about the laws of nature and, essentially, no interest in the epistemological question (although, as we have also noted, there was plenty of subtle and sophisticated mystical exploration). India was different: the sheer luxuriance of Indian philosophy meant that any European perspective on the self and on its relationship to the external world can find an echo somewhere in the extraordinarily rich heritage of Indian Sanskrit literature. For the most part, Indians – both Hindu and Buddhist – tended to accept that the mind's cognition of external reality is ordinarily reliable and true. But there was an intrinsic tendency in Buddhist thought, given the core doctrine of *anatta* (no soul), to see both the external world and the self as illusory. Against this background, it is hardly surprising to find evidence of the same sort of scepticism about causality and about the self that we have already noted in Hume. But this was not inevitable: one prominent figure – who is arguably the most important in the Indian Buddhist tradition after Gautama Shakyamuni himself – evolved a sophisticated approach to the questions about perception, causality and the self that was consistent with the fundamental Buddhist world view but also enabled practical engagement with ordinary life. This was Nagarjuna, who lived sometime in the second or third century CE, and who founded the so-called Middle Way (Madhyamaka) tradition, which was, in turn, to become highly influential in the development of Chinese and Japanese Buddhist thought. If the Europeans of the eighteenth century had known about his work as they grappled with Hume's questions, they would have nodded sagely in agreement with much of what he said. Nevertheless, there remains one crucial difference between Buddhist and European reflection on the nature of the self: on the whole (with perhaps the exception of Hume), the Europeans of the Enlightenment knew there was a self, but could not satisfy themselves that they could prove it; Buddhist teaching, however, knew that people thought there was a self, but its fundamental task was to dissolve that illusion – because that was the way of release from the cycle of suffering into *nirvana*.

The European journey has a long history, going back at least to Augustine. From the Renaissance onwards, with its renewed focus on the human condition, reflection on the self came to have several dimensions to it. First, the pursuit of knowledge about the material world raised the epistemological question: on what basis can we be sure of judgements we make about that world? Second, the boundless curiosity of this new human spirit turned inwards and focused on the self itself: what is this mysterious self of ours? How does it work? And how does it intersect with the exterior world? Then, third, the pursuit of personal holiness – which had generated a long and rich litany of mystical exploration – also evolved into the Christian humanist pursuit of wholeness in everyday living. For Erasmus, this meant responding with integrity to the teachings of the New Testament and listening to the inner voice of conscience; and this search inevitably broadened out into a question about values and the basis for morality. The result was a new sense of the self, as new 'packages' of understandings developed – about the nature of the good,

220

about the stories that form our memories, and about the basis of social relationships.[12]

Enlightenment philosophizing began with the epistemological question: how can we be sure about what we know of the material world around us? As we have seen, this question did not trouble other cultures so much; and indeed, it frustrated some practical minds even within Europe (famously, Samuel Johnson demonstratively kicked a large stone when confronted with the need to prove that things were real and not just ideas of the mind). Why then was it given such prominence from Descartes onwards? Answer: because they wanted a logically self-sufficient basis for their approach to understanding the world that was not dependent on traditional natural theology or on sacred texts. The philosophers tackled this in different ways. Descartes himself not only deployed his famous *cogito, ergo sum* – 'I think, therefore I am' – as his foundational and indubitable certainty, on the basis of which he could erect a framework of certain knowledge about everything else; but he also believed that the mind was endowed with certain innate ideas (such as the idea of God, or of infinity), which it could bring to bear in analysis. John Locke denied this: all the mind had to work on were the impressions it gained from the senses. Bishop Berkeley used God to underpin the validity and coherence of those sense impressions. And Hume's radical scepticism about this entire project was the famous wake-up call to Immanuel Kant, which 'interrupted his dogmatic slumbers'.[13]

It was Kant who went on to evolve what was by far the most sophisticated response to the question. Kant's great system bears more than a passing resemblance to that of Nagarjuna. For Kant there is indeed no final surety of the kind Descartes sought about the real world; we can never have direct knowledge of 'things-in-themselves'. But the human self – the 'transcendental ego', as Kant called it, whose existence is not in question and is in command of its own rationality – applies a priori principles (notably the frameworks of space and time, without which it is not logically possible to make sense of anything), thus enabling us to make sense of our sense impressions and be pragmatically confident about the real world behind them – the world of 'things-in-themselves'.

In retrospect, we can see how this whole line of questioning began to become less and less interesting to the Europeans of the nineteenth century onwards; it was as if there was nothing much more to say after Kant. In any event, the original motivation to free scientific knowledge from the theology and sacred texts of revealed religion faded as time went by (not least because Christian theology and approaches to interpreting the meaning of the Bible gradually underwent profound changes that removed much of the difficulty in reconciling science with religion). But that was by no means the end of the matter. The next question – and it is a deeper, more enduring, perhaps more mysterious one – is about the 'transcendental ego' itself. And this question, once posed, is a challenge in any metaphysical or cultural context. What precisely is the nature of this self? Hume struggled with it more openly than most:

> For my part, when I enter most intimately into what I call *myself*, I always stumble on some particular perception or other, of heat or cold, light or shade, love or hatred, pain or pleasure. I never can catch *myself* at any time without a perception, and never can observe anything but the perception . . . The mind is a kind of theatre, where several perceptions successively make their appearance, pass, re-pass, glide away, and mingle in an infinite variety of postures and situations. There is properly no *simplicity* in it at one time, nor *identity* in different [times]… [It is merely] the successive perceptions . . . that constitute the mind . . . All my hopes vanish when I come to explain the principles that unite our successive perceptions in our thought or consciousness.[14]

Kant did not believe that the self – the 'I' of Descartes' 'I think' – is a metaphysical certainty in the way Descartes had believed it was, either. Nor was he trying to show that the self was immaterial and immortal as Ibn Sina had sought to do (and as Descartes certainly believed). But he saw the self rather as a necessary presupposition for thought to make any sense, not as something known independently to be real. (Here, in particular, the echo of Nagarjuna is hard to miss.) What he called 'the unity of apperception' was necessary to all thought, and thus he effectively rationalizes away Hume's difficulty. (He does so, arguably, by what is in effect a sleight of language: he is happy to use the first person singular and the possessive pronoun 'my' when talking about these apperceptions.

But such language betrays a more immediate sense of self, not just a necessary presupposition for rational thought. Not for the first time, this reminds us of the fact that the human being is a language animal – a point of profound significance Kant never recognized.)

And whereas the epistemological question may have run out of steam since Kant, what he said about the self was in no way the last word. For one thing, the differing positions staked out by Hume and Kant on how this self should *act* still dominate the debates of moral philosophy to this day. For the former, virtue is in the eye of the judicious observer; morality is based on human nature and what makes for a useful and agreeable life.[15] For Kant, morality is founded in the nature of a rational being and in the overarching autonomy of the transcendental ego.[16] If Hume writes from the perspective of an observer, Kant writes from that of the rational agent. Hume's approach is therefore culturally conditioned (even if he shared with his contemporaries a broad understanding of the specific content of morality that they assumed was universal). Kant's approach, by contrast, makes a much deeper claim to universality because it purports to be grounded in the very principles of reason that any rational being must accept.

It would take us beyond the scope of this book to explore this debate and its history in adequate detail. But it is worth noting that Kant's account of morality is radically different from that of Aristotle or of Confucius. They anchor virtue in an understanding of the human place in the order of things, whereas he derives it from the universal structure of practical reasoning. This sets the bar for moral decision-making much higher: it has to claim universal validity; it has, in fact, to be, as he famously called it, a 'categorical imperative' for any rational being. Hume, however, seems more in tune with the pervasive mood of the modern era, which has become profoundly suspicious of any attempt to derive universal values from some culture-free universal source or first principle.

The phenomenon of the self as such

The fascination with the self was not just with the morality of its motives and actions, but with the nature of the self as such. This was to continue all through the nineteenth century and into the twentieth. Philosophers continued to wrestle with the question: is the self a primal act of will (as argued, for example, by Fichte) or is it a conceptual linkage of many actions and sensations into an overall unity, in the way that, for example, the earth is the unity of a multiplicity of things (as argued by Friedrich Schelling)? The first approach makes the self, the I, the mysterious starting point of all knowledge; the second sees it as essentially derivative – but the result is no less mysterious (as when Schelling argues that 'thinking is not my thinking, and being is not my being, for everything is only of God or the totality').[17] One way or another, they had to explain how the experience of self is actually made up of a variety of acts and sensations from one moment to the next – and yet at the same time is a whole, an identity. In the end, their interpretations had their roots in either Descartes or Hume, though: either the self was primary or it was derivative. All in all, these philosophical endeavours are, perhaps inevitably, unsatisfying (as well as ponderous in many cases) in their efforts to square the circle. But they could never escape from the spell of the self; for so much European thought, the self – the individual self – was and remained the central mystery. The self had become the subject. This was the era of individuality.

By the twentieth century, a new philosophical approach to the self sought to free itself from the straitjacket, by being more descriptive of the actual experience of self and less concerned to set the self into any wider metaphysical system. This approach was *phenomenology* – so called because it is interested, not so much in a priori conceptual structures but, rather, in the actual phenomena of mental activity through which we engage with the external world. In the recondite world of philosophy, this was something of a revolution, comparable, as Ricoeur suggested, to the difference between cubism and impressionism.[18] The philosopher who is most closely identified with this new emphasis was Edmund Husserl, a German who taught and wrote at the University of Freiburg in the early decades of the twentieth century.[19] He developed an intricate approach to the analysis of how humans extend their conscious awareness of the world and impose structures of meaning on their experience. He sought to describe conscious awareness in terms of what he called the 'intentionality' of various types of experience (such as perception, thought, memory, desire and linguistic activity, as well as bodily activity).

'Intentionality' refers to the sense that all such experiences must in some way be *of* or *about* something. Husserl then seeks to analyse the way our minds give meaning and order to these intentional experiences, through the particular concepts or images we impose on them. Thus Husserl starts with the conscious self – with Kant's transcendental ego – but argues that this self can only give meaning to its intentional experiences by processing them through concepts and images, such as temporal awareness, spatial awareness, self-awareness, awareness of bodily activity, and so on, which he analyses in meticulous detail. His debt to Kant is obvious, but his focus is very different. Husserl is not interested in the theoretical question of whether we can know anything about the exterior world – about the 'things-in-themselves' that are beyond our senses, which Kant believed we could never directly access. For Husserl, the key question is how the mind actually processes and gives meaning to its experience of things.

All this is, in some ways, an echo of the detailed analysis of consciousness that was a favourite topic of Indian Buddhist scholars over a thousand years earlier. But it also reminds us of Augustine's pathbreaking discussion of the mind and memory in his *Confessions*, which we looked at in Chapter 5. And this in turn reminds us that the 'intentional structures' of the self may not only be intrinsic to human awareness as such; they may well also be conditioned by culture and by history (both individual and collective). Furthermore, the whole focus of early phenomenology on conscious experience begs an obvious set of questions about *unconscious* mental activity, which the then relatively new discipline of psychology was busy analysing, with varying degrees of plausibility (Freud's work was influential in its time, but now seems almost embarrassing to his successors a hundred years later). It also raises questions about the relationship between mental events (conscious or unconscious) and neural activity in the brain, which takes the analysis into the realms of physics and biology. This in turn poses a new version of an old dilemma: the eighteenth century asked the epistemological question about the relationship between our sense impressions and the external reality they were supposed to correspond to; the new question is about the relationship of the mind to the (physical) brain. Hume's question thus arises all over again: if it is possible to correlate all mental activity with electrochemical activity in the brain, is such correlation good evidence of causality? And if so, what causes what?

Some have been content to say simply that neural activity causes mental activity – and, at least in theory, to accept the determinist implications of this. Thus, for example, no lesser scientist than Francis Crick argued that 'mental activities are entirely due to the behaviour of nerve cells, glial cells, and the atoms, ions and molecules that make them up and influence them.'[20] Others have argued, more subtly and precisely, that personal identity – the self – can be reduced to physical and/or psychological continuity. Derek Parfit was an Oxford philosopher of the late twentieth century who was perhaps the best-known and most careful exponent of this position. In an essay significantly entitled 'The unimportance of identity', he argues that there need not be any personal identity of the kind that Descartes, Kant and Husserl all accepted – a kind that that is other than, or more than, physical and psychological continuity. Personal identity is something we all recognize, but it consists only in that continuity and does not somehow 'stand outside' it. The way we use the language of self may be convenient, socially and psychologically, but it is not more than that. He uses a metaphor to illustrate the significance of this point: if I know that several trees are growing together on some hill and am then told that there is a copse on that hill, I have not learnt any new factual information about the trees – but I have learnt a new linguistic fact. Parfit ends his essay with the conclusion that:

> Even the use of the word 'I' can lead us astray. Consider the fact that, in a few years, I shall be dead. This fact can seem depressing. But the reality is only this. After a certain time, none of the thoughts and experiences that occur will be directly causally related to this brain or be connected in certain ways to these present experiences. That is all this fact involves. And in that redescription, my death seems to disappear.[21]

In his focus on individual identity as a linguistic fact, Parfit follows a practice that would probably have Hume's – and possibly Kant's – approval. In his proposal that we can do without it, he stands in a line which connects him to the great Buddhist philosophers of long ago.

The question of Being: Heidegger et al.

But Parfit's reductionism would certainly not be to the taste of Martin Heidegger. He was probably the most globally influential philosopher of the twentieth century (though surely also the most controversial, because of his public role in the academic life of Nazi Germany). He, like Husserl, spent much of his career at Freiburg, succeeding Husserl there when he retired. Thereafter, he carefully distanced himself from Husserl (who was Jewish) in the middle of the wave of anti-Semitism that swept through German universities in the 1930s.

Heidegger took issue early on with both Kant and Husserl on the grounds that the search for the true meaning of the self cannot begin at the level of the consciousness of objects (Husserl's intentionality) but has to dig deeper into the very conditions of being. Heidegger's *Being and Time* is arguably the greatest work of philosophy of the century. In it, Husserl's focus on the awareness of experience has been replaced by a search for what unites our different human senses of what it is to be. Husserl's starting point in the transcendental ego – or the conscious self – has become, to use Heidegger's German word (which has no convenient translation), *Dasein*. This is at one level the normal word for existence; literally, it means 'being there' or being present. This is Heidegger's way of expressing the inherent involvement of being in that which is external to itself; the *Da* of *Dasein* – the 'there' in 'Being there' – carries a suggestion of openness to, and perhaps even of a resulting vulnerability to, the world. So Husserl's intentionality becomes in Heidegger's hands the concept of 'being-in-the-world', which Heidegger goes on to describe using the word *Sorge* ('care') – a word that carries roughly the same penumbra of meaning in German as it does in English.

This is not the place for a full exposition of Heidegger's complex thinking. Interpreting Heidegger has become something of an industry in a number of philosophy schools. There are those who see his thought as being primarily a description of the human existential dilemma of anxiety about the meaning of life in all its transience and troubles, which means that he can be compared with or contrasted with thinkers such as Kierkegaard, Nietzsche or Sartre. There are others who see his work as a profoundly significant exploration of the mysterious nature of human being as such. This makes him a twentieth-century descendant of the

Greek neo-Platonist and early Christian thought world, digging down below the ordinary processes of consciousness to discover the fundamental stratum of being (and in which affinities to the Buddhist project of dissolving the consciousness of consciousness are obvious). There are still others who regard Heidegger as almost wilfully obscurantist and ponderous (and it is at least true that his writing is often obscure – particularly after he considered that he had 'turned' from the world view set out in *Being and Time*, to a more poetic, less analytic, meditation).

It is sufficient for our purposes to note that, for all his distinctiveness, Heidegger remains anchored in what had by then become a strong European tradition of fascination with questions about the self. Although he is determined to show that *Dasein is* not an independent, transcendent ego or substance (and utterly rejects Descartes' concept of the autonomous 'I'), he is a long way from dissolving the self. Even in his later writings – where he argues that he has not done enough in *Being and Time* to abandon the superficial subjectivity of which he accuses Descartes, Husserl and virtually everyone in between – the discrete self in all its mystery, in all its nebulousness, but in all its inescapability still haunts Heidegger's stage.[22]

His summary point, implicit or explicit all through his writings, is that 'being-in-the-world' is inevitably 'being-with' others and 'being-towards' something else (for example, our objectives, our future and ultimately our death). This 'being-with' is fraught with existential risks, which Heidegger's work addresses in ways that can seem more like quasi-religious reflection than dispassionate analytic philosophy. His use of the word *Sorge* or 'care' in the context of being-in-the-world is evidence of this. And as he articulates this 'care' that is intrinsic to being in the world, he uses such terms as *Geworfenheit* ('thrown-ness') and *Verfallenheit* ('fallen-ness') as ways of showing how *Dasein* finds itself in a world in which it is in some way unavoidably untrue to itself. More than just a faint echo of Heidegger's own early Catholic theological training can be heard in his use of this sort of terminology.

For 'being-with' inevitably involves at least the risk of 'a being-lost in the publicness of the "they"', as he puts it.[23] And this involvement in public triviality, which cannot be avoided, gives *Dasein* its characteristic of unsatisfactoriness or, to use a word he makes much of, inauthenticity:

228

This Being-with-one-another dissolves one's own Dasein completely into a kind of Being of 'the Others' . . . We take pleasure and enjoy ourselves as *they* take pleasure; we read, see, and judge about literature and art as *they* see and judge; likewise we shrink back from the 'great mass' as *they* shrink back; we find 'shocking' what *they* find shocking. The 'they' . . . prescribes the kind of Being of everydayness.[24]

This is one of those points in Heidegger's writing where we can readily identify with what amounts to a description of the vacuousness – or alienation – of much modern urban life. His later writing on modern technology, for example, could easily sound like a twentieth-century version of Wordsworth – or even like a poetic mutation of Marx's attack on the alienation brought about by factory labour.[25]

The problems of 'being-with' in turn raise the possibility of an alternative way of being that is more authentic. Above all, what requires an authentic response is the human experience of death. The anticipation of impending death creates anxiety as – in Heidegger's terms – '*Dasein* finds itself face-to-face with the "nothing" of the possible impossibility of its existence.'[26] But it is that same anxiety that makes possible an authentic 'Being-able-to-be' which is not at risk to the 'they'. It confronts the inauthenticity of ordinary life, because it knows that not all the possibilities of existence can be realized – or, to put it in prosaic terms, life can be wasted. In more Heideggerian terms, it is a 'Being-towards-death'; and this involves an 'anticipatory resoluteness' that makes authentic *Dasein* possible.

Heidegger was highly influential among the French existentialists of the mid-twentieth century, for whom he became the foil they had to respond to. A system that seemed to offer a potential answer to everything was bound to provoke reaction. In particular, Sartre reacts against Heidegger's arguments for a strategy of authenticity in the face of death, essentially on the grounds that it is just too neat. Death is not just inevitable; it is its randomness which hurts. As Sartre puts it (surely echoing the experience of countless human beings across cultures and down the ages), 'the perpetual appearance of chance at the heart of my projects cannot be apprehended as my possibility but, on the contrary, as the annihilation of all my possibilities.'[27]

Still, Heidegger's influence was pervasive, and continued beyond the existentialists of the mid-century into the postmodern era of the last decades. The impetus for Jacques Derrida's famous – or notorious – deconstructionism came from Heidegger. Derrida's writing sometimes seems provocative for the sake of it, but his core purpose is clear. His starting point is the deconstruction of existing structures of thought, of expression and of perceived experience, until the foundations are exposed. Descartes believed he had found a secure foundation for knowledge in the irreducible, indubitable thinking ego. Derrida doesn't accept this, any more than Heidegger does; for him, as for Heidegger, the self is not just in and for itself. Experience of the self is always and unavoidably the experience of the other (not least because the experience of the self always has a temporal dimension to it, including elements of the remembered past and of an intentional future, so that it cannot be just a pure, undifferentiated, present experience of the self). So the self is neither irreducible nor indubitable; Descartes was wrong. There is therefore nothing, not even the self, that cannot be deconstructed – and no secure foundation.

Yet the end result of all his deconstruction – of the self, of literary texts, of ways of thinking about the world inherited from the Greeks – is not the dissolution of the self. On the contrary, and even ironically, Derrida's whole career is an angry, campaigning assertion of the importance of human integrity. Derrida wants the self to be honest with itself and to enlarge our sense of common destiny – even with animals. As he argues in his last book, *The Animal that Therefore I Am*, 'autonomy of the "I" can be neither pure nor rigorous; it would not be able to form the basis for a simple and linear differentiation of the human from the animal.'[28] This is not reductionist; it is not saying that there is no difference between humans and animals. In fact, it is arguably a distant echo of a very ancient theme we have already discussed in Chapter 3 – the pre-modern sense of belonging to a wider world. Derrida is relativist but far from materialist; for him, there is no firm footing to be had. But in a sense he is like Kierkegaard: he is still swimming, despite the unavoidable uncertainty – as if over waters that are seventy thousand fathoms deep.[29] He, just as much as Heidegger, is shaped in that European mould: he is fascinated by the human self.

Different Asian starting points

It is certainly not the case that other Eurasian cultures have been uninterested in the human self. So far as mainstream Indian thought is concerned, the Vedantic philosophers of Hinduism have typically believed that the existence of the self – the *atman* – cannot be proved or deduced from sacred texts, but that it is known intuitively by the individual: we simply are conscious of ourselves. But the crucial difference between this and the European perspective is that the *atman* is generally understood not only as the individual self but also as the Universal Self – the *Brahman*. Hinduism assumes, in fact, that the existence of this Universal Self is known directly from the existence of the individual self.[30] It was this sense of direct access to the One that so appealed to the European Romantics of the nineteenth century, but the mainstream of European thought was focused ever more sharply on the individual (Kierkegaard, Nietzsche) or on social forces (Marx).

The Chinese and Japanese thought worlds start from a very different perspective on the individual from that of either Hinduism or the Europeans. In the case of China, mainstream Confucianism has always had a vantage point outside the individual and sees identity in essentially relational terms, as we have noted. Yet from the seventeenth century onwards, new currents of thought were developing – even before the impact of European ideas, initially mediated by the Jesuits, had begun to change China irrevocably. After the Qing Dynasty had brought the tired and moribund Ming era to an end in 1644, more and more scholars were looking for a new practicality in the official approach to the world of real affairs. In particular, Dai Zhen, the most important Confucian scholar active in the eighteenth century, began to pick apart Zhu Xi's ruling system of metaphysics. He was particularly interested in confronting the moral and political implications of the arrogant complacency that had set in. He was no revolutionary and, to the contrary, saw himself as looking back to a purer form of the Confucian truth, which was discernible by careful reading of the Classics.

Dai Zhen couches his argument in traditional Chinese metaphysical terms, but his reasoning amounts to an echo of the nominalism of William of Ockham. So what he wrote paved the way for a more analytical, more evidential approach to the actual conditions of human experience – just as Ockham's razor did in Europe. He himself was something of a polymath: an expert in engineering, astronomy, philology and mathematics. He never abandoned the basic Confucian belief that there is moral purpose in the order of things; in fact, it was this very belief that drove him to his researches. What is new is his unremitting focus on the minutely detailed and objective study of concrete things, not on intellectual speculation (following Zhu Xi) nor on introspection of the mind (following Wang Yangming).[31] This was to describe the relation between subject and object in ways that would have been broadly familiar to his European contemporaries; but it amounted to a radical departure from – or at least a fundamental modification of – the traditional Confucian view.[32]

This analytical separation of subject and object was in effect a potential challenge to the venerable concept – rooted in the teachings of Mencius – of 'heart/mind'. This held that all knowledge involves self-knowledge, and all self-knowledge is a relationship with the wider order of things. It is not that this principle is anti-rationalistic per se. But it did allow for a subtle deprecation of objective knowledge (rather as the classical education for the British upper classes stressed the humanism of Greek and Roman learning and spurned the applied sciences). Thus, for example, the neo-Confucian Zhang Zai, writing in the eleventh century (some hundred years before Zhu Xi), argues:

> The mind of ordinary people is limited to the narrowness of what is seen and heard. The sage, however, fully develops his nature and does not allow what is seen or heard to fetter his mind. He regards everything in the world to be his own self. This is why Mencius said that if one exerts one's mind to the utmost, one can know nature and Heaven . . . Knowledge coming from seeing and hearing . . . is not knowledge obtained through one's moral nature. Knowledge obtained through one's moral nature does not originate from seeing or hearing.[33]

As the contemporary Chinese philosopher Tu Weiming remarks, 'this possibility, that one can enter into all things in the world, and that one can obtain knowledge through one's moral nature without . . . seeing and hearing, is never allowed in Kant's philosophy.'³⁴ Nor was it allowed by Dai Zhen, whose conceptual separation of subject and object potentially meant the elevation of evidence and reason over all reference to received authority in the understanding of the objective world. It was an early step in the journey towards modernism.

There was another consequence of this new approach to epistemology; but it would become clear only more gradually, with the onset of modernity amidst China's traumas of the nineteenth and twentieth centuries. This second implication is even more radical, for a clearer focus on the subject and on objective knowledge brings potential consequences for the application of rational principles to *the individual's place in the order of things*. This in turn potentially unleashes the individual conscience to question the whole metaphysics of the received order and to explore rights and responsibilities from the perspective of the individual self, and not simply that of orthodoxy. In short, it has ethical, social and political implications. It is not, of course, that eighteenth-century Confucians like Dai Zhen saw all the implications of the emerging new thought world. There was no Rousseau among them. But the gradual development – partly self-generated and partly influenced by the growing impact of European thought patterns – of a phenomenology more akin to European ideas was bound to have an impact on all areas of life, not just on the long-standing and rather scholastic Chinese approach to the 'investigation of things'. It would be hard to avoid a full-scale threat to the time-honoured Chinese understanding of the cosmic and social order. As Tu Weiming comments, 'Promethean defiance and Faustian restlessness are not at all compatible with the cherished value of harmony.'³⁵ Yet this is what came with the European discovery of the self and individuality. The revolutionary turmoil of the twentieth century was one consequence of this in Chinese history. But there will be others too, both for China and for Eurasia as a whole; we will explore some of the metaphysical implications of the rise of the self further as we look at broader patterns of history in the next chapter.

But before doing so, we need to explore the different experience of Japanese engagement with European phenomenology. We have already seen in Chapter 2 how Japan was developing its own cultural patterns in the newly urbanized society of the seventeenth century. For all that it was a controlled police state, this was a time of intellectual vibrancy, debate and entertainment. It was a period that saw the rise of a new Confucianism, whose primary concern was to promote the traditional Confucian vision of a harmonious society based on appropriate societal and personal relationships. This was, for obvious reasons, convenient to the authorities. Like their Chinese contemporaries, the Japanese Confucians focused primarily on the ancient classics. The most important figure was Ogyu Sorai, a scholar from around the turn of the eighteenth century. He took the same view as Dai Zhen of the metaphysics of Zhu Xi; but all his attention was focused on ethics and politics rather than on the natural sciences; and he was no champion of the individual.

However, Confucianism never had the same authority in Japan that it had achieved in China. And already in the eighteenth century a very different movement was gaining momentum under the powerful influence of Motoori Norinaga, born just after Ogyu Sorai died and a close contemporary of Kant. Significantly, Norinaga was born into a merchant family, whereas Sorai had come from a samurai background. In a sense, Norinaga was the future, while Sorai was the past. It was he who did more than anyone else to create the story about Japan's origins and past, and to provide the intellectual underpinnings for what would later become State Shinto. In some ways his influence on subsequent developments in Japan can be compared with that of Herder in Germany. The difference is that Herder came from a Lutheran background, in which in the final reckoning the individual stands before God alone. Norinaga inherited all the Japanese instincts that tended to dissolve the subjectivity of the individual into an emotional and existential commitment to the wider whole, as well as Zen-based principles of action focusing on the how more than on the what. Through Herder and through Norinaga, both countries became more and more aware of the *Volk*, its story and its destiny. And in the end, Japan and Germany were to travel remarkably similar roads in the late nineteenth and the early twentieth centuries – roads that took both of them to disaster.

By the end of the nineteenth century, Japan had begun to engage with European philosophy, particularly in what became known as the Kyoto school. The leading figure was Kitaro Nishida, most of whose work was done during the first half of the twentieth century; he died just before the end of the Second World War. He is certainly the most prominent Asian scholar to have engaged with the European world of phenomenology; and he was the first to do more than re-express European ideas in different cultural clothing. In particular, he brought to the examination of the nature of human experience the concept of 'absolute nothingness' that has become something of a hallmark of modern Japanese philosophy. Europeans were used to ideas of relative nothingness (Sartre's famous counter to Heidegger's *Being and Time* was deliberately entitled *Being and Nothingness* – but this very title arguably demonstrates that the concept of nothingness is relative rather than absolute). The roots of the idea of absolute nothingness can be traced deep in Buddhist thought (itself perhaps taking a cue from the Hymn of Creation in the *Rig Veda*). There is a sense in which the concept is a method rather than a principle; for it invites us to probe ever more deeply into the self, and to face all the contingency and anxiety that the threat of absolute nothingness poses to it.

But nevertheless, the Kyoto philosophers were in many ways fellow travellers of Heidegger. Tetsuro Watsuji lived through and beyond the Pacific War. He, in contrast to Nishida, developed the phenomenological project in a much more anthropological direction, wanting to understand human experience from within the specific cultural tradition of Japan. He saw Heidegger as too cerebral (and was surely not wrong in this!); he evolved an alternative concept of being-in-the-world that he called *fudo* – a Japanese word meaning 'climate', including not only the natural climate of a region but also the ways humans there respond to their experience of nature. The attraction of this is obvious as a basis for philosophical enquiry into the human experience of being; it enabled him to explore the close nexus between human being and human culture in specific contexts. He made central use of the Japanese word for human being – *ningen* – which has two poles to it: *nin* on its own is the word for an individual human; *gen* on its own means a shared space. The combined term means for Watsuji that neither an individualist nor a wholly corporatist account of human experience is adequate.[36]

As we have seen, this is not a radically new thought in itself. Watsuji goes on to use it in a more specifically ethical and political context than does Heidegger. The risk lies in the dialectic he describes between the individual and society – between individuals and a specific society with a given 'climate' – which he sees as the essence of being human. Heidegger mostly avoided the risks of particularity, but not always, and he was at his worst when he talked of the people – of the German people, the *Volk* – and of its special spiritual mission to transform the experience of being. For Heidegger, this transformation was needed because of the threat posed by instrumentalist technology to the nature of being. He believed that the German spirit, because of its Romantic awareness (particularly as expressed in its subtlest and deepest form in the poetry of Hölderlin), was uniquely positioned for this mission.

Watsuji walked a different path, but just as near to the cliff edge. For he argued not only that the individual self is not an isolated being (that is, the *nin* only acquires individuality as part of what he called the 'betweenness' of *ningen*), but also that its referent (or its identity) expands as we surrender autonomy – from the individual to the family, to the neighbourhood, to the city and to people at large. At the highest level, it becomes all Japanese people – that is, the nation. Watsuji's concept specifically rejected any external or transcendent vantage point from which to make any judgement at all about the value of the human experience he seeks to analyse: the court of last resort could only be the judgement that resulted from the dialectic within *ningen*. But when both poles of *ningen* were, in effect, subsumed by the state, the dialectic was silenced and totalitarianism was the result. And deep below all of this flowed the current of absolute nothingness, which created the perennial bias towards the surrender of individual autonomy. Heidegger became too involved with Nazi ideology (even though his vision was not, in fact, consistent with the Nazi belief – shared with the Soviet Union – in the power of the machine); Watsuji became too much the proponent of the Greater East Asian Co-Prosperity Sphere, because he allowed the individual to be too completely subsumed in the whole. Neither ever expressed any regret about where the argument had taken them.

A brave new post-war world?

The question about a transcendent vantage point – about universals – is one we shall come back to in the next chapter. But first we need to look at the effect of all the catastrophes of the twentieth century on the sense of self and subjectivity. Japan's Co-Prosperity Sphere has gone; so has Germany's Thousand-Year Reich. The Soviet Union lasted another half century; Maoism lasted for a generation in China, but that too has now gone. In all cases, the artificial distortion of behaviour patterns, brutally imposed both by force, by information control and by systematic indoctrination, has given way to new social orders. And in the new world, new expectations have been set for the role of the individual in society. But there are some striking differences in the response among the various Eurasian cultures – differences born partly of their actual experiences of the twentieth century and, much more deeply, of their different stories about themselves. The past is never quite dead.

To begin with, we should note a profound underlying continuity in the Japanese identity. All through from the very earliest times, the tendency to dissolve the autonomous ego into a set of internal and external relationships has left a sense of the 'no-I' or 'not-I' in the Japanese identity. Internally, the self is something of a relationship – between body and mind, between heart and mind. Externally, the relationship with the other (the object or the other person) is shared between subject and other, such that the self cannot be separated out and is not autonomous in its being or its decisions. This is not the same as a lack of agency: the Zen tradition going back to Dogen made sure of that. But it could and did imply a tendency for responsiveness to displace responsibility, and a propensity to focus on the how rather than on the what. It is not in the least surprising that it was a Japanese philosophical school that set the theme of absolute nothingness at the heart of its phenomenology. Nothingness is the continuing whisper of Buddhism in the Japanese inner ear. As a post-war member of the Kyoto School, Shizuteru Ueda, put it, 'I, not being I, am I.'[37] This is not something Heidegger would ever quite have said; and it is certainly different from the defiance of the European existentialists.

Meanwhile, in the modern China, the language of harmony is in the air again. China has never tolerated nothingness for very long; the individual self always reasserts itself after repression. It is a self that is always conscious of relationships and of their value. *Guanxi*, the pervasive system of networking that criss-crosses Chinese social life beyond the family, is the informal outworking – or, it could even be said, the democratization – of the Confucian order. This networking self has existed for millennia. It was extensively disrupted by Maoist collectivism and by the cult of struggle, but we can now see, with the benefit of a generation's hindsight, that it was never rooted out. Not surprisingly, given the travails of the twentieth century, and particularly of the Maoist era, there has been – in contrast to Japan – virtually no systematic philosophical engagement in the Chinese thought world with the phenomenology that so radically changed Europe. But it is equally unsurprising, given that deeply entrenched Chinese understanding of the self, that one of the most extraordinary religious phenomena of history, the expansion of Christianity in the modern China, has occurred there rather than in the modern Japan. A strong sense of the self is compatible with Confucianism – the Chinese have proven this down the ages – and it is essential to Christianity; Japan's diffused self is much less fertile ground.

In fact, Japan's 'agency of the no-I'[38] is not something that would resonate in post-war European thought, any more than it would resonate in China. Europe in the wake of the Second World War became viscerally suspicious of any appeal to group identities dependent on stories about what binds individuals together. But at the same time, it retains – from its ancient Christian roots and from its Renaissance rediscovery of its Classical Greek heritage – a sense of self that is as strong as China's. Europe may have become the most secular culture on the planet, but its heritage forms its present more than it acknowledges. For Europeans, the individual ego is as assertive as it has ever been in the last five centuries. So much so, indeed, that it is less inclined than ever to accept external moral constraints on its decisions and its actions. Just as Watsuji's Japanese system denies any transcendent vantage point, so does the European post-war mentality. The difference is that Europe's relativism cuts the *individual* adrift. The continuity in Europe's focus on the self and subjectivity is just as striking as the continuity of the Chinese networked self and of the Japanese diffused self that fades into nothingness.

Yet the Europeans face a dilemma: in this sense, unlike *both* the Chinese *and* the Japanese, the European self has lost trust in its external relationships. It first lost its metaphysical framework; it then began to lose its trust in any external authority. In the limit, it loses trust even in Rousseau's sublimated general will. Thus it has become less sure than ever about what it holds to be universal; all that is left is to swim above seventy thousand fathoms of water, but Europe is less and less ready to take Kierkegaard's leap of faith. Europe's most influential contemporary philosopher is probably Jürgen Habermas, who argues passionately against any form of patriotism based on histories, and prosaically calls for a 'communicative rationality' that seeks to discover universals through dialogue among cultures.[39] This may or may not result in a consensus, and he has no answer to what happens if it doesn't. This sums up the bewilderment that is the hallmark of Europe's lost soul – the bewilderment of the individual who is alone. Luther saw the individual as standing alone before God; Kant saw the individual as standing alone, without direct knowledge about God or anything else in the noumenal world. What happens, then, when God seems to have left the stage and when Kant's transcendental ego loses faith in reason? This was Foucault's question about what he called the modern *episteme*.

One answer lies in European literature. Long before most other Eurasian cultures, Europe showed a fascination with the antihero – the figure of satire, defiance and tragedy who asserts the human self, in all its dignity, either in the face of authority that abuses its position or in the face of the randomness of things. The antihero is the quintessential individual. Don Quixote, whom we have already encountered in Chapter 3, was one of the earliest, and was certainly the most influential. But the antihero takes many different forms in the varied European traditions over the period during which the common medieval Christian framework of belief was fragmenting. Grimmelshausen created not one but two great antiheroes: Simplicissimus, whom we met in Chapter 6, and Mother Courage, who then has a second life in all her ambiguity, in the hands of the great German Marxist poet and playwright, Bertolt Brecht.

In the novels of such diverse writers as Balzac, Dickens, Hardy, Zola, Heinrich Mann and Günter Grass, antiheroes fill the pages. And in Camus, the antihero becomes the classic prophet of existentialist defiance, when the central figure of *The Outsider* (is this murderer a hero or a villain?) goes to his death celebrating the 'sublime indifference of the universe'.[40] Meursault's end is a long way from Kant's sense of wonder at the stars above him; and his self feels tortured and meaningless. But it is still fundamentally the transcendental ego that Kant knew, even if unconscious of – or rejecting – the moral law, which Kant believed was in him just as surely as the stars were above him. They are both inheritors of the European consciousness of self.

The antihero not only defies authority (divine or human) but also flirts with evil, which has a special place in European culture. Only Russia shares this fascination with evil: for Confucian China, human nature is essentially good; for Buddhist Japan, the nothingness at the centre of being drains both good and evil of ultimate meaning; for Indian philosophy, the illusory nature of experience has a similar effect, with the difference that ultimate being is not illusory and the end of it all is the blissful and ineffable union of *moksha*; for Islam, the devil seeks to tempt the faithful to turn away from God's path of goodness, but in the end all is from God. In all these cultures there is plenty of room for the devils, demons and malevolent spirits that derive from humanity's ancient sense of enchantment – all of which have also been features of popular belief in Christian cultures down the ages. Nevertheless, there is a profoundly important difference: for the Christian cultures, uniquely, the evil is not just 'out there'; it is also deep within the self. Theologians, both Western and Orthodox, have seen the self-centredness of the self as at the core of this story ever since the earliest phases of Christian history (in fact, from the writings of Paul onwards[41]). It is therefore hardly surprising that a culture that puts the individual self at the centre of its attention is also so conscious of the power of evil.

Three emblematic figures of the European tradition betray its continuing flirtation with evil: the Satan of Milton's *Paradise Lost*; Goethe's *Faust*; and Nietzsche's *Übermensch*. In *Paradise Lost*, it is Satan who plays the role of antihero: Satan defies the ultimate authority of God and knowingly – even happily – accepts the price:

> Hail horrors, hail Infernal world, and thou profoundest Hell,
> Receive thy new Possessor: One who brings
> A mind not to be changed by Place or Time.
> The mind is its own place, and in itself
> Can make a Heav'n of Hell, a Hell of Heav'n . . .
> Here we may reign secure, and in my choice

To reign is worth ambition though in Hell:
Better to reign in Hell, than serve in Heav'n.[42]

This is the clearest possible assertion of the right of the self to self-rule. The mind is its own place, and it can make its own heaven out of hell. No other character in *Paradise Lost* is as interesting and alive as is Satan.

Goethe's Faust is a child of the Enlightenment, created over a century later than Milton's Satan. For Goethe, the project is not to 'justify the ways of God to men', as it was for Milton.[43] Rather, it is an extraordinary journey in search of experience. This time it is the human, not the tempter Mephistopheles, who is interesting and unquestionably alive. The journey includes the tragedy of Faust's fatal seduction of the innocent young Gretchen. As this story unfolds in painful intensity, she goes to her death for the murder of her baby; yet, as she does, somehow she grows in stature, while he is diminished. But he continues his journey, becoming less a specific flesh-and-blood figure and more a symbol of the spirit of his age – restless, this-worldly, inquisitive, domineering, acquisitive and action-orientated. The purpose of life is not just to philosophize but to taste the world and leave a mark.

His journey is crammed full of allusion and allegory. After the tragedy of Gretchen, he continues through scenes that represent the corrupt and decadent world of the European *ancien régime*; through his encounter with Helen of Troy (in whom he discovers a bliss that he knows cannot endure, because it is ideal and unreal); through a plunge back into a prescient allegory of the tempestuous upheavals of nineteenth-century Europe; to a final act that has Faust undertaking what is at one level a banal engineering project (at the cost of innocent lives) and at another level a metaphor for the human desire to subdue the earth. His final apotheosis is strange and ambiguous: his soul is taken up to a heaven where the figure of God now seems absent, but where the Mater Gloriosa, the Queen of Heaven from Catholic piety, receives him and where he is transformed and redeemed. Goethe was in no sense a conventional Christian; but this vivid, mysterious ending is certainly not pure irony, either. Goethe's highly unorthodox use of the iconography of grace and redemption is ambivalent and open-ended, as is the very final 'mystical chorus':

Everything transient
Is only an image;
The unattainable
Is happening here;
What cannot be described
Is now being done;
The eternal feminine
Draws us on.[44]

Faust is a Protean figure. The original Faust, the one captured by Christopher Marlowe, is one of the great medieval myths and morality plays; in Goethe's hands, he becomes a metaphor for the ambivalent outworkings of the European Enlightenment, for the spirit of the modern urbanized era. From the vantage point of two centuries later, he can be seen as the incarnation of the German tragedy, or of the European identity, or even of the human spirit more generally. And his ending in an ambiguous redemption by the spirit of the feminine is a parable whose full depth of meaning we are only now beginning to discover. The ambivalence is the key: is Faust a hero? Not in the Classical Greek sense. Is he an antihero? Yes, and no. He defies easy categorization. Is he the unruly schoolchild, kicking over the traces for the hell of it? Is he the 'rebel without a cause'?[45] Is he Dionysus? Or is he just Nietzsche's Übermensch?

Just Nietzsche's Übermensch? Friedrich Nietzsche was the brilliant son of a German Lutheran pastor, raised in what seems to have been a devout and gentle household. His father died of some kind of brain disease when he was just thirty-five and Friedrich was just five. It was a hammer blow he never quite got over.[46] Later, in his early forties but only three years before his own mental collapse, he came into some money as a result of a court judgement. The first thing he did, after paying off some debts, was to buy a tombstone for his father, engraved with the quotation 'Love never fails', from one of Paul's most famous purple passages.[47] This from the man who had pronounced that God is dead, and who had condemned Christianity for its cult of weakness and its hypocritical value system. It is hard not to believe that Nietzsche's anger with God is an anger whose seed was sown by the painful death of his father.

The Übermensch is Nietzsche's embodiment of his credo: God is dead; human beings have a will to power; this will – this drive – is the governing principle of the healthy life; it is also a will to truth (the truth that fulfilment of human potential lies not in the conventional Christian morality of weakness but – to quote the title of one of his most compelling books – beyond good and evil). The authentic person is a free spirit, self-determined and self-creating; thus the healthy life creates itself, which in turn means that aesthetics are an expression of the will to power (and in particular Nietzsche sees architecture as 'the intoxication of the great will that is demanding to become art'[48]).

And, finally, the healthy life is to be affirmed, not denied. In this, Nietzsche stakes out a position against Schopenhauer, who is the other major *enfant terrible* of nineteenth-century European thought about the human self. Arthur Schopenhauer was not widely known in his lifetime, but after his death in 1860, his major work, *The World as Will and Representation*, seemed suddenly to strike a chord that resounded throughout the rest of the century. Nietzsche was at first an enthusiastic convert to Schopenhauer's view that the world is driven by the will to live (which became, of course, Nietzsche's will to power), and also to his conclusion that this inevitably leads to dissatisfaction or to disillusionment (for either our will is not satisfied – or if it is, we lose interest). Schopenhauer's way out from this dilemma was through the aesthetic contemplation of nature and art (especially music). Famously, his influence on Wagner led Nietzsche to an early fascination with Wagner in his turn.

Nietzsche's enthusiasm for Schopenhauer's Indian-inspired life-denial did not last (nor did his adulation of Wagner). He ends by being the most powerful advocate of a very assertive individualism that, in the end, became sinister in its implications. In one of his most provocative works, for example, he asks:

Who will attain anything great if he does not find in himself the strength and the will to *inflict* great suffering? Being able to suffer is the *least* thing; weak women and even slaves often achieve virtuosity in that. But not to perish of internal distress and uncertainty when one inflicts great suffering and hears the cry of this suffering – that is great, that belongs to greatness.[49]

Nietzsche is not a consistent writer of systematic philosophy, but his main theme is clear, and he writes his polemics with unrivalled brilliance. He cannot reasonably be blamed for the Nazi world view; but some of what he said was kindling for the fire. And Leni Riefenstahl's unnervingly powerful film about the Nazi Nuremberg rallies, *The Triumph of the Will*, has a title that cannot help but evoke Nietzsche's central thesis.

Was all this just a European sickness, born of the European fascination with the self and subjectivity? No: the will to power is hardly just a European phenomenon. Nietzsche's analysis of the drives of the human psyche uncovered some difficult truths that have shown themselves in behaviour in all the cultures of Eurasia. His arguments for going 'beyond good and evil' are different from those of Tetsuro Watsuji; but the end result was equally disturbing. And the will to power, together with the readiness for violence, runs through the writings and actions of Lenin, Stalin and Mao.

All of this begs an obvious question. Nietzsche was a cultural relativist:

> Since humans no longer believe that a God is guiding the destinies of the world as a whole, . . . humanity must set itself ecumenical goals, embracing the whole earth. The older morality . . . demands from the individual those actions that we desire from all people – a nice, naive idea, as if everyone without further ado would know which sort of action would benefit the whole of humankind . . . Rather, in the interest of ecumenical goals, for whole stretches of human time, special tasks, perhaps even evil tasks, would have to be set. In any event, . . . we must discover first a *knowledge of the conditions of culture*, a knowledge surpassing all previous knowledge, as a scientific standard for ecumenical goals. This is the enormous task of the great minds of the next century.[50]

There is something uncomfortably prescient about this. The Third Reich saw itself as carrying out special – even evil – tasks in the interest of its definition of ecumenical goals. The Leninist, Stalinist and Maoist hand also fits all too neatly into that glove. As Mao notoriously put it:

a revolution is not like inviting people to dinner, or writing an essay, or painting a picture or doing embroidery ... To right the wrong it is necessary to exceed the proper limits; the wrong cannot be righted without doing so.[51]

Nietzsche would have nodded his agreement.

At the same time, beyond the dreadful twentieth century, we find that the task of setting what Nietzsche called ecumenical goals is more urgent than ever; and though we should certainly reject his call to do evil in pursuit of them, he was surely right about the essential need for a knowledge of the conditions of culture as a precondition for those goals. One century later than he envisaged, this is still the task – in what is, however, a much more open, connected, pluralistic world than he could ever have imagined or desired. The task is to move from the first person singular to the first person plural – without dissolving the person.

9

The end of history?

So this is where we are now: Eurasia is the world's largest land mass, has the bulk of the world's population and produces the bulk of the world's economic output. It has become again the political centre of gravity of the world. All the great cultures of the world have their origin in Eurasia, and – except for one – still have their centre of gravity there. (The exception is Christianity, whose centre of gravity is now in the Americas and Africa; what is left behind is a Europe profoundly unsure about its identity.) As Eurasia becomes more and more connected, both physically and virtually, those cultures are becoming increasingly aware of one another. Eurasia is also becoming urbanized. The majority of Eurasians – from Ireland to Vladivostok – now live in cities, with less and less direct connection to the natural world that used to be their ancestors' home. The ancient cultures were all imbued with an unquestioning sense of belonging to the natural order of things; but city life and the resulting spread of knowledge has slowly broken down the integrated metaphysics that framed the thought worlds of East Asia, South Asia, the Muslim *ummah* and Christendom. Now, most of us are migrants, uprooted from where we grew up, even if we still carry our individual memories of home and our folk memories of a lost way of life.

We are ambivalent about our new urban life, which seems simultaneously to offer so much opportunity and so much uncertainty. Yet our urban selves are not just unrelated, disconnected molecules. Urban life is not simply a rupture from the past. In fact, the way we think about our individual identity – in terms of such categories as gender, ethnicity, occupation and our culture (or religion) – may not have changed fundamentally. These categories:

> necessarily constitute the collective identities that most saliently
> define us to ourselves and to others, as in different historical versions

246

they always have . . . The 'only' difference from the past, which however makes all the difference, is that knowing this enables us to distinguish what is fixed and what is not in our identities, and to exercise our freedom to choose and to create accordingly.[1]

So *what* we think about each of these elements in the identities of ourselves and others has been, and will continue to be, deeply affected by urbanization. There is surely no more dramatic evidence of this than the empowerment of women, as we noted in Chapter 2. At the same time, our identities continue to be shaped by collective cultural experience; and it is equally striking that national cultural identities have grown stronger even as the pace of urbanization and connection has quickened. Those cultural identities are shaped by a past that is partly mythical but never dead; the only question is whether it is recognized or not. And we know – from both our individual development and from our national histories – that a past that is not recognized or confronted honestly is dangerous to our identity. These national cultural identities have remained stronger than the universals that might have been expected to emerge from the common experience of urbanization. Nationhood is not dead (only among Europe's intelligentsia is it regarded as a dangerous spectre from the past) and, in fact, it has never been more alive.

So, once again, we live in a Westphalian world, with Eurasia at its centre. The world stage is now dominated by a group of major powers, all of which – except one – are Eurasian. The exception is America, which is not only a major global power but also a major Eurasian power. Westphalia is an order that in effect calls into question universal values: *cujus regio, ejus religio.* Indeed, for all the connectivity – indeed, precisely because of that connectivity – we are in some ways more conscious of differences than ever. The threats to stability are obvious: the geopolitical stresses as the tectonic plates rub against one another; the problem of the commons; and deeper still, the differences in world view that are in effect apparently competing universals. In particular, the great question about America and China and the second great question about China and India involve all three of these levels of threat.

Yet there are also profound commonalities of human experience – across cultures and down the ages. Humans everywhere know what it is to experience joy, love, loss, transience, tragedy and the pity of things. We also know what it is to be on a spiritual journey with a sense that the destination is unclear and that the risks on the way are many and varied. In all cultures, we know about odysseys. All cultures also know that the world was once enchanted, and still is for many as they seek to control their daily lives; and we also know about the ubiquitous human need for rituals that take us beyond ourselves. And some, at least, in all cultures know the pull of the mystical, which manifests itself in remarkably similar ways everywhere. Not all of this is lost in translation.

But not all is the same either. In particular, the Europeans have been on a journey of discovery of the self and subjectivity. This is a journey that has produced much philosophizing, as well as a remarkable outpouring of artistic creativity – particularly in literature from the seventeenth century onwards. The philosophy is perhaps as much a reflection as a shaper of the intellectual mood; it has always had a limited audience, and most people most of the time have just got on with their lives. Yet that intellectual mood has surely been the eddy on the surface of a deeper current, the most visible literary manifestation of which has been the rise of the antihero, who is the would-be embodiment of everyone.

So where next on the journey? Have we reached the end of history? Notoriously, Francis Fukuyama posed the question when, in 1989, he argued that the world was living through the early stages of the final triumph of the liberal democratic order. His essay was written before the full extent of the Chinese resurgence became clear. Three decades later, it is far less obvious that the world is converging on a common set of universals, even in the political and economic domains with which Fukuyama was concerned – let alone at the deeper level of the metaphysical questions about individuality, individualism and human relationships. And if no such convergence is to be expected, then the implication is that the world faces a Westphalian stasis for the rest of this century – with all its fragility, even brittleness, and with all the consequent risks of violent breakdown.

But, in fact, there is no reason to believe that Eurasia's order will be static. Indeed, many have argued that the prospect is for the opposite of what Fukuyama posited: that the rise of Asia in general (and of China in particular) is inexorable; and that the West in general (and Europe in particular) is doomed. All roads seem to lead to Beijing[2] and America's day is done.[3] There are plenty of contrary voices, of course: prognoses of dire trouble ahead for China are readily available.[4] Conversely, there are those who look through the extreme dysfunctionality of American politics at the country's immense creative dynamism.[5] But the general impression is of an Asia in the ascendant and of a West in decline, at least relatively.

The sense of malaise and of decline in the West is not new. Cultural pessimism could be smelt in the atmosphere of Europe and Russia in the late nineteenth century and is clearly evident, for example, in the plays and stories of Chekhov and in the novels of Thomas Mann. Then, in the wake of the shattering impact of the First World War, came the book that was emblematic of the new mood – Oswald Spengler's *Der Untergang des Abendlandes* (*The Decline of the West*), whose first volume was published in a Germany reeling under the weight of the huge human and economic cost of the war, in the summer of 1918. Spengler was a philosopher of history: his overall thesis was that history is the story of cultures, which are like biological organisms in that they grow and decay and have limited lifespans. In the case of Europe, he argued that the rationalism of the Enlightenment had moved from excessive optimism to excessive scepticism, and the religious impulse that had formed the culture in the first place was giving way to what he called a 'second religiousness' in which the broader population would rebel against the intellectual elite and its rationalism. The final step would be the rise of a new 'Caesar'; however, this is not a sign of rejuvenation but of a culture in its death throes. Spengler was no friend of the open society and had fascist – though not Nazi – leanings. His ideas became immensely influential in the turbulent decades between the two World Wars, not just in Germany, and indeed not just in Europe. Few would now resonate with his sweeping judgements; but some of what he said sounds remarkably prescient in a world of social media and fake news.

His was a time when historians searched for the patterns of history. Spengler had a marked influence on others who were in their turn formative figures of their time. Perhaps the most obvious example is the British historian Arnold Toynbee. He is little read now; but in the mid-twentieth century, this prolific writer may well have been one of the most widely read scholars in any discipline. The centrepiece of his work was his ten-volume *Study of History*, published over a period of three decades up to 1961. This magnum opus looked at the rise and fall of civilizations in every continent from the very earliest to those that were prominent in his own day. His overarching thesis was that civilizations grow through an energetic response to specific challenges led by a 'creative minority' and that they decline as that creative minority degenerates into a comfortable dominant minority and becomes too complacent to face the next challenge. It is not necessary to accept Toynbee's world view to acknowledge the continuing relevance of some of this to the Europe of the twenty-first century, as it looks back to the heady days of the visionaries who brought the post-war European project into being. And his template for growth under the leadership of a creative minority could be applied without much difficulty to the modern China (but if so, then his scheme of things also represents a longer-term challenge for China).

Both Spengler and Toynbee sought long-term patterns and what they saw in those patterns was alarming for the European culture within which they worked. Others have also sought for patterns that span centuries, but have reached more sanguine views about the present. Thus, the French historian Fernand Braudel adopted a carefully articulated approach to history based on three layers of time; the very long-term effects of the particular geographic environment; the centuries-long effects of culture, sociology and power structures; and the much shorter term – and relatively evanescent – effects of specific historical events. But Braudel was no Spenglerian pessimist; on the contrary, he was above all unabashed in his love of his own country. For him, '*la France profonde*' had something eternal – or at least, eternally precious – about it.

Meanwhile, in the Islamic thought world, the Algerian moral philosopher Malek Bennabi, a contemporary of both Toynbee and Braudel, evolved a theory of the rise and fall of civilizations that focused on the critical generative role of a new religious impulse in the birth of a new culture. What he termed the 'age of the spirit' was then followed by an 'age of reason' as a civilization expanded. In this age of reason, the religious impulse weakens and society begins to lose its moral base, even as it develops intellectually and politically. Bennabi traced the decline of

Islam to the gradual loss of impetus in Spain. He had no magic wand; his approach to renewal called for individual human commitment, honest appropriation of the Muslim cultural heritage – and a recognition that this would all take time.[6] Bennabi wrote against the background of the Algerian experience of colonization; but the challenge of securing the moral base in the age of reason – to use his terminology – resonates well beyond the *ummah*, from Europe at one end of the continent to Japan at the other in the twenty-first century.

None of these historians had a theory so overarching as to entail a theory of human history as a whole. In fact, all this fits with a cyclical – or even just an episodic – view of the longer-term story of humanity as a whole. It is of a piece with the famous opening sentence of China's *The Romance of the Three Kingdoms*: 'empires wax and wane, states cleave asunder and coalesce' – or perhaps with the opening passage of the early thirteenth-century Japanese *Tale of the Heike*:

> the hue of the flowers of the teak tree declares that they who flourish must be brought low. Yes, the proud ones are but for a moment, like an evening dream in springtime. The mighty are destroyed at the last, they are but as dust before the wind.[7]

The end of the age – again and again

In fact, every major Eurasian culture had some inkling that empires would not continue ad infinitum. In most cases, however, this took the form not of a sophisticated philosophy of history but of religious forebodings of one form or another. Even in Japan, there have been periods when a mood of decay – *mappo*, as the Japanese called it, meaning a strong sense of the decay of the *dharma*, as foreseen in the traditional Buddhist scheme of things – was pervasive. Both the individual salvation promised by the Pure Land School and the social gospel of Nichiren Buddhism were responses to this *mappo*; only Zen, for which the specific moment and the action were all that counted, blithely ignored it. And particularly in China and in Europe, it took the form of millenarianism: sectarian movements with inspirational leaders who foretold a coming crisis of cosmic significance that would usher in a new age. Religious millenarianism represented a continual threat to the political and social order. Certain themes occur again and again in both cultures. In both, for example, there is a repeated tendency to see history as having three phases. One variant has a first age of long-lost innocence and equality, followed by the present age of corruption and oppression, then a final age that is about to irrupt and bring an end to all the sufferings of the present age. Another variant has a first phase in which there is an impending cosmic crisis because of the presence of so much evil in the world, followed by a great battle between a supernatural saviour and the forces of evil, before a final age of joy, peace and plenty.

Repeatedly over the last two millennia of Chinese history, both Daoism and Buddhism produced millenarian movements that proclaimed a threefold view of history along one or other of those lines. Thus, for example, as long ago as the second century of the Common Era, a widespread and violent uprising against the Han government took its inspiration from a Daoist text known as the *Taiping jing* ('Scripture of the heavenly peace'). This describes the ideal society and implies that heavenly forces are poised to renew the world and bring about a mystical new order in which all will be well. In later centuries, both Daoist and Buddhist movements produced visions of saviours who would change history. The most significant was Maitreya, the Buddha 'who is yet to come' to redeem the world. Maitreya gained prominence, in the early Indian Mahayana conception, as the Buddha who would appear at the zenith – in the far distant future – of the great cosmic cycle of growth and decay. Chinese Buddhism reimagined this pattern (as it reimagined so much else in the Buddhism it took from India): Maitreya would appear not at the zenith but at the nadir, when the cycle was on the turn from decay and decline. And not in the far distant future. In China, a sense of imminence – born, as in the case of earlier Daoist movements, of economic distress and suffering – turned this figure of Buddhist eschatology into the standard bearer of repeated millenarian movements that threatened to upend society in defiance of the ruling Confucian orthodoxy.

All through the medieval period in China, Maitreya lurked as the forthcoming saviour; and every now and then someone would take it on themselves to foment rebellion in his name. The most successful was the rebel who overthrew the Yuan (Mongol) regime and became the first Ming emperor in 1368. He had carried the colours of the secret White Lotus Society, which was dedicated to watching for the revelation of Maitreya. But the typically Chinese habit of syncretization ensured that Buddhist and Daoist millenarian sects gradually intermingled; gradually, their motifs and ideas fused together (absorbing themes from other millenarian sources too, notably from Manichaeism, which had filtered into China from Iran during the Tang Dynasty). They became known collectively as the White Lotus. At the centre of the cluster of beliefs that loosely connected them emerged the figure of the Eternal Mother, who would rescue those of her children who turned to her, bringing them to her Native Land of True Emptiness, where they would enjoy perfect bliss. Maitreya eventually becomes just an emissary or agent of this Mother with her background in folk religion.[8] White Lotus movements continued to be active until well into the twentieth century; they were regularly suppressed by the authorities, who clearly understood the challenge they represented to the Confucian order. But while they never lost their revolutionary potential, the Buddhist eschatology with its enormous cyclical patterns of cosmic growth and decay of the *dharma* was submerged beneath the figure of the Eternal Mother. What was left was the continuing struggle between order – Confucian order – and inspired but anarchic upheaval.

By far the deadliest challenge of all to the Confucian order came in the nineteenth century, at a time when the Qing Dynasty was already struggling to survive the onslaught of the Europeans and was in severe danger of losing the Mandate of Heaven. This time, it was a crude Christian heresy that provided the initial religious impulse. Hong Xiuquan was from a poor rural background; mystical visions experienced while he was ill persuaded him that he was the younger brother of Jesus Christ. His charisma founded a movement of rebellion – the Taiping ('Great Peace') – which gained momentum through some early victories over Qing government forces. It spread rapidly, took Nanjing and made it the capital of the new Heavenly Kingdom of Great Peace. The Taiping belief system was a strange amalgam of recast Christian ideas, some Buddhist themes and a strong component of Confucianism redescribed in theistic rather than in humanistic terms.[9] The combination of a radical millenarianism, total mobilization of the population of areas they controlled, and large-scale fighting over wide areas led to loss of life in the tens of millions. It was by far the worst human catastrophe of the nineteenth century anywhere on the planet.

After fourteen years of devastation, the Heavenly Kingdom of Great Peace collapsed in mayhem when government forces finally recaptured Nanjing. The Taiping seared the folk memory of China. Its mobilization of the peasantry was the harbinger of what was to come under the communist insurgency of the twentieth century; in the end its millenarianism was less important than its social radicalism. Viewed through a modern Chinese prism, after the restoration of order following the Cultural Revolution, it is one more reason to keep a wary eye on any metaphysical system – Buddhist, Christian or Muslim – which claims supernatural insight about the end of history.

Yet modern Chinese thought, both before and after the rise of the Communist Party, has imbibed a strong dose of eschatology – of the sense that history has a direction of travel and is heading to a climax – from European sources. Thus, for example, soon after the First World War the philosopher Liang Shuming at Peking University was expounding a three-phase view of history, in the first phase of which the European 'orientation of the human will' strove to subdue nature; the second phase would be the era of the Chinese orientation of the will, which sought conformity to the natural order; and the third would be the Indian orientation, which sets aside the human will altogether and seeks union with the true inner nature and the whole cosmic will.[10] Mao, needless to say, did not accept such a non-materialist and passive view of China's place in history. His eschatology was fundamentally conflictual and violent: the future was contained in the contradictions of the present and would be created through trial and error, using the art of war.[11] There is nothing completely new under the sun: the direct and indirect parentage of this view of history is traceable in Chinese thought to the Qin Emperor and to Sun Tzu, and draws on wellsprings in European thought from Rousseau to Hegel, and from Darwin to Spencer.[12]

India tells a markedly different story: there has been little in the way of millenarian upheaval at any stage in its history. There was always plenty of peasant distress, just as there was in China or in Europe. India certainly did not lack the mythological source-material to create millenarian visions. In the *Mahabharata*, the monkey god Hanuman describes four ages of the cosmos: an age of perfection and equality; followed by two more ages of successive decline, of weakening in the moral order of the *dharma*, leading to the breakdown of the *varnas* (the divinely ordered structure of human occupations that underpinned the caste system); and in the final age, the *kaliyuga*, chaos and suffering are the result of a world turned upside down. But then the cycle of ages starts all over again; the forces of chaos are defeated (in one of the Indian texts an emanation of Vishnu descends to earth to defeat evil and to strengthen the *dharma*), and the *varna* structure is restored. The ages come and go, and all remains the same. Everything unfolds over huge timescales; the sense of imminence that is so characteristic of Chinese millenarianism has been all but entirely missing in India. This encouraged a tendency for communities to seek religious emotional release through *bhakti*, and for the individual to seek *moksha* through a personal journey of mysticism. Some have also argued that the social structure of traditional rural India militated against the egalitarian bonds that are so crucial to the formation of millenarian movements. There was thus no millenarian pathway from misery. Or as Max Weber put it, Hinduism has no 'last day'.[13]

The only significant movement in Indian history that did have some of the characteristics associated with millenarianism was Sikhism. This extraordinary phenomenon was not born of an overwhelming sense that the age was coming to an end. Rather, it was Guru Nanak's inspiration that there was only one world truth ('there is no Hindu, there is no Muslim', he declared). But he founded a commune that became a movement, which in later generations evolved a military presence and built up an empire in the Punjab, in defiance of the Mughals of the late seventeenth and early eighteenth centuries. Internal disorder contributed to its collapse later on in the nineteenth century as the British consolidated their control. The Sikh Khalsa – a collective body of initiated Sikhs – perhaps bears some comparison with the Japanese samurai in its recognition of a military duty sitting alongside a spiritual focus on the purity of the mind. As one modern Sikh commentator describes it, Sikhism is 'not about hearing voices from God, but it is about changing the nature of the human mind, and anyone can achieve direct experience and spiritual perfection at any time'.[14] But one of the five items of clothing traditionally worn by an initiated Sikh is the *kirpan* – the dagger, which was to be carried at all times. Nevertheless, the Sikh Khalsa was not millenarian: it was not founded on the conviction of an imminent cosmic change in history. Sikhism is – notwithstanding doctrinal differences from mainstream Hinduism – deeply rooted in Indian metaphysics.

Its great opponents, the Mughals, were of course inheritors of a very different world view. Islam, like Christianity, has its imagery of a last day of history, namely the Day of Reckoning, when all will be judged according to their deeds. Its traditions – though not the Qur'an itself – have vivid imagery of an apocalypse. Jesus, who, according to the Qur'an, was not crucified but taken up into heaven (this difference on a question of history being arguably the fundamental point of divergence between Christianity and Islam), returns to fight the final great battle against the forces of evil, symbolized by the figure of the *dajjal*, the evil being whom Jesus slays near Jerusalem. The traditions also speak of the Mahdi (the rightly guided one), a role at first credited to religious and political leaders, but which later became a messianic figure who would appear in the east with a mighty army to purify the *ummah* and establish peace and justice. Mahdis have repeatedly appeared in Muslim history (including the one who brought down General Gordon at Khartoum in a famous and dramatic episode of British colonial history). Meanwhile, Shiite Islam has its own specific millenarian vision, of the time when the Twelfth Imam, who went into 'occultation' in the ninth century, returns to right the wrongs of the *ummah* and avenge the oppression of the Shiites. There have been times in history when the *ummah* has seethed with expectation and a sense that the apocalypse is imminent. This was the case, for example, at the first millennium of the Islamic calendar in 1591/2 CE; and about a century earlier than that, a respected scholar forecast the end of all things in the Muslim year 1500 (2076 CE) – in an intriguing parallel to the messianic fervour that swept Europe at about the same time, in the run-up to the year 1500 of the Christian calendar.[15]

Notwithstanding this and other points of contact between Christian and Islamic millenarianism, there is a profound difference between the

Muslim and Christian perspectives on the end of history. Right from the first, Christianity nurtured an expectation of the imminent return of Jesus Christ: his coming would inaugurate a thousand-year kingdom of the just, over which he would reign in glory; and at the end, he and all the saints would enter heaven, while the wicked would be condemned to eternal damnation. Millenarianism remained widespread in the Christian churches of the first three centuries – the details of what was expected might vary somewhat but the imminence of Christ's coming was the essential theme. The expectation is clear in the New Testament, whose Greek text took over without translation what appears to be the original Aramaic chant of the early Christians: *Maranatha!* (Come!).[16] So central was this expectation of Christ's return that it became one of the tenets of the Nicene Creed; thus it is embedded in the doctrine of the Christian churches to this day. There is no parallel to this either in the early history of Islam or in the metaphysics of India and China.

But gradually, expectations were adjusting, at least with regard to the imminence of Christ's coming. Moreover, the growing influence of Greek philosophy in Christian thought, as the religion spread out from its origins in Judaea and into the wider Mediterranean world, moved the centre of gravity of its theology towards a much more spiritual and allegorical interpretation of its foundational texts. In the eastern churches, millenarianism largely died out in the fourth century. This took longer in the Latin churches, but in the end, the result was similar. Augustine sees the great battle that pitted Christ and his saints against the wicked as being the struggle of the Church against the world, and in *The City of God* he allegorizes the book of Revelation's depiction of the thousand-year reign of Christ, rather than treating it as literal truth. Augustine's immense authority sets the tone for subsequent theology; so did the fact that the Roman Catholic Church was to become the moral authority of empire. As in the east, millenarianism was largely marginalized.

Not entirely, however. As the year 1500 approached, the Dominican friar Savonarola stirred the passions of Florence with sermons condemning the corruption of the Church and the evils of tyrants, and with promises of power and glory through God's special blessing if the city reformed itself and lived a life worthy of its calling. He was an extraordinarily charismatic figure who crammed the cathedral with listeners to his sermons. Among his followers, if Vasari is to be believed, was the artist Botticelli.[17] But in the end Savonarola proved to be a shooting star and died at the stake as the secular powers regained their grip.

In the last analysis, although Savonarola used vivid mystic imagery, he was a proclaimer of reform, not of the end of history. And indeed, by his time the demand for reform was becoming unstoppable. Within two decades of his death, Luther's ninety-five theses against indulgences unleashed the events that culminated in the break-up of the Catholic Christian world in Europe. Protestantism brought a renewed interest in millenarian thought, and several movements on its margins opted out of secular life in order to be in the right community, or place, at the right time to welcome the return of Christ. But with one spectacular exception, such groups did not for the most part even try to impose a new messianic kingdom on the world. The exception was the bizarre takeover in the early sixteenth century of the city of Münster (scene of treaty-making, as we have seen in Chapter 6, in the following century). A group of radical millenarians proclaimed a Kingdom of Zion in which all adults were compulsorily rebaptized, property was to be held in common and polygamy legalized – all in anticipation of the new Kingdom of Christ. The experiment did not last long, and Münster was retaken by the forces of the bishop they had expelled. The secular order was soon restored.

But Europe was prone to agrarian uprisings just as China was. The marginalization of millenarianism meant that the leaders of movements like the Jacquerie in France or the Peasant Rebellion in England – both in the late fourteenth century – were largely motivated by economic, social and political demands rather than by any belief that they were bringing on the end of the age. So were the leaders of the largest such uprising in Western Europe before the French Revolution – the German Peasant War of the early sixteenth century. This was the first war of the printing age, so that their manifestos were distributed in their tens of thousands across the areas of conflict. In particular, the 'Twelve Articles', written by a preacher and a furrier, used the idea of godly law to critique the present conditions of their own society. This certainly made their demands radical, but its central focus was not on proclaiming the imminence of the coming millennial Kingdom of Christ.

The age of the Spirit: Hegel and his enduring influence

But the thought world of Christian Europe was nonetheless alive – not so much with apocalyptic visions of the end time as with discussion about the shape and direction of history under the aegis of God. Three hundred years before all the excitement around the year 1500 and the following century of vicious religious wars, an Italian mystic, biblical commentator, theologian and philosopher named Gioacchino da Fiore (Joachim of Fiore) proposed a theory of history that has echoed down the ages ever since. A slender but recognizable thread connects his ideas with human experience as apparently far removed as that of twentieth-century China. For he saw history as unfolding in three phases, which – on the analogy of the Christian doctrine of the Holy Trinity – he called the ages of the Father, the Son and the Holy Spirit. The age of the Father was the time of the Old Testament, when humanity was subject to the laws of God; the age of the Son was inaugurated by the incarnation of Christ and represented by the teachings of the New Testament. What was new was that Joachim believed he was living through the transition from this age to a third age – that of the Holy Spirit – when humanity would come into direct contact with God and enjoy the glorious freedom promised to the children of God in the New Testament. A new dispensation of universal love would make the letter of New Testament teaching redundant; and the institutional Church would be governed by the 'order of the just', which some of his followers later identified with the new Franciscan order.

It is easy to see why this vision of the future would be controversial; and, in fact, his ideas were attacked repeatedly after his death in 1202 (by Thomas Aquinas among others). But he himself was never condemned; he was popular in his lifetime and enjoyed a lively dialogue with more than one pope as well as with other church heavyweights. His description of life in the age of the Holy Spirit is not far from Augustine's vision of the City of God: his contrast between the freedom of the just in the perfect society and the reign of justice in an imperfect society has clear parallels in classical Chinese thought; it would also become a familiar theme of Enlightenment debate about society and the individual. But the most strikingly distinctive and enduring aspect of his thought was his scheme of history – the idea that history has a discernible pattern and direction *and not merely an eventual end*. The existing Christian scheme had already moved beyond the millenarianism of the early churches to an acceptance that the experience of living 'in the last days' would, for all practical purposes, last for the foreseeable future. But Christianity – like Islam but unlike Indian or Chinese metaphysics – still presumed there would be an end to all things. It also presumed that the revelation of God's truth and purposes was already complete. Joachim gave this a new twist: the New Testament might be the final revelation, but the age of the Holy Spirit would see humans understanding the deep meaning of God's words for the first time. History, in other words, had a future to it. This future would not be a reversion to some past golden age, as in the immense cycles of the Indian cosmic view; nor would it be a process of continuous coming into being as envisaged in the neo-Confucian metaphysics of Zhu Xi (for whom *yin* and *yang* come into mysterious union such that the multiplicity of things is produced and reproduced).[18] The future would be different from the present as well. In short, there is a forward momentum to history and the present is not the last word.

The question of the future and of the direction of history was thus coming into focus – as an essential concern, in fact, for the new learning of the Renaissance. This question would not go away, even as Europe began to leave behind the medieval consensus it had built on a blend of Christian eschatology and Aristotelian metaphysics. And a jump forwards to the early nineteenth century brings us face to face with a thinker whose debt to the conceptual framework first fashioned by Joachim is obvious, and whose ideas have arguably done more than any others to shape the deep structure of the way the modern world thinks about its history: Georg Wilhelm Friedrich Hegel.

Hegel was a philosopher through and through, with a convoluted and turgid style of writing that makes his thought hard to access. A good deal of what he argued now looks very passé: his views on law and the role of the state, for example, could make him seem almost like a propagandist for the Prussian state. But his most striking achievement came in his first major book, *Phänomenologie des Geistes*, whose very title poses a problem of translation, as it can mean either 'The Phenomenology of Spirit' or

'The Phenomenology of *the* Spirit'. (As a further complication, *Geist* can mean 'mind' as well as 'spirit'.) This book, together with his *Encyklopädie der Philosophischen Wissenschaften im Grundrisse* (*Encyclopaedia of the Philosophical Sciences in Basic Outline*), set the terms of debate from then onwards. It influenced even those who rejected it outright (Schopenhauer and Nietzsche, for example) in that it was impossible simply to ignore it. Marx rejected its metaphysics, substituting his own materialist alternative, and yet worked within the conceptual framework of Hegel's dialectics; Mao radically upended Marx's materialist dynamic, using a Hegelian conceptual framework in so doing. When Mao met Kissinger in 1973 as America and China felt their way towards establishing normal relations, their three-hour conversation covered almost all the geopolitical issues of the day, but they also found time to touch on Hegel's view of freedom and his dialectic approach.[19] When Francis Fukuyama asked his famous question about whether the end of history had been reached with the collapse of the Soviet Union, he was asking a Hegelian question.

Hegel's ideas are complex and wide ranging, and this is not the place to give them and the controversies they caused anything like a comprehensive treatment. But underlying all his work was a principle that turns out to be of profound importance in interpreting the human journey of self-discovery. In the 'Phenomenology' he looks at the way human self-consciousness develops, beginning from what he calls '*sense*-certainty' (the basic information we receive through our senses). Consciousness then recognizes that there are general properties or qualities that are applicable to what is perceived through the senses. This recognition leads to understanding; and this in turn underpins *self*-certainty. Hegel then looks at how this individual consciousness with its self-certainty relates to other human consciousnesses. For Aristotle (as for Confucius), humans are by nature social beings,[20] but for Hegel, the self is unavoidably torn between attraction and estrangement in its relationship to the 'other'. This contradiction is resolved by recognizing that other conscious selves have the same need for self-certainty. But this recognition can only succeed in confirming our own self-certainty if it is reciprocal and equal; in this way we come through to a higher reality in which, to use his term, consciousness 'universalizes' itself.

Underlying this pattern of development is a dialectic in which the contradictions inherent in something given are exposed by something other, and they are resolved only by what is given and what is other *both* being subsumed into something higher. Essential to this dialectic is the negation; *human development can never be linear and has an intrinsic element of conflict and struggle*. But this opposition between subject and object, between the self and the other, between the thesis and the antithesis – is always taken up into a higher synthesis. And in that synthesis, the essence of earlier stages is preserved, not lost or cancelled out, even as they are subsumed into the higher truth. Thus, for example, self-certainty is enriched, not lost, in the process of universalizing consciousness – individuality is developed, not cancelled out, by the mutual recognition of community. Hegel applies this dialectical principle in a variety of areas: in the study of the human mind and its consciousness of the exterior world; in his description of human family and societal relationships, and in his analysis of the development of the state.

And he applies it above all to human history. For Hegel, history is, in effect, the story of the human consciousness universalizing itself through mutual recognition of other consciousnesses. Hegel describes this process as what he calls 'subjective spirit' encountering 'objective spirit', resulting in both of them being subsumed in the emergence of 'absolute spirit'. The full consummation of history will see all individuality fully realized because fully subsumed in the higher reality of this absolute spirit – which is usually written with initial capitals in English as Absolute Spirit (even though the original German does not highlight it in this way). Thus the history of humanity is the story of the realization of Absolute Spirit through all the twists and turns of individual and cultural interaction. From the point of view of the individual, the experience of history is therefore both of free and rational self-certainty and of a kind of higher necessity (which was the point Mao made to Kissinger). As Hegel writes in his 'Encyclopaedia':

World history is the necessary development, out of the concepts of mind's freedom alone, of the motives of reason and so of the self-consciousness and freedom of the mind.[21]

Yet at the same time:

> All actions, including world-historical actions, culminate with individuals as . . . the living instruments of what is in substance the deed of the world spirit, and they are therefore directly at one with that deed though it is hidden from them and is not their aim and purpose.[22]

A key role in this process is played by religion. Hegel saw the Roman Stoics as having a clear enough doctrine of what makes for the good life but as lacking any exemplar they could point to. Christianity, however, provided the particular historical exemplar in the person of Jesus. Medieval Catholicism had been caught up too much in a literal understanding of its 'representations' – its pictures and stories – whereas by his time, he believed, Protestantism had properly conceptualized the truths about the human condition that are implied by Christian doctrines about incarnation, forgiveness, death and resurrection. Thus, Christian belief pointed the way to the emergence of Absolute Spirit, the culmination of which is a shared common life of reason and love based on those truths.

It is easy to see why the concept of Absolute Spirit sits uncomfortably in the modern European thought world. To many it is nothing but a throwback to a pre-critical era – a sort of pseudo-religious non-explanation that adds nothing to the understanding of history. From the perspective of Christian theology, it is usually regarded as a highly unorthodox distortion of its central doctrines. Furthermore, Hegel's discussion of particular historical situations – of what he considered to be the four 'world-historical' epochs – is Europe-centred and betrays a very superficial view of the history of other Eurasian cultures. Thus, he defines the four epochs as: the oriental world, in which individuals have no consciousness of individuality; the classical Greek city states, where the individual is self-conscious but the relation to the *polis* is based solely on custom and tradition, not on free, rational decision; the Roman state, where the universal dominates the individual but where the Stoics hold out for individuality; and finally what he calls the Germanic world – meaning, in practice, most of western Europe – in which there is a mature balance between the exterior and the interior, between the individual and society, a balance facilitated by the rise of Christianity. These four epochs he describes respectively as the periods of the Spirit's childhood, adolescence, adulthood and maturity.

From the vantage point of the twenty-first century, this seems little more than patronizing, ignorant nonsense. And for the most part, modern commentary on Hegel has taken his metaphysics at face value and rejected it outright. But some have argued that he can be understood as using a convenient language of vaguely Christian metaphysics to explore cultural relativities and patterns in history.[23] And there is a growing recognition that his dialectic can also be seen as throwing light on the way we use language to (using Rowan Williams's phrase) 'posit, critique and re-found' what we say about anything at all.[24] All fruitful dialogue, in fact, is dialectic. The influential German philosopher Hans-Georg Gadamer (who died in 2002 at the ripe age of 102) has argued, in essentially Hegelian terms, that experience is always a matter of interpretation which *changes* us; and our experience is never just a clean slate – interpretation always involves tradition, which is always expressed in language and therefore involves relationship. The relationship with what we experience is always with a 'thou' and not an 'it'. Therefore, 'we cannot have experiences without asking questions.'[25]

In any event, whether or not the modern mind finds Hegel's Absolute Spirit appealing, three things are clear about his world view. First, his understanding of the underlying processes and principles of historical development has been widely influential, not only because of its adoption by Marx but also because it seems to fit the actuality of history so much better than the optimism about straightforward progress that enthused so many of his contemporaries. And, as the conversation with Mao demonstrates, it is not necessary to subscribe to Hegel's doctrine of Absolute Spirit to understand the power of his dialectic in explaining history. Second, and unlike Marx, Hegel would never have taken the view that a change in social and economic relationships alone was enough to complete the universalization of the human consciousness (or, to use his language, for the full realization of Absolute Spirit). On the contrary, he was clear that 'it is a modern folly to alter a corrupt ethical system, its constitution and law, without changing the religion, to have a revolution without a reformation.'[26] In this, too, Mao was on his side – even if it was a very different reformation he had in mind when he launched the Cultural Revolution.

Third, Hegel himself saw in the language of Christianity some important truths about the nature of human individual and historical development. His use of Christian terminology was in no way just a sort of poetic flourish or a genuflection to his own cultural milieu. This is not the place for a full discussion of how his theological background informs his philosophy of history. Suffice it to note here how, for example, in the final few paragraphs of the 'Phenomenology' he writes of the Absolute Spirit 'sacrificing' itself as it embodies itself in nature, and 'emptying' itself (here quoting the actual Greek word used by Paul as he articulated his understanding of the divine significance of Jesus Christ in his letter to the Philippians[27]) in order to come into being in the unfolding of history, the totality of which is the 'calvary' of the Spirit.[28]

What in all of this gives us insight into the historic challenges of the next century? Can we imagine a dialectic among the great Eurasian world cultures in which our individuality is confirmed as it comes to recognize the other? Can we envisage a resulting synthesis as something that embraces but also goes beyond our present experience of difference? Is there *any* sense in which we can talk in Hegel's language about growth towards maturity for the individual-in-community? And, with or without Hegel's metaphysics – with or without reifying or even personalizing his absolute spirit as Absolute Spirit – can we accept that there is something necessary, something inevitable, about such a dialectic of development? What, in short, can we reasonably hope for?

The answer must of course begin, at least, by recognizing that there can be no certainty. Hegel may have unearthed a pattern of human development that is deeply significant for our history, but he himself, as well as plenty of other prophets before and since his time, misread the dialectic. His judgement that the Europe of the nineteenth century had reached maturity looks embarrassingly naive. Marx's communist manifesto turned into a tragic nightmare for millions. And Fukuyama's question now rings hollow, as the individualism that underlies liberal market economics seems radically compromised. Furthermore, the challenges seem daunting indeed. This book has argued that the geopolitics of Eurasia are more complex and more potentially conflictual than ever, and that

Eurasia's Westphalian approach to governance and international relations is unstable and dangerous. It would be easy to be pessimistic about the prospects for progress on some of the most important 'ecumenical goals' – to use Nietzsche's term – for the next century, goals, for example, that relate to the climate and to the environment in which we live and move and have our being.

The great dialectic: individuality and individualism

Yet arguably there are also signs of the times, which give reason to believe that some form of dialectic is indeed in process and may possibly bring us to maturity before it is too late. This is the great dialectic of individuality and individualism. We have argued that individuality is the great fact of the modern era, driven above all by urbanization as it breaks down older more communal identities and as it facilitates the spread of knowledge about the world. But, to use Hegelian terminology, we increasingly see in *individualism* the negativity that exposes the contradictions of individuality. Individualism is the self-centredness that self-certainty can so easily become. The question is how the contradictions will be resolved through growth into the maturity of a better way of being. This is the deep question that lurks beneath all the geopolitical tensions and cultural differences we have looked at in preceding chapters. It has been forced towards the surface more than anything else by the ambiguities of the urbanization that is radically transforming our experience of being. The challenge it represents is even more profound and existential than the problems of the commons that now intrude on all our consciousnesses – because it lies at their root. And it is a challenge for all: no individual and no culture has reached maturity and all will have to learn if they are to grow. This is not a matter of the rise and fall of civilizations, of the sun rising in the east and setting in the west.

First then, *there is the clear evidence of a spreading awareness – and expression – of individuality throughout all of the cultures of Eurasia.* Individuality is deeper than individualism: the latter can be a political orientation, a social attitude, psychological self-centredness or even an existentialist credo; the former is the self-certainty of which Hegel wrote, which underpins a healthy human self-consciousness and reaches maturity only through engagement with the other. So this is not just the first person singular writing itself into the sentence as the subject, with the other only as object. As we saw in the last chapter, this has historically been in many ways a peculiarly European journey of discovery, and one with plenty of twists and turns. But the self-conscious self was never unique to Europe and is making its presence felt more and more assertively in all Eurasia's now urbanized cultures.

It would not be difficult to point to powerful expressions of individuality in modern storytelling, in both novels and in film, from specific and very different contexts such as Japan, India, Turkey and Iran – in the so-called 'I-novels' of nineteenth- and twentieth-century Japan, or in such films as those of Satyajit Ray, of Nuri Bilge Ceylan and of Asghar Farhadi. But to look in more detail at just one pair of examples, two of the best-known Chinese novels of recent decades are *Fortress Besieged* (Qian Zhongshu, 1947) and *Red Sorghum* (Mo Yan, 1986). In both these novels the author is clearly processing his own experience of the ups and downs of twentieth-century Chinese history, albeit in very different ways and contexts. The central figure in both is a classic antihero. *Fortress Besieged* is a product of pre-Communist China, and tells the satirical but poignant story of an ineffectual young man who wastes his time studying abroad, gets a fake degree, returns to China and lands a university teaching post on the basis of this degree; meanwhile, his love life is vacuous and he eventually marries disastrously. His wife ends up leaving him as he listens to the sound of a clock ticking. This is the China of the late 1930s, but it could be anywhere in the modern urban, bourgeois world; its central character is a classic modern antihero. Towards the end, he turns an unblinking gaze on himself:

When his wife had fallen asleep, he began reflecting on how cold and indifferent he felt now at the thought of possibly meeting [a former girlfriend] T'ang Hsiao-fu again. If he really did meet her, it would be just the same. That was because the self that had loved her a year ago had long since died. The selves that had loved her, who had been afraid of Su Wen-wan and had been seduced by Miss Pao, had all died one after another. He had buried some of his dead selves in his memory, erected a monument to them and occasionally paid them homage, such as by a moment of feeling for T'ang Hsiao-fu. Others seemed to have died by the wayside and been left there to rot and decompose or be devoured by birds and beasts – but never to be completely obliterated – such as the self which had bought the diploma . . .[29]

Red Sorghum tells the story of a Shandong family who live through the Japanese occupation, civil war and chaos, and is written with the hindsight of an unnamed narrator who has lived through the Great Leap Forward and the Cultural Revolution. It is earthy and violent: the central figure, the grandfather of the narrator, is a murderer, freebooter, unfaithful lover and tireless fighter against the Japanese forces who roam the countryside. It is deeply rooted culturally – shot through both with the brutal realism of the times and also with elements of enchantment that reflect the reality of Chinese provincial life. Yet, in the midst of the savagery, the preciousness of the human is never quite lost. When the grandmother, killed in an encounter with the Japanese army, is buried amid the sorghum, the grandfather and teenage son (father of the narrator) react intensely and differently:

Grandma was the last to be interred. Once again, her body was enshrouded in sorghum. As Father watched the final stalk hide her face, his heart cried out in pain, never to be whole again throughout his long life. Granddad tossed on the first spadeful of dirt. The loose clouds of black earth thudded against the layer of sorghum like an exploding grenade shattering the surrounding stillness with its lethal shrapnel. Father's heart wept blood.[30]

Though the setting of *Red Sorghum* is a poorly educated and chaotic rural environment, it is of course urbanization that makes possible the expression of the individual human significance of it all. Mo Yan may have come from the rural world he describes, but his writing career has been lived out in the urban world of the modern China. In fact, the growing consciousness of individuality is closely related to the spread of urbanization, and to the connectivity and education – in its broadest sense – that comes with it. Moreover, this seems to be a one-way street. Does education – at least, formal education – lag the experience of urbanization? Yes, surely, for many millions of people. Can governments block access to wider sources of information and connectivity that are essential to full development of the individual? Yes, we know that they can. Could a culture turn backwards and *reduce* educational connectivity? Yes, and we suspect that this is happening in some conservative areas of the Muslim *ummah*, for example. Thought control remains a weapon of disturbing power. Yet it is hard to see this dyke holding in the end. This means that overall knowledge of the other will continue to expand. As that happens – through education, virtual connectivity and travel – human individuality is developed and enriched through the deepening relationship with the other. If we want to use Hegel's terminology, self-certainty becomes subjective spirit encountering objective spirit. But whatever terminology we prefer, he was right to see this as something profoundly important for human history. There is no cultural relativity about this; it is a human universal, born of the experience of urbanization that is now the universal norm and not reversible.

But then there are the contradictions of individuality. Again, as Hegel saw so clearly, the self's experience of the other involves ambiguities; the self reacts to the other in a mixture of attraction and estrangement. The self can engage or retreat; it can relate or reject. The mature self will engage and relate; the insecure self will retreat and reject. So in response to those ambiguities, individuality elides all too easily into individualism. A Europe that explored the individual self and expressed individuality in all its mystery thereby loosened its chains – and freed it to be individualistic. In the myth of Prometheus, the Titan who stole fire from the gods and gave it to the humans is chained to a rock in torment by Zeus, before being freed by Heracles. The European Romantics saw in Prometheus a figure who stood for human defiance of external restraints, moral or physical. For the likes of Goethe and Shelley (whose *Prometheus Unbound* is the fullest and most uncompromising assertion of this defiance) this was a humanist manifesto loosed from humanism's earlier Christian reference points. But freed thus from its chains, the human spirit was discovering – again, through urbanization – not just its individuality but the excitements and temptations of *individualism*. The literary emblems of individualism, as we have noted in Chapter 8, were such antiheroes as Satan, Faust and the Übermensch.

Individualism became, above all, an American credo: life, liberty and the pursuit of happiness. But not a dream only for Americans: it is and always has been the magnet for millions from around the world, to an extent that surpasses all others. At its best, it is exhilarating and the sense of liberation can be almost tangible. But then the excitement palls – as it has done in Europe over a century of trauma. The world has learnt that the individualism of the market society produces instability, inequality, materialism, short-termism and a degree of obsessive self-centredness that is in the end dangerous to the self. The dream, in short, becomes a nightmare.

Discontent with individualism has now become pervasive. The pursuit of happiness has turned into the pursuit of pleasure, which has become the purpose of life. Aristotle saw the fulfilment of life's *telos*, or its goal, as being *eudaimonia* – literally, wellness of spirit. Confucius saw the highest stage of individual human development as sagehood. Thomas Aquinas saw it, in an explicit theological context, as *beatitudo* or blessedness. These notions are not identical to one another and have differing metaphysical backgrounds. But they have all understood something about the nature of individuality: its healthy development necessarily entails something more than self-interest and self-centredness. This is not just a challenge for America and if there is a crisis of individualism, it is not just a Spenglerian decline of the West. It is no coincidence that the Chinese authorities worry expressly about the values of young modern urbanites. In earlier times, in China and elsewhere, the Marxist alternative of an imposed materialist collectivism appeared to be an available option. But no longer. *The uncomfortable truth is that the experience of individualism is as much a human universal as is the growth of individuality.*

So how will – or should – the dialectic unfold? What is it that will resolve the contradictions of individualism and subsume human individuality into some greater human reality? One answer lies in that sense, which we have already noted, that international dialogue on values needs to focus not just on human rights but also on shared responsibilities. This is certainly a voice that has become increasingly persistent in East Asian cultures in recent decades; but it is also a theme of the discourse of

Islam – the only explicitly theocratic culture of the modern world – and even in a Europe that is as convinced of the sanctity of human rights as any other culture on the planet. In China, the government has in recent decades responded to its own dismay about the effects of what the state media called 'mammonism and extreme individualism' by emphasizing the importance of a social harmony to be achieved by a balance between government and individual virtue – between the perennial Chinese instincts of *fazhi* (rule by law) and of what is in effect Confucian self-cultivation, which we noted in Chapter 4.[31] In fact, China has now systematized this approach, approving an official statement of 'core socialist values', to be taught in schools and to be promoted by party members and by popular artists. The list includes three groups of values: national, social and individual. Each group is a blend of rights and duties, and their Confucian underpinnings are very obvious (in fact, the absence of any identifiably Marxist themes is striking). Thus the list includes: at the national level, prosperity, democracy, civility and harmony; at the social level, freedom, equality, justice and the rule of law; and, at the individual level, patriotism, dedication, integrity and friendship.

It would be easy to view this cynically and to point out the obvious areas where rhetoric parts with reality. But there are many Europeans who would acknowledge how much better their own societies would be if some such set of values were their own social charter too. Various European governments – including the British – have sought in recent decades to introduce citizenship teaching into their educational systems in one way or another; but the underlying motive has often been to facilitate integration of immigrants, rather than to tackle the individualism that has troubled the Chinese so much.

Meanwhile, philosophical circles have continued to wrestle with the problem they have confronted ever since Prometheus was loosed by the Enlightenment from the chains of Zeus. If values are not divinely ordained or implied by the inherent nature of human beings, and cannot be convincingly based on some transcendent principle of rationality (as Kant sought to do), then on what basis can they be deemed to be universal? Many have simply accepted that this is not theoretically possible and have been happy to argue that there is enough agreement on particular ethical issues to work with in practice. For those left uneasy by such pragmatism, however, there have, in broad terms, been two kinds of alternative. The first works back from the Aristotelian/Confucian answer to what makes for a spiritually healthy life – for *eudaimonia*, in Aristotle's terms. What is valuable is what is implied by – or promotes – well-being in this holistic sense. But this begs the question of whether Aristotle was right (neither Christianity nor Islam could accept *eudaimonia* as a sufficient definition of human fulfilment; nor, for different reasons, would it be compatible with Hinduism or the core teachings of Buddhism). The fact is that history has been riven with strong disagreements about the good life and, hence, about the virtues that it calls for. Some of these disagreements predate by a long way the breakdown of integrated metaphysics in the European Enlightenment.[32] The second approach, associated in particular with Jürgen Habermas, is to avoid the substance of the question and instead focus, as we noted in Chapter 8, on the process of arriving at an answer – on the cross-cultural dialogue needed to ensure 'communicative rationality'.

The inconclusiveness of this search for universal values – for a set of rights and duties that is not culture bound and by which the development of all cultures can be measured – is, in the end, the consequence of the age-old philosophical truism that we cannot deduce what ought to be from what is. In the final analysis, *the potential resolution to the contradictions of individualism lies not in finding this holy grail but in the full development of human individuality in society.* This development is a process that – unsurprisingly – has significant parallels to the growth of the individual human personality from childhood to mature adulthood. Hegel's judgements on the various particular cultures he examined may seem unwise, to say the least; but that does not invalidate his basic insight. We know how individuals grow through engagement with others; we know how the past that weighs on the present has to be faced up to; and we know how in extreme cases of psychological trauma the development of the mature adult can be badly distorted. We also know that the journey of individual human life is one of continuous learning – from others about the other – and about the self. 'Talking introduces us to ourselves.'[33] When this happens, knowledge always eventually triumphs over prejudice. There is every reason to believe that all this is equally true, not just of humans as individuals but of humans in society – of cultures and of nations. The cultures of Eurasia will find themselves on this journey, not because of explicit national or societal decisions *but because urbanized human individuality cannot avoid it.* This is the basis for the synthesis that is the final movement of the dialectic. It is final because – absent some massive cataclysm – we cannot reverse urbanization: the human species is changing irrevocably under its impact. This is the sense in which we are coming to the end of history.

Three final points about this final movement of the dialectic. First, this end will take a long time to reach full fruition. The human odyssey will not be free of dangers and diversions. There is every reason to fear that the process of reaching civilizational maturity will be fraught with tension and possible violence. Conflict and struggle are an inevitable element in the dialectic of development. In this, Hegel would not have accepted the optimism of the later nineteenth century – whether in the form of the positivism of French post-revolutionary thought (Saint Simon and Comte) or of the confident assumptions of British liberal history (Macauley). The evidence of the twentieth and the twenty-first centuries is surely that Hegel's understanding of the dynamics of human history was more profound than either of these other intellectual traditions. The resolution of the great historical dialectic of individuality will, in other words, play itself out at one level in the recognized form of geopolitics; and these have, as we have seen in Chapter 5, plenty of stress points in today's Eurasia. There could well be setbacks, some of which could be horrendous, enough even to delay consummation by generations – it is all too easy to conjure up the nightmares. But to the question we asked in Chapter 6 – whether in today's Westphalian Eurasia the human journey has reached some kind of stasis – the answer is clearly negative. There is something inexorable – but absolutely not straightforward – about the direction of travel on the human odyssey towards the end of history.

Second, all will be challenged and changed in this process. It will certainly have implications for the institutions of society, of nations and of the international order (though specific speculation about institutional developments would take us well beyond the scope of this book). And, at a deeper level, it will have implications for the way individuals understand their identities. No culture has arrived at the goal of its human development – the full flowering of human individuality. We have noted in Chapter 2, for example, the deep and wide-ranging consequences of urbanization for the identity of women (and therefore also of men). To put the point still more broadly, no culture will have reached the goal of this journey while so many are denied the flowering of their individuality (which is, however, not the same thing as rampant individualism). The end of the dialectic will not be the triumph of any one ideology; for this is a dialectic of the human self, not of doctrines. The challenge will be felt most deeply by the two most dominant powers on the Eurasian stage – America and China. But all others, including Muslims troubled by modernity; Europeans troubled by their heritage; Japanese troubled by their individuality and gnawed at by their past; Indians troubled by fears of encirclement and uncertain about the relationship of their future to their Hindu identity; and Russians troubled by loss of empire and prestige and, like others, living with an unrecognized past – all will be challenged in the process.

Third, the open question is whether or not enough progress will be made quickly enough to prevent the problem of the commons causing widespread and irreversible damage to the environment and human living conditions. The omens are not good at present: we are a long way from a carbon-free growth model for the global economy; and environmental degradation continues apace. What happens to human societies and to human self-consciousness when average temperatures climb several degrees in less than a century is not yet clear, but many of the people who will have to live through the upheavals and tensions it will surely produce are already alive. It could well be that the third and final phase of the dialectic of human history will be more like a wartime economy of managed shortages than a cornucopia, because of what we are doing to our planet.

And one coda on metaphysics. We will never cease to wonder at our experience of life; no metaphysical system we have ever lived with has provided all the answers. In fact, there is no possibility of a closed and complete system, since we have no firm vantage point outside of ourselves from which to view all things. Our metaphysical systems – whether theist, monist or materialist – are acts of faith, grounded more or less rationally or intuitively, and they can never be more than that. But we cannot do without a system; our human individuality demands

274

some coherence in its understanding of the other, even if the coherence were to lie in accepting that all is blind chance. Eurasia has spawned all the great cultures of the world and all of its great metaphysical systems. Whichever one we choose to live by, we will gain immeasurably in our individuality and in our humanity if we are open to learning the wisdom of others. As the great Catholic thinker Hans Küng once remarked, we should look for the human, not just the inhuman, in other world views, and judge other people's systems by their best, not just their worst – just as we hope that they would judge ours by our best, not just by our worst.[34]

Notes

1 Eurasia: the next hundred years

1 Pierre Teilhard de Chardin's *Le Phénomène Humain* was originally published by Éditions du Seuil in 1955.

2 From the last line of W. B. Yeats's famous and uncannily prescient 1919 poem, 'The Second Coming'.

3 Barry Cunliffe, *By Steppe, Desert and Ocean* (Oxford University Press, 2015), p. 113.

4 Isaiah 45.

5 See Jonathan E. Hillman, *The Rise of China–Europe Railways* (Center for Strategic and International Studies, 2018).

6 Henry Kissinger, *World Order* (Penguin, 2014), pp. 23–31.

7 Speech by President Xi Jinping at the UN Office in Geneva, 18 January 2017.

8 Samuel P. Huntington, *The Clash of Civilizations and the Remaking of the World Order* (Simon & Schuster, 1997).

2 Cities: immediacy, connectivity, freedom, alienation – and identity?

1 Urban population projections are regularly published by the UN Population Division, Department of Economic and Social Affairs.

2 World Bank and International Labour Office (ILO) official statistics, 2018.

3 See Sunil Khilnani, *The Idea of India* (Penguin, 2012), Chapter 3, for an insightful discussion of the Indian experience of cities.

4 Friedrich Engels, *Die Lage der arbeitenden Klasse in England* (*The Condition of the Working Class in England*), 1845.

5 Frank McLynn, *Genghis Khan* (Vintage, 2016), pp. 300–2.

6 Jeremiah 39—40.

7 Luo Guanzhong (Lo Kuan-Chung) (C. H. Brewitt-Taylor, tr.), *The Romance of the Three Kingdoms* (Vol. 1) (Tuttle Publishing, 2002), p. 63.

8 Rashid al-Din (W. M. Thackston, ed. and tr.), *Jami'u't-tawarikh: Compendium of chronicles* (Harvard University Press, 1998).

9 Steven Runciman, *The Fall of Constantinople 1453* (Cambridge University Press, 1990).

10 Friedrich Schiller, *Die Geschichte des Dreißigjährigen Krieges* (*The History of the Thirty Years War*), 1805.

11 See Wayne A. Meeks, *The First Urban Christians* (Yale University Press, 2003), pp. 15–16, for a summary of urban social life in the Eastern Mediterranean at the time of the apostle Paul's famous journeys.

12 See Igor de Rachewiltz, 'Some remarks on the ideological foundations of Chingis Khan's empire', *Papers on Far Eastern History* (1973, available online at: <www.altaica.ru>).

13 See Peter Frankopan, *The Silk Roads* (Bloomsbury, 2015), p. 177.

14 See Kenneth Ch'en, *Buddhism in China* (Princeton University Press, 1973), p. 16.

15 Revelation 21.2–5, 16, 18, 22, 25.

16 Augustine (Henry Bettenson, tr.), *The City of God* (Vol. 22) (Penguin, 1984), pp. 1087–91.

17 William Wordsworth, 'Composed upon Westminster Bridge' in *Poems, in Two Volumes* (Longman, Hurst, Reese & Orme, 1807).

18 Frankopan, *The Silk Roads*, p. 262.

19 Charles-Louis de Secondat, baron de La Brède de Montesquieu, *De l'Esprit des Lois* (*The Spirit of the Laws*) (Vol. 1, originally published in 1748); and his 'Notes sur l'Angleterre' ('Notes on England'). See especially Iain Stewart, 'Montesquieu in England: His "Notes on England"', with commentary and translation, *Oxford University Comparative Law Forum*, 6 (2002, available online at: <www.ouclf.iuscomp.org>).

20 Francis Fukuyama, *The Origins of Political Order* (Profile Books, 2012), pp. 410–13.

21 Christopher I. Beckwith, *Empires of the Silk Road* (Princeton University Press, 2011), pp. 245–62.

22 Adam Smith, *The Wealth of Nations* (William Strahan, Thomas Cadell, 1776).

23 See R. Taggart Murphy, *Japan and the Shackles of the Past* (Oxford University Press, 2014), p. 44.

24 Tim Blanning, *The Romantic Revolution* (Weidenfeld & Nicolson, 2010), pp. 8–9.

25 William Wordsworth, 'The world is too much with us' in *Poems, in Two Volumes.*

26 Genesis 1.28–9.

27 Augustine (R. S. Pine-Coffin, tr.), *Confessions* (Penguin, 1961), Book 10, Chapter 8.

28 See, for example, the Swiss historian Jacob Burckhardt's *The Civilization of the Renaissance in Italy* (SMK Books, 2012) from 1860, which specifically highlights the significance of nature for Petrarch.

29 William Wordsworth, 'Lines written a few miles above Tintern Abbey, on revisiting the banks of the Wye during a tour' in *Lyrical Ballads*, 1798.

30 Adam Smith, *The Wealth of Nations*, Book 5, Chapter 1.

31 Karl Marx, in a note appended to Part I of 'The German Ideology', quoted in Leszek Kołakowski, *Main Currents of Marxism* (Norton, 2008), pp. 141–2.

32 Karl Marx, 'The German Ideology', quoted in Kołakowski, p. 129.

3 So who do we think we are now?

1 From Immanuel Kant, *The Critique of Practical Reason*, 1788, quoted in Paul Guyer, 'Introduction: the starry heavens and the moral law' in Paul Guyer (ed.), *The Cambridge Companion to Kant* (Cambridge University Press, 1992).

2 Wing-tsit Chan, *A Source Book in Chinese Philosophy* (Princeton University Press, 1973), p. 136.

3 Wing-tsit Chan, *A Source Book in Chinese Philosophy*, p. 136.

4 'The Laozi', Chapter 25, in Wing-tsit Chan, *A Source Book in Chinese Philosophy*, p. 153.

5 'The Zhuangzi', Chapter 12, in Wing-tsit Chan, *A Source Book in Chinese Philosophy*, p. 202.

6 'The Zhuangzi', Chapter 2, in Wing-tsit Chan, *A Source Book in Chinese Philosophy*, p. 181.

7 Alasdair MacIntyre, *After Virtue* (University of Notre Dame Press, 2007), pp. 52–3.

8 See Johanna Lidén, 'Buddhist and Daoist influences on Neo-Confucian thinkers and their claim of orthodoxy', *Orientalia Suecana* (2011), 60, pp. 163–84.

9 See Catherine Hudak Klancer, *Embracing our Complexity* (State University of New York Press, 2015).

10 See, for example, Wing-tsit Chan, *A Source Book in Chinese Philosophy*, p. 640.

11 Oliver Leaman, *Islamic Philosophy* (Polity Press, 2009), p. 45.

12 See P. M. Holt, Ann K. S. Lambton and Bernard Lewis (eds), *The Cambridge History of Islam* (Vol. 2B) (Cambridge University Press, 1977), p. 619.

13 Michael Axworthy, *Iran: Empire of the Mind: A history from Zoroaster to the present day* (Penguin, 2008), p. 133.

14 Ockham's 'razor' has appeared in several different formulations down the centuries. He himself wrote that 'plurality must never be posited without necessity' in his discussion of the work of Peter Lombard. The most commonly quoted version of his 'razor' is, in fact, attributable to the Franciscan philosopher John Punch, whose commentary on Duns Scotus from 1639 states that 'entities should not be multiplied without need'.

15 Maurice Walshe (tr.), *The Complete Mystical Works of Meister Eckhart* (Crossroad Publishing, 2008), Sermon 13b.

16 Michel Foucault, *Les Mots et les Choses*, published in English as *The Order of Things* (Routledge, 2002), p. 183.

17 Foucault, *The Order of Things*, p. 35.

18 Foucault, *The Order of Things*, p. 357.

19 N. K. Sandars (tr.), *The Epic of Gilgamesh* (Penguin, 1983), p. 63.

20 *The Epic of Gilgamesh*, p. 107.

21 Miguel de Cervantes (John Rutherford, tr.), *Don Quixote* (Penguin, 2003), p. 982.

22 Victor Hugo (Norman Denny, tr.), *Les Misérables* (Penguin, 1982), p. 318.

23 Victor Hugo, *Les Misérables*, p. 1232.

4 'What is a nation?'

1 Adam Smith, *The Theory of Moral Sentiment*, 1759, opening paragraph.

2 Karl Marx and Friedrich Engels, *The Communist Manifesto*, 1848.

3 Ferdinand Tönnies, *Gemeinschaft und Gesellschaft* (*Community and Society*), 1887.

4 Ernest Renan, 'Qu'est-ce qu'une nation?' ('What is a Nation?'), 1882 (available online at: <www.bmlisieux.com/archives/nation01.htm>).

5 Johann Gottlieb Fichte, *Reden an die Deutsche Nation* (*Addresses to the German Nation*), 1808.

6 From an address by W. S. C. Copeman in the Chelsea Physic Garden, 1960.

7 See, for example, Benedict Anderson, *Imagined Communities* (Verso Publications, 1983); Ernest Gellner *Nations and Nationalism* (Blackwell, 1983); Eric Hobsbawm and Terence Ranger (eds), *The Invention of Tradition* (Cambridge University Press, 1983).

8 See Gerald Izenberg, *Identity* (University of Pennsylvania Press, 2016), pp. 217–24, for a useful summary of the debate about national identity.

9 See selections from 'The Mozi' in Wing-tsit Chan, *A Source Book in Chinese Philosophy* (Princeton University Press, 1973), pp. 211–31.

10 See Chris Fraser, 'Major rival schools: Mohism and legalism' in J. Garfield and W. Edelglass (eds), *The Oxford Handbook of World Philosophy* (Oxford University Press, 2011).

11 Confucius (Edward Slingerland, tr.), *The Analects* (Hackett Publishing, 2003), Book 17, verse 2.

12 'Book of Mencius', Book 6, Part 1, in Wing-tsit Chan, *A Source Book in Chinese Philosophy*, pp. 51–60.

13 'The Xunzi', Book 23, in Wing-tsit Chan, *A Source Book in Chinese Philosophy*, pp. 128–35.

14 John Locke, *Second Treatise of Government*, 1690.

15 Voltaire, *Candide ou l'Optimisme*, 1759.

16 See Julia Simon-Ingram, 'Rousseau and the problem of community: Nationalism, civic virtue, totalitarianism', *History of European Ideas* (1993), 16(1–3), pp. 23–9.

17 C. Bertram, 'Rousseau's legacy in two conceptions of the general will: Democratic and transcendent', *Review of Politics* (2012), 74(3), pp. 403–20.

18 See Charles Taylor, *The Language Animal* (Harvard University Press, 2016), especially pp. 12–25.

19 See Mads Qvortrup, 'A civic profession of faith: Rousseau's and nationalism' in *The Political Philosophy of Jean-Jacques Rousseau* (Manchester University Press, 2003), Chapter 4.

20 See the definition of nationalism articulated by Ernest Gellner as quoted by Mads Qvortrup.

21 Natsume Soseki (Meredith McKinney, tr.), *Kokoro* (Penguin, 2010).

22 See Christopher de Bellaigue, *The Islamic Enlightenment* (Vintage, 2018) for an overview of the struggle for modernization in the *ummah* in the nineteenth and twentieth centuries.

23 Amartya Sen, *The Argumentative Indian* (Farrar, Straus & Giroux, 2005).

24 Jürgen Habermas, *Between Facts and Norms* (MIT Press, 1998), pp. 491–515 and 566–7.

5 The past that is never dead

1 Quoted in Yoshiro Tamura (Jeffrey Hunter, tr.), *Japanese Buddhism* (Kosei Publishing, 2005), p. 53.

2 Shuichi Kato (Don Sanderson, tr.), *A History of Japanese Literature* (Vol. 2) (Kodansha International, 1990), p. 126.

3 Junichiro Tanizaki (Edward G. Seidensticker, tr.), *The Makioka Sisters* (Vintage, 2000), p. 91.

4 Dick Davis (tr.), *Faces of Love: Hafez and the poets of Shiraz* (Penguin, 2013).

5 *Li Po and Tu Fu: Poems selected and translated by Arthur Cooper* (Penguin, 1973), p. 188.

6 See Shuchen Xiang, 'The irretrievability of the past: Nostalgia in Chinese literature from Tang-Song poetry to Ming-Qing *san-wen*', *International Communication of Chinese Culture* (2015), 2(3), pp. 205–22.

7 Rabindranath Tagore, *Gitanjali*, Song 21 (originally published by Macmillan, 1917).

8 Augustine, *Confessions*, Book 10, Chapter 17.

9 Augustine, *Confessions*, Book 11, Chapter 28.

10 See Rowan Williams, *On Augustine* (Bloomsbury, 2016), p. 13.

11 Paul Ricoeur, *Anthropologie Philosophique, Écrits et Conférences* (Vol. 3) (Éditions du Seuil, 2013), p. 345.

12 Augustine, *Confessions*, Book 10, Chapter 16.

13 From Marcel Proust, *A la Recherche du Temps Perdu, Volume 1: Du côté de chez Swann*, author's own translation.

14 L. P. Hartley, *The Go-Between* (1953).

15 William Faulkner, *Requiem for a Nun* (1950), Act I, Scene 3.

16 Eric Hobsbawm and Terence Ranger (eds), *The Invention of Tradition* (Cambridge University Press, 1983).

17 George Orwell, *Nineteen Eighty-Four* (1949), Book 3, Chapter 2.

18 Sunil Khilnani, *The Idea of India* (Penguin, 2012), p. 164.

19 See, for example, Romila Thapar, *Somanatha* (Penguin India, 2005).

20 Kenneth Ch'en, *Buddhism in China* (Princeton University Press, 1973), pp. 338–50.

21 Gene Reeves (tr.), *The Lotus Sutra* (Wisdom Publications, 2008), ch. 4.

22 D. T. Suzuki, *Zen and Japanese Culture* (Tuttle Publishing, 1988), p. 78.

23 From the title of Ruth Benedict's famous book, *The Chrysanthemum and the Sword*, published in 1946 at the invitation of the US Office of War Information.

24 Hugh Kennedy, *The Caliphate* (Penguin, 2016), p. 149.

25 Kennedy, *The Caliphate*, p. 228.

26 Michael Axworthy, *Iran* (Penguin, 2008), pp. 120–1.

27 See Peter Frankopan, *The Silk Roads* (Bloomsbury, 2015), pp. 285–6.

28 See, for example, Georges Minois, *La Guerre de Cent Ans* (Perrin, 2010).

6 Westphalian Eurasia?

1 Samuel P. Huntington, *The Clash of Civilizations and the Remaking of the World Order* (Simon & Schuster, 1997), pp. 19–39.

2 Henry Kissinger, *World Order* (Penguin, 2015).

3 Zbigniew Brzezinski, *The Grand Chessboard* (Basic Books, 1997).

4 See Kissinger, *World Order*, p. 235.

5 Edward Said, *Orientalism* (Penguin, 2003).

6 See, for example, Robert Irwin, *For Lust of Knowing* (Allen Lane, 2006).

7 Said, *Orientalism*, p. 259.

8 Huntington, *The Clash of Civilizations*, pp. 20, 28.

9 Amartya Sen, *The Argumentative Indian* (Farrar, Straus & Giroux, 2005), p. 290.

10 Francis Fukuyama, 'The end of history?', *The National Interest* (Summer 1989), 16, pp. 3–18.

11 See Huntingdon, *The Clash of Civilizations*, p. 306.

12 Johann Wolfgang von Goethe, *Faust, Part 1* (1808, rev. edn, 1828–29), line 1112.

13 See Kissinger, *World Order*, p. 289.

14 Kissinger, *World Order*, p. 295.

15 Universal Declaration of Human Rights (1948), Articles 23–7.

16 See, for example, Ali Allawi, *The Crisis of Islamic Civilization* (Yale University Press, 2009), pp. 193–7.

17 Cairo Declaration on Human Rights in Islam (1990), Articles 1, 24.

18 Final declaration of the Regional Meeting for Asia of the World Conference on Human Rights (1993), Clause 8.

19 Francis Fukuyama, *Political Order and Political Decay* (Profile Books, 2014), p. 394.

20 Huntington, *The Clash of Civilizations*, p. 108.

21 See Graham Allison, 'The Thucydides trap', *FP* (9 June 2017, available online at: <www.foreignpolicy.com/2017/06/09/the-thucydides-trap>).

7 Not lost in translation

1 Johann Peter Eckermann (John Oxenford, tr.), *Gespräche mit Goethe in den letzten Jahren seines Lebens* (*Conversations with Goethe in the Last Years of his Life*) (North Point Press, 1984), p. 132.

2 See, for example, David Damrosch, *How to Read World Literature* (Wiley-Blackwell, 2008).

3 Johann Wolfgang von Goethe, *Maxims and Reflections*, 1833.

4 Damrosch, *How to Read World Literature*, pp. 21–2.

5 Murasaki Shikibu (Edward G. Seidensticker, tr.), *The Tale of Genji* (Alfred A. Knopf, 1987), p. 135.

6 Dick Davis (tr.), *Faces of Love: Hafez and the poets of Shiraz* (Penguin, 2013), p. 8.

7 'Pied Beauty' by Gerard Manley Hopkins, in Robert Bridges (ed.), *Poems of Gerard Manley Hopkins* (Humphrey Milford, 1918).

8 Damrosch, *How to Read World Literature*, p. 50.

9 A. L. Basham, *The Wonder That Was India* (Picador, 2004), p. 422.

10 Shuichi Kato (Don Sanderson, tr.), *A History of Japanese Literature* (Vol. 2) (Kodansha International, 1990), p. 67.

11 R. H. P. Mason and J. G. Caiger, *A History of Japan* (Tuttle Publishing, 2001), p. 239.

12 André Lévy, *Chinese Literature, Ancient and Classical* (Indiana University Press, 2000), p. 84.

13 Horace, *Odes*, Book 3, 30, author's translation.

14 N. K. Sandars (tr.), *The Epic of Gilgamesh* (Penguin, 1983), p. 107.

15 Donald Keene (ed. and comp.), *Anthology of Japanese Literature* (Grove Press, 2007), p. 236.

16 See, for example, Sukumari Bhattacharji, 'Sanskrit drama and the absence of tragedy', *Indian Literature* (1978), 21(3), pp. 6–17.

17 Basham, *The Wonder That Was India*, p. 442.

18 See Jennifer Wallace, 'Tragedy in China', *The Cambridge Quarterly* (2013), June, 42(2), pp. 99–111.

19 See Caroline Jansen, 'Mind the gap? Some observations on the study of tragedy from an international perspective' in Freddy Decreus and Mieke Kolk (eds), 'Rereading Classics in "East" and "West": Post-colonial perspectives on the tragic', *Documenta Jaargang* (2004), 22(4), pp. 316–31 (available online at: <www.academia.edu>).

20 See Rowan Williams, *On Augustine* (Bloomsbury, 2016), pp. 95–101, for a discussion of the possibility of the tragic in a fundamentally rationalistic Augustinian universe.

21 Ruth Benedict, *The Chrysanthemum and the Sword* (Mariner Books, 2005), p. 222.

22 James Joyce, *A Portrait of the Artist as a Young Man* (1916). See Penguin Classics edition (2000), pp. 109–58.

23 See Ian Buruma, *The Wages of Guilt* (Jonathan Cape, 1994), p. 128, for the reaction of a Japanese visitor to the Museum in Nanjing on the notorious 'Rape of Nanking' of 1937/1938.

24 Natsume Soseki (Meredith McKinney, tr.), *Kokoro* (Penguin, 2010), p. 229.

25 Deuteronomy 26.

26 See Arye Zoref, *Journeys for God in Sufi and Judeo-Arabic Literature* (Potsdam University, 2016), p. 110.

27 Matsuo Basho (Donald Keene, tr.), *The Narrow Road to Oku* (Kodansha International, 1996), p. 19.

28 T. S. Eliot, 'Little Gidding' in *Four Quartets* (Harcourt, Brace & Company, 1943).

29 Ian Johnson, *The Souls of China* (Allen Lane, 2017), p. 50.

30 David Palmer, Glenn Shive and Philip Wickeri (eds), *Chinese Religious Life* (Oxford University Press, 2011).

31 John Breen and Mark Teeuwen, *A New History of Shinto* (Wiley-Blackwell, 2010).

32 Max Weber, *The Sociology of Religion*, 1920.

33 Keith Thomas, *Religion and the Decline of Magic* (Penguin, 2003).

34 Jörg Lauster, *Die Verzauberung der Welt* (*The Enchantment of the World*) (C. H. Beck, 2016).

35 Quoted in Wendy Doniger, *The Hindus* (Oxford University Press, 2010), p. 356. Compare Isaiah 49 or Psalm 139.

36 Jalal al-Din Rumi, 'I died as a mineral' in Reynold A. Nicholson (ed. and tr.), *The Mystics of Islam* (Routledge & Kegan Paul, 1963), and quoted in A. L. Basham (ed.), *A Cultural History of India* (Oxford University Press, 1997), p. 468.

37 Dogen (Robert Aitken and Kazuaki Tanahashi, tr.), *Genjokuan* (available online at: <www.theZensite.com>).

38 2 Corinthians 12.

39 Sura 53.

40 Basham, *A Cultural History of India*, p. 254.

41 Basham, *A Cultural History of India*, p. 304.

42 Basham, *A Cultural History of India*, p. 249.

43 Wing-tsit Chan, *A Source Book in Chinese Philosophy* (Princeton University Press, 1973), p. 202.

8 First person singular

1 Alasdair MacIntyre, *After Virtue* (University of Notre Dame Press, 2007), p. 61.

2 See Ray Huang, *1587, a Year of No Significance* (Yale University Press, 1981).

3 Francis Fukuyama, *Political Order and Political Decay* (Profile Books, 2014), pp. 230–1.

4 Tom Holland, *Dominion: The making of the Western mind* (London: Little, Brown, 2019).

5 Diarmaid MacCulloch, *Reformation: Europe's house divided, 1490-1700* (London: Penguin, 2004), p. 131.

6 Sasha Becker and Ludger Woessmann, 'Was Weber wrong? A human capital theory of Protestant economics history', *The Quarterly Journal of Economics* (2009), 124(2), pp. 531-96.

7 Max Weber (Talcott Parsons, tr.), *The Protestant Ethic and the Spirit of Capitalism* (Blackwell, 1992), p. 125.

8 Julien Offray de La Mettrie, *Système d'Epicure*, 1750, quoted in Norman Hampson, *The Enlightenment* (Penguin, 1982), p. 94.

9 Denis Diderot, *Pensées sur L'Interprétation de la Nature*, 1754, quoted in Hampson, *The Enlightenment*, pp. 95-6.

10 David Hume, *The Natural History of Religion*, 1757, quoted in Hampson, *The Enlightenment*, p. 121.

11 See Hajime Nakamura and Philip P. Wiener (eds), *Ways of Thinking of Eastern Peoples* (University of Hawaii Press, 1985), p. 608, note 21.

12 Charles Taylor, *Sources of the Self* (Harvard University Press, 1989), p. 105.

13 Immanuel Kant, *Prolegomena to any Future Metaphysics*, 1783.

14 David Hume, *A Treatise of Human Nature*, 1738.

15 David Hume, *An Enquiry Concerning the Principles of Morals*, 1751.

16 Immanuel Kant, *The Critique of Practical Reason*, 1788.

17 From Friedrich von Schelling, *Collected Works*, Vol. 7, Section I. See Andrew Bowie (Edward N. Zalta, ed.), 'Friedrich Wilhelm Joseph von Schelling' in *The Stanford Encyclopedia of Philosophy* (2016, available online at: <https://.plato.stanford.edu>).

18 Paul Ricoeur, *Anthropologie Philosophique, Écrits et Conférences* (Vol. 3) (Éditions du Seuil, 2013), p. 73.

19 Donn Welton (ed.), *The Essential Husserl* (Indiana University Press, 1999).

20 Francis Crick, *The Astonishing Hypothesis* (Scribner, 1994).

21 Derek Parfit, 'The unimportance of identity' in Henry Harris (ed.), *Identity* (Clarendon Press, 1995), p. 45.

22 See Gerald Izenberg, *Identity* (University of Pennsylvania Press, 2016), pp. 62-86, for one of the most accessible summaries of Heidegger's thought on identity.

23 Martin Heidegger (John Macquarrie and Edward Robinson, tr.), *Being and Time* (Blackwell, 1990), p. 220.

24 Heidegger, *Being and Time*, p. 164.

25 See, in particular, Martin Heidegger (Fred D. Wick and J. Glenn Gray, tr.), *What Is Called Thinking?* (Harper & Row, 1968).

26 Heidegger, *Being and Time*, p. 310.

27 Jean-Paul Sartre, *Being and Nothingness* (New York Philosophical Library, 1956), p. 537.

28 Jacques Derrida (Marie-Louise Mallet, ed., and David Wills, tr.), *The Animal that Therefore I Am* (Fordham University Press, 2008).

29 Søren Kierkegaard (Howard V. Hong and Edna H. Hong, tr.), *Concluding Unscientific Postscript to Philosophical Fragments*, 1846 (Princeton University Press; rev. edn, 1992).

30 Nakamura, *Ways of Thinking of Eastern Peoples*, pp. 98–102.

31 See Wing-tsit Chan, *A Source Book in Chinese Philosophy* (Princeton University Press, 1973), pp. 709–10.

32 See Jana Rosker, 'Epistemology in Chinese Philosophy' in *The Stanford Encyclopedia of Philosophy* (2018).

33 Wing-tsit Chan, *A Source Book in Chinese Philosophy*, p. 515.

34 Tu Weiming, *Confucian Thought* (State University of New York Press, 1997), pp. 163–4.

35 Tu Weiming, *Confucian Thought*, p. 21.

36 See Thomas Kasulis, *Engaging Japanese Philosophy* (University of Hawaii Press, 2018), Chapter 13.

37 Shizuteru Ueda, quoted in Bret W. Davis, 'The Kyoto School' in *The Stanford Encyclopedia of Philosophy* (2017).

38 See Kasulis, *Engaging Japanese Philosophy*, p. 585.

39 Jürgen Habermas (W. Hohengarten, tr.), *Post-Metaphysical Thinking* (MIT Press, 1992), pp. 28–57.

40 Albert Camus, *L'Etranger* (Gallimard, 1942), translated and published as *The Outsider* (Hamish Hamilton, 1946).

41 See, in particular, Romans 7.

42 John Milton, *Paradise Lost*, Book 1.

43 Milton, *Paradise Lost*, Book 1.

44 Johann Wolfgang von Goethe, *Faust, Part Two*, author's translation.

45 From the 1954 film of that name directed by Nicholas Ray.

46 See Julian Young, *Friedrich Nietzsche* (Cambridge University Press, 2010).

47 1 Corinthians 13.8.

48 Friedrich Nietzsche, *Twilight of the Idols* in Keith Ansell Pearson and Duncan Large (eds), *The Nietzsche Reader* (Blackwell, 2014).

49 Nietzsche, *The Gay Science* in *The Nietzsche Reader*, p. 232; emphasis in original.

50 Nietzsche *Human, All Too Human* in *The Nietzsche Reader*, p. 168; emphasis in original.

51 Alexander V. Pantsov with Steven I. Levine, *Mao* (Simon & Schuster, 2013), p. 174.

9 The end of history?

1 Gerald Izenberg, *Identity* (University of Pennsylvania Press, 2016), p. 426.

2 Peter Frankopan, *The New Silk Roads: The present and future of the world* (Bloomsbury, 2018).

3 See, for one of many examples, Alfred W. McCoy, *In the Shadows of the American Century* (Ateneo de Manila University Press, 2017).

4 See, for example, George Magnus, *Red Flags* (Yale University Press, 2018).

5 See, for example, Alan Greenspan and Adrian Wooldridge, *Capitalism in America* (Allen Lane, 2018).

6 See Ali Allawi, *The Crisis of Islamic Civilization* (Yale University Press, 2009), pp. 68–73.

7 R. H. P. Mason and J. G. Caiger, *A History of Japan* (Tuttle Publishing, 2001), p. 127.

8 Richard Shek, 'The alternative moral universe of religious dissenters in Ming-Qing China' in James D. Tracy and Marguerite Ragnow (eds), *Religion and the Early Modern State* (Cambridge University Press, 2010).

9 See Vincent Yu-chung Shih, *The Taiping Ideology* (University of Washington Press, 1967).

10 Jeanne-Marie Gescher, *Becoming China* (Bloomsbury, 2017), p. 277.

11 Gescher, *Becoming China*, p. 646.

12 Gescher, *Becoming China*, pp. 294–5.

13 Erik af Edholm, 'The problem of Millenarism (sic)', *Scripta Instituti Donneriani Aboensis*, 1975 (available online at: <https://doi.org/10.30674/scripta.67080>).

14 Arvind-Pal Singh Mandair, *Sikhism: A guide for the perplexed* (Bloomsbury, 2013), pp. 132–4.

15 See David Cook, *Contemporary Muslim Apocalyptic Literature* (Syracuse University Press, 2005).

16 See 1 Corinthians 16.22. There is an ambiguity about the meaning. Grammatically, it could be either in the imperative tense or in the past: 'Come, O Lord' or 'The Lord has come.' It is usual to read it as in the imperative tense, however, which is consistent with the clear expectation of Christ's imminent return, evident both in the writings of Paul and in the book of Revelation.

17 Giorgio Vasari (George Bull, tr.), *Lives of the Artists: Volume 1* (Penguin, 1987), p. 227.

18 Catherine Hudak Klancer, *Embracing Our Complexity* (State University of New York Press, 2015), pp. 56–7.

19 See US Department of State Memorandum of Conversation, 12 November 1973.

20 Klancer, *Embracing Our Complexity*, p. 113.

21 G. W. F. Hegel, *Encyklopädie der Philosophischen Wissenschaften im Grundrisse* (*Encyclopaedia of the Philosophical Sciences in Basic Outline*) (1830; G. Lasson and O. Pöggler (eds), Hamburg, 1959), paragraph 342, author's translation.

22 Hegel, *Encyklopädie*, paragraph 348, author's translation.

23 See, for example, Terry Pinkard, *Hegel's Phenomenology* (Cambridge University Press, 1994).

24 See Rowan Williams, *The Edge of Words* (Bloomsbury, 2014), p. 42.

25 Hans-Georg Gadamer (Joel Weinsheimer and Donald G. Marshall, tr.), *Truth and Method* (Bloomsbury, 2014), pp. 363–70.

26 Hegel, *Encyklopädie*, paragraph 436.

27 Philippians 2.

28 A. V. Miller (tr.), *Hegel's Phenomenology of Spirit* (Oxford University Press, 1977), pp. 492–3.

29 Qian Zhongshu (Jeanne Kelly and Nathan K. Mao, tr.), *Fortress Besieged* (Penguin, 2006), p. 371.

30 Mo Yan (Howard Goldblatt, tr.), *Red Sorghum* (Penguin, 2003), p. 142.
31 See Stephen C. Angle, *Contemporary Confucian Political Philosophy* (Polity Press, 2012), p. 67.
32 See Alasdair MacIntyre, *After Virtue* (University of Notre Dame Press, 2007), pp. 168–9, on the difference between the Aristotelian and Stoic conceptions of virtue.
33 Williams, *The Edge of Words*, p. 151.
34 In conversation with the author, 2009.

Select bibliography

A list of all the books I have read that relate to the human odyssey would include a large proportion of the books I have ever read. It would, furthermore, be hard to find a clear basis for selection. So I have chosen a simpler, more limited, approach: this bibliography includes all the works cited in this book.

Allawi, Ali, *The Crisis of Islamic Civilization* (New Haven, CT: Yale University Press, 2009).

Allison, Graham, 'The Thucydides trap' in *FP* (9 June, 2017, available online at: <www.foreignpolicy.com/2017/06/09/the-thucydides-trap>).

Anderson, Benedict, *Imagined Communities: Reflections on the origin and spread of nationalism* (London: Verso Publications, 1983).

Angle, Stephen C., *Contemporary Confucian Political Philosophy* (Cambridge: Polity Press, 2012).

Augustine (R. S. Pine-Coffin, tr.), *Confessions* (London: Penguin, 1961).

Augustine (Henry Bettenson, tr.), *The City of God* (London: Penguin, 1984).

Axworthy, Michael, *Iran: Empire of the Mind: A history from Zoroaster to the present day* (London: Penguin, 2008).

Basham, A. L. (ed.), *A Cultural History of India* (New Delhi: Oxford India Paperbacks, 1997).

Basham, A. L., *The Wonder that was India* (London: Picador, 2004).

Basho, Matsuo (Donald Keene, tr.), *The Narrow Road to Oku* (Tokyo: Kodansha International, 1996).

Becker, Sasha and Wössmann, Luther, 'Was Weber wrong? A human capital theory of Protestant economics history', *The Quarterly Journal of Economics* (2009), 124(2), pp. 531–96.

Beckwith, Christopher I., *Empires of the Silk Road: A history of Central Eurasia from the Bronze Age to the present* (Princeton, NJ: Princeton University Press, 2011).

Bellaigue, Christopher de, *The Islamic Enlightenment: The modern struggle between faith and reason* (London: Vintage, 2018).

Benedict, Ruth, *The Chrysanthemum and the Sword: Patterns of Japanese culture* (New York: Mariner Books, 2005).

Bertram, C., 'Rousseau's legacy in two conceptions of the general will: Democratic and transcendent' in *Review of Politics* (2012), 74(3), pp. 403–20.

Bhattacharji, Sukumari, 'Sanskrit drama and the absence of tragedy' in *Indian Literature* (New Delhi: Sahitya Akademi, 1978).

Blanning, Tim, *The Romantic Revolution* (London: Weidenfeld & Nicolson, 2010).

Bowie, Andrew, 'Friedrich Wilhelm Joseph von Schelling' in *The Stanford Encyclopedia of Philosophy* (2016, available online at: <https://.plato.stanford.edu>).

Breen, John and Teeuwen, Mark, *A New History of Shinto* (Hoboken, NJ: Wiley-Blackwell, 2010).

Brzezinski, Zbigniew, *The Grand Chessboard: American primacy and its geostrategic imperatives* (New York: Basic Books, 1997).

Buruma, Ian, *The Wages of Guilt: Memories of war in Germany and Japan* (London: Jonathan Cape, 1994).

Camus, Albert, *L'Etranger* (Paris: Gallimard, 1942; published in English as *The Outsider*, Stuart Gilbert (tr.), London: Hamish Hamilton, 1946).

Cervantes, Miguel de (John Rutherford, tr.), *Don Quixote* (London: Penguin, 2003).

Chan, Wing-tsit, *A Source Book in Chinese Philosophy* (Princeton, NJ: Princeton University Press, 1973).

Ch'en, Kenneth, *Buddhism in China: A historical survey* (Princeton, NJ: Princeton University Press, 1973).

Confucius (Edward Slingerland, tr.), *The Analects* (Indianapolis, IN: Hackett Publishing, 2003).

Cook, David, *Contemporary Muslim Apocalyptic Literature* (Syracuse, NY: Syracuse University Press, 2005).

Crick, Francis, *The Astonishing Hypothesis: The scientific search for the soul* (New York: Scribner, 1994).

Cunliffe, Barry, *By Steppe, Desert and Ocean: The birth of Eurasia* (Oxford: Oxford University Press, 2015).

Damrosch, David, *How to Read World Literature* (Oxford: Wiley-Blackwell, 2008).

Decreus, Freddy and Kolk, Mieke (eds), 'Rereading Classics in "East" and "West": Post-colonial perspectives on the tragic' in *Documenta Jaargang* (2004), 22 (available online at: <www.academia.edu>).

Derrida, Jacques (Marie-Louise Mallet, ed., and David Wills, tr.), *The Animal that Therefore I Am* (New York: Fordham University Press, 2008).

Diderot, Denis, *Pensées sur L'Interprétation de la Nature* (1753; published in English as *On the Interpretation of Nature*, 1754).

Doniger, Wendy, *The Hindus: An alternative history* (Oxford: Oxford University Press, 2010).

Eckermann, Johann Peter, *Gespräche mit Goethe in den letzten Jahren seines Lebens* (1848; published in English as *Conversations with Goethe in the Last Years of his Life*, John Oxenford (tr.), San Francisco, CA: North Point Press, 1984).

Edholm, Erik Af, 'The problem of Millenarism (sic)' in *Scripta Instituti Donneriani Aboensis* (1975, available online at: <https://doi.org/10.30674/scripta.67080>).

Eliot, T. S., 'Little Gidding' in *Four Quartets* (New York: Harcourt, Brace & Company, 1943).

Engels, Friedrich, *Die Lage der arbeitenden Klasse in England* (1845; published in English as *The Condition of the Working Class in England*, 1885).

Epic of Gilgamesh, The (N. K. Sandars, tr.) (London: Penguin, 1983).

Faces of Love: Hafez and the poets of Shiraz (Dick Davis, tr.) (New York: Penguin, 2013).

Faulkner, William, *Requiem for a Nun* (1950).

Fichte, Johann Gottlieb, *Reden an die Deutsche Nation* (1808; published in English as *Addresses to the German Nation*, Gregory Moore (tr.) (Cambridge University Press, 2009).

Foucault, Michel, *Les Mots et les Choses* (1966; published in English as *The Order of Things*, Abingdon: Routledge, 2002).

Frankopan, Peter, *The Silk Roads: A new history of the world* (London: Bloomsbury, 2015).

Frankopan, Peter, *The New Silk Roads: The present and future of the world* (London: Bloomsbury, 2018).

Fraser, Christopher, 'Major rival schools: Mohism and legalism' in
J. Garfield and W. Edelglass (eds), *The Oxford Handbook of World
Philosophy* (Oxford: Oxford University Press, 2011).

Fukuyama, Francis, 'The end of history?', *The National Interest* (Summer
1989), 16, pp. 3–18.

Fukuyama Francis, *The Origins of Political Order: From pre-human times
to the French Revolution* (London: Profile Books, 2012).

Fukuyama, Francis, *Political Order and Political Decay: From the Industrial
Revolution to the globalization of democracy* (Profile Books, 2014).

Gadamer, Hans-Georg (Joel Weinsheimer and Donald G. Marshall, tr.),
Truth and Method (London: Bloomsbury, 2014).

Gellner, Ernest, *Nations and Nationalism* (Oxford: Blackwell, 1983).

Gescher, Jeanne-Marie, *Becoming China: The story behind the State*
(London: Bloomsbury, 2017).

Goethe, Johann Wolfgang von, *West-östlicher Diwan* (1819; published in English
as *West-Eastern Diwan*, Eric Ormsby (tr.), London: Gingko Library, 2019).

Goethe, Johann Wolfgang von, *Faust, Part 1* (1808, rev. edn, 1828–1829).

Goethe, Johann Wolfgang von, *Maxims and Reflections* (1833).

Greenspan, Alan and Wooldridge, Adrian, *Capitalism in America: A
history* (London: Allen Lane, 2018).

Guyer, Paul (ed.), *The Cambridge Companion to Kant* (Cambridge:
Cambridge University Press, 1992).

Habermas, Jürgen (W. Hohengarten, tr.), *Post-Metaphysical Thinking:
Philosophical essays* (Cambridge, MA: MIT Press, 1992).

Habermas, Jürgen, *Between Facts and Norms: Contribution to a discourse
theory of law and democracy* (Cambridge, MA: MIT Press, 1998).

Hampson, Norman, *The Enlightenment: An evaluation of its assumptions,
attitudes and values* (London: Penguin, 1982).

Harris, Henry (ed.), *Identity: Essays based on Herbert Spencer lectures given
in the University of Oxford* (Oxford: Clarendon Press, 1995).

Hartley, L. P., *The Go-Between* (1953).

Hegel, G. W. F., *Encyklopädie der Philosophischen Wissenschaften im
Grundrisse* (Berlin, 1830; G. Lasson and O. Pöggler (eds), Hamburg,
1959; published in English as *Encyclopaedia of the Philosophical Sciences
in Basic Outline*, Klaus Brinkmann (tr.), Cambridge: Cambridge
University Press, 2015).

Hegel, G. W. F. (A. V. Miller, tr.), *Hegel's Phenomenology of Spirit* (Oxford: Oxford University Press, 1977).

Heidegger, Martin, *Sein und Zeit* (1927; published in English as *Being and Time*, John Macquarrie and Edward Robinson (tr.), Oxford: Blackwell, 1990).

Heidegger, Martin, *Was heißt Denken?* (1952; published in English as *What Is Called Thinking?*, Fred D. Wieck and J. Glenn Gray (tr.), New York: Harper & Row, 1968).

Hillman, Jonathan E., *The Rise of China–Europe Railways: The dawn of a new commercial era?* (Washington, DC: Center for Strategic and International Studies, 2018).

Hobsbawm, Eric and Ranger, Terence (eds), *The Invention of Tradition* (Cambridge: Cambridge University Press, 1983).

Holland, Tom, *Dominion: The making of the Western mind* (London: Little, Brown, 2019).

Huang, Ray, *1587, a Year of no Significance: The Ming Dynasty in decline* (New Haven, CT: Yale University Press, 1981).

Hugo, Victor (Norman Denny, tr.), *Les Misérables* (London: Penguin, 1982).

Hume, David, *A Treatise of Human Nature* (1738).

Hume, David, *An Enquiry Concerning the Principles of Morals* (1751).

Hume, David, *The Natural History of Religion* (1757).

Huntington, Samuel P., *The Clash of Civilizations and the Remaking of the World Order* (London: Simon & Schuster, 1997).

Husserl, Edmund (Donn Welton, ed.), *The Essential Husserl: Basic writings in transcendental phenomenology* (Bloomington, IN: Indiana University Press, 1999).

Huxley, Aldous, *The Perennial Philosophy* (London: Harper, 1945).

Irwin, Robert, *For Lust of Knowing: The Orientalists and their enemies* (London: Allen Lane, 2006).

Izenberg, Gerald, *Identity: The necessity of a modern idea* (Philadelphia, PA: University of Pennsylvania Press, 2016).

Johnson, Ian, *The Souls of China: The return of religion after Mao* (London: Allen Lane, 2017).

Joyce, James, *A Portrait of the Artist as a Young Man* (1916).

Joyce, James, *Ulysses* (1922).

Kant, Immanuel, *Prolegomena to any Future Metaphysics* (1783).

Kant, Immanuel, *The Critique of Practical Reason* (1788).

Kasulis, Thomas, *Engaging Japanese Philosophy: A short history* (Honolulu, HI: University of Hawaii Press, 2018).

Kato, Suichi (Don Sanderson, tr.), *A History of Japanese Literature: From the Manyoshu to modern times* (Tokyo: Kodansha International, 1990).

Keene, Donald (ed.), *Anthology of Japanese Literature* (New York: Grove Press, 2007).

Kennedy, Hugh, *The Caliphate* (London: Penguin, 2016).

Khilnani, Sunil, *The Idea of India* (London: Penguin, 2012).

Kierkegaard, Søren (Howard V. Hong and Edna H. Hong, tr.), *Concluding Unscientific Postscript to Philosophical Fragments* (1846 rev. edn, Princeton, NJ: Princeton University Press, 1992).

Kissinger, Henry, *World Order: Reflections on the character of nations and the course of history* (London: Penguin, 2014).

Klancer, Catherine Hudak, *Embracing Our Complexity: Thomas Aquinas and Zhu Xi on power and the common good* (New York: State University of New York Press, 2015).

Kołakowski, Leszek, *Main Currents of Marxism: The founders, the Golden Age, the breakdown* (New York: Norton, 2008).

La Mettrie, Julien Offray de, *Système d'Epicure* (1750).

Lauster, Jörg, *Die Verzauberung der Welt: Eine Kulturgeschichte des Christentums* (2014; published in English as *The Enchantment of the World: A cultural history of Christendom*, Munich: C. H. Beck, 2016).

Leaman, Oliver, *Islamic Philosophy* (Cambridge: Polity Press, 2009).

Lévy, André, *Chinese Literature, Ancient and Classical* (Bloomington, IN: Indiana University Press, 2000).

Li Po and Tu Fu: Poems (selected and tr. Arthur Cooper) (London: Penguin, 1973).

Lidén, Johanna, 'Buddhist and Daoist influences on Neo-Confucian thinkers and their claim of orthodoxy' in *Orientalia Suecana* (2011), 60, pp. 163–84.

Locke, John, *Second Treatise of Government* (1690).

Lotus Sutra, The (Gene Reeves, tr.) (Somerville, MA: Wisdom Publications, 2008).

Luo, Guanzhong (Lo Kuan-Chung) (C. H. Brewitt-Taylor, tr.), *The Romance of the Three Kingdoms* (Vol. 1) (Clarendon, VT: Tuttle Publishing, 2002).

McCoy, Alfred W., *In the Shadows of the American Century: The rise and decline of US global power* (Manila: Ateneo de Manila University Press, 2017).

MacCulloch, Diarmaid, *Reformation: Europe's house divided, 1490–1700* (London: Penguin, 2004).

MacIntyre, Alasdair, *After Virtue* (Notre Dame, ID: University of Notre Dame Press, 2007).

McLynn, Frank, *Genghis Khan: The man who conquered the world* (London: Vintage, 2016).

Magnus, George, *Red Flags: Why Xi's China is in jeopardy* (New Haven, CT: Yale University Press, 2018).

Marx, Karl and Engels, Friedrich, *The Communist Manifesto* (1848).

Mason, R. H. P. and Caiger, J. G., *A History of Japan* (Clarendon, VT: Tuttle Publishing, 2001).

Meeks, Wayne A., *The First Urban Christians: The social world of the apostle Paul* (Yale University Press, 2003).

Meister Eckhart, The Complete Mystical Works of (Maurice Walshe, tr.) (New York: Crossroad Publishing, 2008).

Minois, Georges, *La Guerre de Cent Ans: Naissance de deux nations* (Paris: Perrin, 2010).

Mo, Yan (Howard Goldblatt, tr.), *Red Sorghum* (London: Penguin, 2003).

Montesquieu, Charles-Louis de Secondat, baron de La Brède de, *De l'Esprit des Lois* (1748; published in English as *On the Spirit of the Laws*, 1750).

Montesquieu, Charles-Louis de Secondat, baron de La Brède de, *Notes sur l'Angleterre* (1879; published in English as *Notes on England* (commentary and tr. Iain Stewart), Oxford University Comparative Law Forum, 2002, 6; available online at: <www.ouclf.iuscomp.org>).

Murasaki, Shikibu (Edward G. Seidensticker, tr.), *The Tale of Genji* (New York: Alfred A. Knopf, 1987).

Murphy, R. Taggart, *Japan and the Shackles of the Past* (New York: Oxford University Press, 2014).

Nakamura, Hajime (Philip P. Wiener, ed.), *Ways of Thinking of Eastern Peoples: India, China, Tibet, Japan* (Honolulu, HI: University of Hawaii, 1985).

Nietzsche Reader, The (Keith Ansell Pearson and Duncan Large, eds) (Oxford: Blackwell, 2014).

Orwell, George, *Nineteen Eighty-Four* (1949).

Palmer, David, Shive, Glenn and Wickeri, Philip (eds), *Chinese Religious Life* (New York: Oxford University Press, 2011).

Pantsov, Alexander V. with Levine, Steven I., *Mao: The real story* (New York: Simon & Schuster, 2013).

Pinkard, Terry, *Hegel's Phenomenology: The sociality of reason* (Cambridge, NY: Cambridge University Press, 1994).

Proust, Marcel, *A la Recherche du Temps Perdu, Volume 1: Du côté de chez Swann* (Paris: Bernard Grasset, 1913).

Qian, Zhongshu (Jeanne Kelly and Nathan K. Mao, tr.), *Fortress Besieged* (London: Penguin, 2006).

Qvortrup, Mads, Chapter 4, 'A civic profession of faith: Rousseau's and nationalism' in *The Political Philosophy of Jean-Jacques Rousseau: The impossibility of reason* (Manchester: Manchester University Press, 2003).

Rachewiltz, Igor de, 'Some remarks on the ideological foundations of Chingis Khan's empire', *Papers on Far Eastern History* (1973; available online at: <www.altaica.ru>).

Rashid al-Din (W. M. Thackston, ed. and tr.), *Jami'u't-tawarikh: Compendium of chronicles: A history of the Mongols* (Cambridge MA: Harvard University Press, 1998).

Renan, Ernest, 'Qu'est-ce qu'une nation?' ('What is a Nation?') (1882; available online at: <www.bmlisieux.com/archives/nation01.htm>).

Ricoeur, Paul, *Anthropologie Philosophique, Écrits et Conférences* (Paris: Éditions du Seuil, 2013).

Rosker, Jana, 'Epistemology in Chinese philosophy' in *The Stanford Encyclopedia of Philosophy* (2018, available online at: <https://.plato.stanford.edu>).

Runciman, Steven, *The Fall of Constantinople 1453* (Cambridge: Cambridge University Press, 1990).

Said, Edward, *Orientalism* (London: Penguin Books, 2003).

Sartre, Jean-Paul, *L'Etre et le Néant: Essai d'ontologie phénoménologique* (1943; published in English as *Being and Nothingness: An essay in phenomenological ontology*, New York Philosophical Library, 1956).

Schiller, Friedrich, *Die Geschichte des Dreißigjährigen Krieges* (1805; published in English as *The History of the Thirty Years War*, A. J. W. Morrison (tr.), London: Bell & Daldy, 1873).

Sen, Amartya, *The Argumentative Indian: Writings on Indian history, culture and identity* (New York: Farrar, Straus & Giroux, 2005).

Shih, Vincent Yu-chung, *The Taiping Ideology: Its sources, interpretations and influences* (Seattle: University of Washington Press, 1967).

Simon-Ingram, Julia, 'Rousseau and the problem of community: Nationalism, civic virtue, totalitarianism', *History of European Ideas* (1993), 16(1–3), pp. 23–9.

Singh Mandair, Arvind-Pal, *Sikhism: A guide for the perplexed* (London: Bloomsbury, 2013).

Smith, Adam, *The Theory of Moral Sentiments* (1759).

Smith, Adam, *The Wealth of Nations* (London: William Strahan, Thomas Cadell, 1776).

Soseki, Natsume (Meredith McKinney, tr.), *Kokoro* (New York: Penguin, 2010).

Spengler, Oswald, (C. F. Atkinson, tr.) *Decline of the West: An abridged edition* (Oxford: Oxford University Press, 1991).

Suzuki, D. T., *Zen and Japanese Culture* (Rutland, VT: Tuttle Publishing, 1988).

Tagore, Rabindranath, *Gitanjali*, song 21 (originally published by Macmillan, 1917).

Tamura, Yoshiro (Jeffrey Hunter, tr.), *Japanese Buddhism: A cultural history* (Tokyo: Kosei Publishing, 2005).

Tanizaki, Junichiro (Edward G. Seidensticker, tr.), *The Makioka Sisters* (London: Vintage, 2000).

Taylor, Charles, *Sources of the Self: The making of the modern identity* (Cambridge MA: Harvard University Press, 1989).

Taylor, Charles, *The Language Animal: The full shape of the human linguistic capacity* (Cambridge, MA: Harvard University Press, 2016).

Teilhard de Chardin, Pierre, *Le Phénomène Humain* (Paris: Éditions du Seuil, 1955; generally translated into English as *The Phenomenon of Man*).

Thapar, Romila, *Somanatha: The many voices of a history* (New Delhi: Penguin India, 2005).

Thomas, Keith, *Religion and the Decline of Magic* (London: Penguin, 2003).

Tönnies, Ferdinand, *Gemeinschaft und Gesellschaft* (1887; published in English as *Community and Society*, C. P. Loomis (tr.), London: Transaction Publishers, 1988).

Toynbee, Arnold (abridged D. C. Somervell), *A Study of History* (Oxford: Oxford University Press, 1987).

Tracy, James D. and Ragnow, Marguerite (eds), *Religion and the Early Modern State: Views from China, Russia and the West* (New York: Cambridge University Press, 2010).

Tu, Weiming, *Confucian Thought: Selfhood as creative transformation* (Albany, NY: State University of New York Press, 1997).

Vasari, Giorgio (George Bull, tr.), *Lives of the Artists (Volume 1)* (London: Penguin, 1987).

Voltaire, *Candide ou l'Optimisme* (1759).

Wallace, Jennifer, 'Tragedy in China', *The Cambridge Quarterly* (2013), June, 42(2), pp. 99–111.

Weber, Max, *Gesammelte Aufsätze zur Religionssoziologie* (1920; published in English as *The Sociology of Religion*, Talcott Parsons (tr.) (Boston, MA: Beacon Press, 1993).

Weber, Max, *Die Protestantische Ethik und der Geist des Kapitalismus* (1905; published in English as *The Protestant Ethic and the Spirit of Capitalism* (Talcott Parsons, tr.), Oxford: Blackwell, 1992).

Williams, Rowan, *The Edge of Words: God and the habits of language* (London: Bloomsbury, 2014).

Williams, Rowan, *On Augustine* (London: Bloomsbury, 2016).

Wordsworth, William, *Lyrical Ballads* (1798).

Wordsworth, William, *Poems, in Two Volumes* (London: Longman, Hurst, Reese & Orme, 1807).

Xiang, Shuchen, 'The irretrievability of the past: Nostalgia in Chinese literature from Tang-Song poetry to Ming-Qing *san-wen*', *International Communication of Chinese Culture* (2015), 2(3), pp. 205–22.

Young, Julian, *Friedrich Nietzsche: A philosophical biography* (New York: Cambridge University Press, 2010).

Zoref, Arye, *Journeys for God in Sufi and Judeo-Arabic Literature* (Berlin: Potsdam University, 2016).

Index

family, role of 101
fascism 113–14
Faulkner, William, on the
   past 122
Faust (antihero) 241–2
Ferdinand, Archduke Franz
   88
feudalism 86
Feuerbach, Ludwig 50
financial power 172–3
Fiore, Gioacchino da *see*
   Joachim, of Fiore
Fitche, Johann Gottlieb, on
   language 92
fluidity (in urban life) 54
folklore 60, 123–4
'footloose urbanite' 58
Fortress Besieged (Qian)
   267–8
Foucault, Michel 73–4
France
   agrarian economy 28
   autonomous cities 39
   national identity 87
   past, relationship with
      146
   vernacularization 96
Frederick II, King of Prussia
   100, 151
freedom 101–3
freemasonry 110
French language, use in
   England 93
French Revolution 14, 103
fudo 235
Fukuyama, Francis 160, 248
Fukuzawa, Yukichi 108

Gandhi, Indira 128
Gandhi, Mahatma
   nationalism 112–13
   on the past 124–5
geisha 45
Germany
   national identity 87
   past, relationship with 146
   unification 87
   vernacularization 96
   weakness at the centre 39

Geworfenheit ('thrown-ness')
   228
Ghazali, Abu Hamid
   Muhammad al- 34,
   69–70, 72
Gilgamesh 76–7
Go-Between, The (Hartley)
   122–3
God
   existence of 64–6
   sovereignty of 69
Goethe, Johann Wolfgang
   von 179–80, 241–2
Gökalp, Ziya 112
Great Learning 68
great powers 154–7, 162
Greater East Asia Co-
   Prosperity Sphere 135, 236
Greece 87
grief and loss, artistic
   expression of 187–8
Grimmelshausen, Hans Jakob
   Christoffel von 150
Guan, Hangqing 192
Guangxu, Emperor of China
   109
guilt, artistic expression of
   194–5

Habermas, Jürgen 239
   on nationhood 114
Habsburg Empire 40
   decline of 105–6
   national identities within
      87
Hafez 34, 185
   on memories 117
Hanseatic League 39, 149
happiness, pursuit of 270
Harappans (Indus Valley) 8–9
Hartley, L. P. 122
Heavenly Kingdom of Great
   Peace 253–4
Hegel, Georg Wilhelm
   Friedrich 24, 260–5
   historical dialectic 50–1,
      246, 273–4
Heidegger, Martin 227–9,
   235–6

Herder, Johann Gottfried
   102–3
heritage, makes nation 90–1
hero 182
Hindi 96–7
Hinduism
   antithetical to tragedy 192
   and enchantment 201–2
   inspirational texts 125–6
   national identity 127–8
   self, concept of 231
   traditions 18
Hiroshima 135
history
   end of 273
   impact on America 155–6
   importance of 105, 116
   as a journey 50
   patterns of 249–51, 260
Hitler, Adolph 107
Hobbes, Thomas 99
Hobsbawm, Eric 123–4
Hội An 44
Holy Roman Emperor 10, 39
Holy Roman Empire 73, 149
Hong, Xiuquan 253–4
Hong Kong 25
   as migrant city 58
Hopkins, Gerard Manley
   185–6
Horace 188–9
Hugo, Victor 80–2
human rights 173–6, 270–1
humanism 214, 220–1
humanity
   culture 90–2
   in Eurasia 7–11
   fulfilment 270–3
   naturally religious
      199–201
   nature 98–103
   shared experience 1, 22
Hume, David 217–18
   on nature of self 222–3
Humphrey, John Peters 173
Hungary 87
Huntington, Samuel 155,
   159–60
Husserl, Edmund 224–5

Index

kabuki 45
Kalidasa 186–7
Kang, Youwei 109
Kant, Immanuel 59, 225
  on nature of self 221–3
karma 23, 126, 190
Kautilya 161
Khan, Genghis 33
Kissinger, Henry 13–14,
  155–6, 261, 262
knowledge
  spread of 212–14
  thirst for 214–16
Kobayashi, Issa 188
Kokoro (Soseki) 108, 194–5
kokutai 107–8
Korea *see* North Korea; South
  Korea
Korean War 172
kremlins, ancient 143
Krishna 126
Kyoto 44

La Mettrie, Julien Offray de
  217, 218
labour, value of 43
languages 35
  dividing factor in nation
    state 106–7
  forming nation 90, 91,
    95, 97
  fringe 96
  national identity 92–4,
    138
  translations 181–4
Laozi (Lao Tzu) 60–2
Latin, decline of 92–3
Latin Christianity, influence
  213–14
Latium 32
law, divinely ordained 66
League of Nations 153–4
Lenin 28
  use of Marxism 52
Leninism 16
Les Misérables (Hugo) 80–2
Leviathan (Hobbes) 99
Liang, Qichao 109
Liang, Shuming 254

liberal
  democratic order 17–18,
    20, 160
  economics 17
life, ruptured 73–5
life-in-nature 63–4, 73
  in China 67–8
Lin, Daiyu 79
Linnaeus, Carl 93
literature
  antihero motif 239–44,
    267–8
  and culture 91–2, 182
  fall of cities 31
  hero motif 182
  and nationhood 91–2
  use of vernaculars 94
Locke, John 221
  on human nature 99–100
London 39–40
  extoled by Wordsworth 37
  as migrant city 58
Lord Mayor (London) 40
loss and grief, artistic
  expression of 187–8
Lotus Sutra, The 134
Louis XIV (of France) 151
love, artistic expression of
  186–7
lunar men, Birmingham 38
Luoyang 30
Luther, Martin 72
Lutheran Protestantism 151

Machiavelli, Niccolo 161
Madhi 256
Mahabharata 125–6
Maitreya 252–3
male privilege 53
Malthus, Thomas 168–9
Mandarin Chinese 95
Mandate of God 138
Mandate of Heaven 10, 16,
  33, 108, 132, 253
Mao, Zedong
  eschatology 254
  mistakes 16
  use of Marxism 52
mappo 251

markets 17
Marx, Karl 42–3, 49
  and capitalism 52
  God, existence of 50–1
  on industrialization 85
  on nation states 86–7
  on world literature
    179–80
Marxism 52, 131
  controlling the past 124
Masaryk, Thomas 106–7
materialism 7, 51
Meiji Restoration 107
memories 116–22
  communal 123
  identity, building blocks
    of 119–21
  problem for national
    identity 146–8
Mencius 99
Mencius (writings) 68
merchants 45
Merv 32
Mesopotamia 76
metaphysical systems
  199–201, 274–5
  differences 209–10
Middle East
  and Europe 158–9
  national identities 136–41
migrants 56, 246
  experiences 56–7
  question of identity 58
migrations 58
  patterns 56–7
  rural to urban 28–9
military competition 105
millenarianism
  China 251–4
  Christianity 257
  India 254–6
  Islam 256
  Protestantism 258
  Sikhism 255–6
Milton, John 240
Mo, Yan 267, 268
Mohenjo-daro 29, 30
moksha 23, 126
monarchy 38